Gaspar Noé: Interviews

Conversations with Filmmakers Series
Gerald Peary, General Editor

GASPAR
NOÉ

I N T E R V I E W S

Edited by Geoffrey Lokke

University Press of Mississippi / Jackson

The University Press of Mississippi is the scholarly publishing agency of
the Mississippi Institutions of Higher Learning: Alcorn State University,
Delta State University, Jackson State University, Mississippi State University,
Mississippi University for Women, Mississippi Valley State University,
University of Mississippi, and University of Southern Mississippi.

www.upress.state.ms.us

The University Press of Mississippi is a member
of the Association of University Presses.

Library of Congress Cataloging-in-Publication Data

Names: Lokke, Geoffrey, editor.
Title: Gaspar Noé: interviews / Geoffrey Lokke.
Other titles: Conversations with filmmakers series.
Description: Jackson : University Press of Mississippi, 2024. | Series: Conversations
with filmmakers series | Includes bibliographical references and index.
Identifiers: LCCN 2024022654 (print) | LCCN 2024022655 (ebook) |
ISBN 9781496854247 (hardback) | ISBN 9781496854223 (trade paperback) |
ISBN 9781496854230 (epub) | ISBN 9781496854254 (epub) | ISBN 9781496854261 (pdf) |
ISBN 9781496854216 (pdf)
Subjects: LCSH: Noé, Gaspar, 1963—Interviews. | Noé, Gaspar, 1963—Criticism and
interpretation. | Motion picture producers and directors—Interviews. | Motion picture
producers and directors—France. | Motion pictures—Production and direction.
Classification: LCC PN1998.3.N635 A5 2024 (print) | LCC PN1998.3.N635 (ebook) |
DDC 791.4302/33092—dc23/eng/20240610
LC record available at https://lccn.loc.gov/2024022654
LC ebook record available at https://lccn.loc.gov/2024022655

British Library Cataloging-in-Publication Data available

Contents

Introduction

As Gaspar Noé notes in these conversations, he is painfully aware of how his reputation as a "provocateur" precedes him. (He finds Americans' use of the French word characteristically tacky.) For many viewers and critics, the Buenos Aires–born French filmmaker remains, above all, the director of *Irréversible* (2002), a short-circuited, arthouse "revenge-o-matic" modeled, somewhat surprisingly, on Harold Pinter's 1978 play *Betrayal*. Before the release of Noé's 2020 "Straight Cut" of the film, *Irréversible*'s scenes ran in reverse order, beginning with a gruesome killing at a nightclub, climaxing with a notorious, nine-minute rape scene, followed by an almost shockingly tender dénouement (or prologue) between the two lovers at the heart of the film (played by Monica Bellucci and Vincent Cassel). And it's these intimate moments—soundtracked by an Étienne Daho record—that have somehow stayed with me the longest, rather than the horrors that precede them.

Those acquainted with Noé's body of work know that images of extreme violence are inextricable to his cinema, but these should hardly define him as a person or artist. Noé's many enthusiasts and followers remain in steady awe of the director's vertiginous camerawork, immersive visuals, and expressionistic editing that greet the diminished attention spans of digital life with displays of extreme acts and endurance for both performers and audiences alike. The conversations brought together here, many appearing in English for the first time, reveal Noé as a monomaniacal, restless student of cinema whose often contradictory drives and beliefs have sustained him as one of the most daring European directors of his generation.

In December 2019, weeks before the COVID pandemic brought much of the globe to a halt, Noé suffered a near-fatal cerebral hemorrhage on the streets of Paris. Yet he doubts the experience will push him to make films any faster—he has produced only six feature-length films over the last thirty years. Although he frequently notes how waiting for funds to materialize is a particularly agonizing process—Noé had conceived of his films *Enter the Void* (2009) and *Love* (2015) long before he wrote *Irréversible*—he admits that he needs this time to ensure he has something new on offer, to push himself to engage and develop new forms. Noé is something of a "signature" artist, but he has never made the same film twice. His early diptych of *Carne* (1991) and *Seul contre tous* [*I Stand Alone*, 1998], featuring actor Philippe Nahon, is routinely compared to the logorrhea of Céline and the pessimism of philosopher Emil Cioran (although Noé insists here that neither were conscious influences). *Irréversible*, by comparison, was his calculated attempt to create a brutishly unedifying exploitation film, an overdetermined revenge fantasy that somehow gives audiences both everything and none of which they had come to expect. As with Quentin Tarantino, Noé seems to have been shaken by watching Sam Peckinpah's 1971 thriller *Straw Dogs* in his youth. While revenge films seem to be an enduring (and lucrative) obsession for the American director, Noé appears to have exhausted this narrative in one go.

Climax (2018), a house music and dance film gone wrong and his closest collaboration with Daft Punk musician Thomas Bangalter, was inspired in large part by the 1970s arthouse horror of Andrzej Żuławski and Dario Argento. Noé later convinced an octogenarian Argento to appear in his 2021 masterwork *Vortex*, alongside actress François Lebrun, which shadows the final weeks of an elderly couple's deteriorating lives. Lebrun, who starred in Jean Eustache's *The Mother and the Whore* (1973), evidently one of Noé's enduring favorites, is predictably heartrending as an old woman fraught by dementia, as language and memory slowly come to fail her. Argento, in seemingly his first film role, is a staggering presence. (Noé reveals here that he had cast Argento after attending a lecture his friend had delivered years before.) *Enter the Void* and *Love*, which directly follow on from each other, are radically different films—the latter a sardonic, dissociative dream before the empty void of death, the other a melodrama punctuated by explicit sex shot and projected in 3D.

The vagaries of Noé's influences and obsessions, explored in these wide-ranging conversations, help elucidate and complicate the filmmaker's varied oeuvre. The volume collects Noé's interviews taken from both major and underground publications: conversations with critics, rabid fans, scholars, and a number of artists, including his fellow directors Abel Ferrara, Matthew Barney, Hubert Sauper, and Harmony Korine. In addition to documenting his wry, good-natured responses to public outrage and habitually mixed reviews, Noé speaks about his process and poetics as a writer, cinematographer, editor, producer, and director; his engagement with past, present-day, and developing film technology; and his fascination, indebtedness, and close study of filmmakers such as Fritz Lang, Stanley Kubrick, and Peckinpah—Noé appears to situate his own aesthetic between their *Metropolis*, *2001: A Space Odyssey*, and *Straw Dogs*, respectively.

Noé also discusses traveling and growing up in Argentina; his use of irony and (black) humor; melodrama, tragedy, and the current state of genre film; as well as modes of filmmaking that captivate him, including movies for children. Other persistent topics include working with actors (and nonactors), his long-standing collaborations with filmmaker Lucile Hadžihalilović (his wife) and cinematographer Benoît Debie, drugs, violence, religion and secularism, electronic music, poster art, the relationship between body and mind, and prevailing norms of spectatorship.

Again, many of Noé's contradictions are laid bare in these conversations. Some of these pertain to his repeated claims that his films are somehow beyond contemporary politics, namely that he works to avoid crude allegories. He clearly balks at the idea that *Climax* says anything about race or racial strife in France, although, like his contemporary Bertrand Bonello's *Nocturama* (2016), it is more or less impossible to ignore the role different bodies play in the violent, tribalized microcosm that he choreographs on screen. Noé claims that his use of the French tricolor at the outset of *Climax* preempts this "racialized" reading (when it quite palpably heightens it). Elsewhere, he reveals that Philippe Nahon's Butcher character, who appears in three of his films, is an examination of the National Front and the particular wounded masculinity that has driven its appeal and continued success. In fact, Noé once considered giving his diptych of *Carne* and *I Stand Alone* the overall title of *France*. (*Le pénis* was also an option, apparently.) Perhaps this disjunction captures Noé's evolving sense of what he believed cinema, or at least his own cinema, could ever accomplish politically. Likewise, the didactic intertitles in *Lux Æterna* that profess his firmly held atheism do little to pall the fact that his films are entrenched in religious motifs and narratives, as Julia Sirmons has explored elsewhere, even if these ritual acts are ultimately performed before an indifferent, godless universe.[1] Further, Noé, a man who bequeathed the cinema an ejaculating 3D penis, says he has little to no interest in pornography (at least since the porn houses were removed from the Champs-Élysées).

Interestingly, Noé seems to frame his fiction filmmaking in terms of documentary work. Noé does not write full-length screenplays; instead, his actors improvise around a short, five-to-six-page scenario. He seems to see his methods as isomorphic to those of early practitioners of cinéma-vérité, that is, in continuously provoking his screen subjects to perform—truth can only be elucidated through performance. At the same time, Noé is also keenly attracted to depicting moments of crisis—like Robert Drew's first visions of direct cinema—in which conscious or even semiconscious presentations of self are no longer possible. In light of his reliance marked interest in nonfiction aesthetics, it comes as no surprise to read that Noé is considering a transition towards making works that are more easily indexed as documentaries, inspired by big-budget Soviet propaganda films from the twenties and thirties.[2]

As one might expect, most of the interviews included here came out of press tours that coincided with the release of his feature films, dating from 1998 to 2022, and more often than not, focused on whatever film Noé was there to promote. But there are also some notable outliers in the volume. Laurent Aknin's 2014 interview, for instance, was conducted in advance of *I Stand Alone*'s fifteenth anniversary and offers an interesting opportunity for Noé to reexamine some of his earliest films. His interviews with other filmmakers tend to be more freewheeling; as Jan-Willem Dikkers, editor of *Issue* magazine, noted to me, Noé tends to do the interviewing whenever he is speaking to other artists. Accordingly, Noé's conversation with Abel Ferrara is more about the latter's *9 Lives of a Wet Pussy* and Pasolini than it is about *Love*. On the other hand, Noé's conversation with Jessica Piersanti for *Apartamento*, an interior design magazine, is remarkable, given Noé clearly has no interest in their remit whatsoever; instead, we get a rare portrait of Noé at work in his editing room. Noé's discussion with Pip Chodorov is exclusively devoted to Kubrick's *2001*, a film Noé has incessantly rewatched, parsed, and anatomized since seeing it upon first release. As well, Frédéric Polizine and Alexis Veille, writing for their exhaustive Gaspar Noé fan site *Le temps détruit tout*, needle Noé with the sort of maniacal questions about foreign Blu-ray errata that only inspired obsessives could dream up.

If the "Straight Cut" of *Irréversible* is anything to go by, Noé recognizes that viewing a film is a kind of deformance (to borrow a phrase from literary critics Lisa Samuels and Jerome McGann); and our individual, idiomatic engagements with his cinema in ways mirror the way his elliptical films often double back on themselves, opening themselves up in different ways.[3] I believe (or at least hope) that this collection of conversations with Noé will further deepen that process and broaden our understanding of one of the more mercurial, dazzling, and willfully frustrating artists working in film today. In light of *Vortex*, one of the most humane, terrifying, and beautiful films I have witnessed in recent years, I am confident Noé's best work lies ahead of us.

I translated five of the interviews included here, which ultimately proved to be something of a challenge. English is one of Noé's first languages—he learned English, in fact, long before he moved to France. But Noé's English is very, shall we say, idiosyncratic, monologuing at hyper-speed in his oddly clipped phrases. (Transcribing verbatim his conversation with Abel Ferrara was a real joy.) I obviously did not try to mimic his English when translating these conversations. All of my conscious betrayals of the French—breaking up sentences, cutting down repetitions—were made in good faith, even if there is occasionally some disconnect between Noé's voice in English and these translations.

I would like to extend my sincere thanks to the University Press of Mississippi, in particular my editor Emily Snyder Bandy, for the very generous opportunity to edit this book, as well as Gerald Peary, editor of the Conversations with Filmmakers Series, whose own interview with Noé is included here. Corley Longmire, my project editor, was a wonderful resource as I prepared the manuscript for publication. I would also like to thank Mitch Parry, my first-year film instructor at the University of Victoria, who (I think jokingly) forbade everyone in the lecture hall from ever watching *Irréversible*. And many thanks to my friends who have watched and talked movies with me over the years, particularly Alex Lane, Sam Richman, Dave Gerardi, Nick Walther, and my partner Lachlan Brooks.

GL

Notes

1. Julia Sirmons, "Bad Trips: Spiritual Agonies and Ecstasies in the Films of Gaspar Noé," *PAJ: A Journal of Performance and Art* 45, no. 2 (2023): 48–55.

2. Martin Dale, "Gaspar Noé Sets His Goals for His Next Film Project after *Vortex*," *Variety*, December 8, 2022, https://variety.com/2022/film/global/gaspar-noe-2-1235454739/.

3. Lisa Samuels and Jerome McGann, "Deformance and Interpretation," *New Literary History* 30, no. 1 (1999): 25–56.

Chronology

1963 Gaspar Noé is born in Buenos Aires, Argentina. His father, Luis Felipe Noé, is a painter and public intellectual; his mother, Nora Murphy, a local activist and social worker.

1976 Noé's family moves to France in order to escape the military dictatorship led by President Jorge Rafael Videla. The dictatorship would last until 1983.

1979 Noé starts making films using a Super 8mm camera, a gift from his father.

1980–83 Noé attends École nationale supérieure Louis-Lumière, a film school in Paris. Although he graduates in two years, he stays on to complete his thesis project.

1984 Noé debuts *Tintarella di Luna* [*Moonlight*], his graduation film, which subsequently airs on Canal+.

1985 Noé assists the director Fernando Solanas on *Tangos, El Exilio de Gardel* [*Tangos, The Exile of Gardel*], a film that depicts Argentinians in Paris. Over the next few years, Noé works on films produced by the company Flagrants Délits, a number of them directed by Bruno Podalydès.

1986 Noé is cinematographer on Lucile Hadžihalilović's film *La première mort de Nono* [*The First Death of Nono*]. The two filmmakers form their own film company, Les Cinémas de la Zone, and later are married. Noé directs a short film, *Pulpe amère* [*Bitter Pulp*], which is acquired by Canal+.

1988 Noé is assistant director on Solanas's film *Sur* [*The South*]. The film is set in Buenos Aires at the end of the dictatorship.

1990 Noé registers *Fleurs* [*Flowers*], a rarely if ever screened short film.

1991 Noé's film *Carne* [*Meat*], produced by Flagrants Délits, wins the top prize in the short film category of the International Critics' Week at the Cannes Film Festival, in addition to the Georges Sadoul Prize and the Prix Très Special.

1993 During this period, Noé first conceives his projects *Soudain le vide* and *Danger*, which eventually materialize as *Enter the Void* (2009) and *Love* (2015), respectively.

1994   Noé writes and directs a short film, *Une expérience d'hypnose télévisuelle* [*A Televisual Hypnosis Experience*], for the Canal+ program *L'oeil du cyclone* [*The Eye of the Storm*], starring actors Marie-France Garcia and Alain Ganas.

1995   Noé directs a forty-five-second television spot, *Le lâcher d'animaux d'élevage* [*The Release of Farm Animals*], as part of an anti-hunting campaign. The short piece features a voiceover by screen legend Alain Delon.

1996   Noé directs a music video and accompanying promotional spots for "Je n'ai pas" ["I Don't Have"] by Les Frères Misère. He is cinematographer for Hadžihalilović's film *La bouche de Jean-Pierre* [*Jean-Pierre's Mouth*], also known as *Parental Guidance*, an official selection at Cannes and winner of the Prix Très Special.

1998   Noé and Hadžihalilović create short films for the French Ministry of Health to be broadcast on Canal+; Noé directs *Sodomites* and is the cinematographer on Hadžihalilović's *Good Boys Use Condoms*. Noé also releases *Seul contre tous* [*I Stand Alone*], a sequel to *Carne*. The film screens at Cannes and wins top honors at the Sarajevo Film Festival. He shoots an additional short, *Intoxication*, during the production of *Seul contre tous*, starring his fellow director Stéphane Drouot. Noé also directs the music video for "Insanely Cheerful" by Bone Fiction.

1999   Noé directs *On derait qu'on serait* [*What We'd Say We'd Be*], a series of twelve promotional films for the fashion designer Agnès B., who had helped finance *Seul contre tous*. Noé also directs the music video for "Je suis si mince" ["I'm So Thin"] by Arielle.

2001   Preproduction for *Enter the Void* comes to a halt. Due to financing issues, the film languishes in "development hell" for nearly a decade.

2002   Noé receives international recognition for *Irréversible* [*Irreversible*], starring Vincent Cassel, Monica Bellucci, and Albert Dupontel, a film lauded and reviled for its depictions of extreme sexual and physical violence, continuous shots, and its exhibition of scenes in reverse order, a structure inspired by Harold Pinter's play *Betrayal* (1978). The film is the third to feature actor Philippe Nahon as a nameless butcher, following *Seul contre tous* and *Carne*. Noé also creates two music videos for Daft Punk musician Thomas Bangalter out of unused footage from *Irreversible*.

2004   *Artforum* critic James Quandt coins the term "The New French Extremity" in order to describe a number of transgressive, graphic, and violent French films, including Noé's. Other filmmakers associated

with the tendency are Claire Denis, Catherine Breillat, Virginie Despentes, Bertrand Bonello, and Coralie Trinh Thi. Noé creates two of
three proposed television spots for AIDS awareness commissioned
by the National Institute for Prevention and Health Education, which
he later abjures (they are credited instead to "Roberto Keller"). Noé
also directs the music video for Placebo's single "Protège-moi" ["Protect Me"].

2005   Noé directs *Eva*, a series of three short films starring model Eva Her-
zigová alongside a fluffy, provocatively placed kitten. The shorts are
broadcast on Canal+ during the 2005 Cannes Film Festival.

2006   Noé creates two short films. *We Fuck Alone* is made for the omnibus
Destricted, a collection of "explicit films" that also features Marina
Abramović, Richard Prince, and Matthew Barney, among other filmmakers and video artists. *SIDA* (AIDS) is part of *8*, an international
omnibus that includes contributions from Gus Van Sant, Jane Cam-
pion, and Wim Wenders. Noé's film depicts a man with AIDS in a
Burkina Faso hospital.

2008–09   Noé directs a series of promotional videos for Yves Saint Laurent's
fragrance La nuit de l'homme starring Vincent Cassel and Bénédicte
Graff. The videos would be the first of several collaborations with the
fashion house. Noé also creates a forty-two-second film for the vodka
42Below as part of the company's "film showcase." Other contributors
are Abel Ferrara, Asia Argento, Charles Burnett, and David Lynch.
Noé's film *42* is crafted out of unused footage from his *Enter the Void*,
which is nearing completion.

2010   *Enter the Void* receives a limited release in France, following its debut at Cannes in an unfinished form. Based loosely on *The Tibetan
Book of the Dead* and Noé's experiences with psilocybin mushrooms,
the psychedelic film is shot from a first-person point of view. Filmed
in Tokyo and Montreal, *Enter the Void* receives fairly mixed reviews.
Noé subsequently releases two more shorts, *DMT* and *Vortex* (unrelated to his 2021 film), made from unused *Enter the Void* footage and
effects.

2011   Noé makes a short film, *Ritual*, for the omnibus *7 días en la Habana*
[*7 Days in Havana*]. Shot in Cuba, the film depicts a young Afro-
Cuban lesbian who is forced to undergo a cleansing ritual by her parents. Noé is nearly kicked off of the project for refusing to present the
producers with a screenplay.

2012–13   Noé directs music videos for Nick Cave & The Bad Seeds ("WE NO
WHO U R"), SebastiAn ("Love in Motion"), and Animal Collective

("Applesauce"). Noé also shoots the explicit cover photograph for Sky Ferreira's album *Night Time, My Time*.

2014   Noé directs the short film *Shoot* for a football-themed omnibus, *Short Plays*. It is first screened at Rio Fest, a few months after the FIFA World Cup in Brazil.

2015   Noé's *Love*, a "sexual melodrama" in 3D starring Karl Glusman, Aomi Muyock, and Kiara Kristin, is an official selection for Cannes. Much like Lars von Trier's *Nymphomaniac* films (2013), initial reception of the film largely focuses on its "unsimulated" sex scenes.

2016   Noé edits the trailer for Guillaume Nicloux's drama *The End*, starring Gérard Depardieu.

2018   Noé shoots his horror-inflected dance film *Climax* in only fifteen days. Choreographed by Nina McNeely, the film marks Noé's second collaboration with Thomas Bangalter, who had provided music for *Irreversible* (Noé also creates a music video for Bangalter's "Sangria" out of footage from *Climax*). Besides actors Sofia Boutella and Souheila Yacoub, the film's cast is comprised of dancers with no previous acting experience.

2019   Shot over one week, Noé directs *Lux Æterna*, commissioned by Saint Laurent. The film stars Charlotte Gainsbourg, Béatrice Dalle, Abbey Lee, and Karl Glusman in a fictional film set in the midst of a witch-burning scene. Using the same crew, Noé also shoots the music video for "Thirst" by SebastiAn. In December, Noé suffers a severe brain hemorrhage and is hospitalized.

2020   Noé reedits his breakout film *Irreversible* into chronological order, following a number of unauthorized and bootleg attempts. The new version is released as *Irreversible: Straight Cut*. Noé also debuts *The Art of Filmmaking*, a short film to accompany screenings of *Lux Æterna*, which repurposes footage from Cecil B. DeMille's *King of Kings* (1927). He also creates a promotional video for Saint Laurent's 2021 summer collection starring Charlotte Rampling.

2021   Noé variously contributes to Fernando Solanas's posthumous documentary *Tres en la deriva del acto creativo* [*Three in the Drift of the Creative Act*], a portrait of Solanas and his friends Eduardo Pavlovsky and Noé's father, Luis Felipe. In addition to working as a camera operator, Noé appears briefly in the film.

2022   Noé's film *Vortex* is released in France, inspired by his near-fatal stroke and the constraints of making a film during the COVID-19 pandemic. Starring horror director Dario Argento and actor François

Lebrun, the chamber play-like drama depicts the final weeks of an elderly couple's shared lives.

2023   Noé directs another promotional video for Saint Laurent to showcase its 2023 men's winter collection.

Filmography

TINTARELLA DI LUNA [*Moonlight*] (1984)
Production companies: Les Productions Nocturnes, ENPC (École Louis-Lumière)
Director: **Gaspar Noé**
Screenplay: **Gaspar Noé**
Camera operators: Gilles Herpin, Magali Raynal, Eric Wild
Editor: **Gaspar Noé**
Cast: Cécile Ricard (Charlotte), Antoine Mosin (Mario), Pierre Bonnafet (Beto), André Dupon (Pepino), J. J. Scheffer (The Thief), Luis Felipe Noé (The Killer), Rafael Gumucio (The Child), Olivier Achard (The Climber), Carlos Kusnir (The Machinist)
18 minutes / Color

PULPE AMÈRE [*Bitter Pulp*] (1987)
Production company: Les Cinémas de la Zone
Director: **Gaspar Noé**
Screenplay: **Gaspar Noé**
Editor: **Gaspar Noé**
Cinematography: Maxime Ruiz
Cast: Norma Guevara, Hector Malamud
6 minutes / Color

FLEURS [*Flowers*] (1990)
Production company: Les Cinémas de la Zone
Director: **Gaspar Noé**
2 minutes / Color

CARNE [*Meat*] (1991)
Production companies: Les Cinémas de la Zone, CNC, Flagrant Délit Productions, Canal+
Producer: Lucile Hadžihalilović
Director: **Gaspar Noé**
Screenplay: **Gaspar Noé**

Cinematography: Dominique Colin
Editor: Lucile Hadžihalilović
Cast: Philippe Nahon (The Butcher), Blandine Lenoir (Cynthia), Frankye Pain
(The Butcher's Mistress), Hélène Testud (The Maid)
38 minutes / Color

L'OEIL DU CYCLONE: "UNE EXPÉRIENCE D'HYPNOSE TÉLÉVISUELLE"
[*The Eye of the Storm: "A Television Hypnosis Experience"*] (1994)
Production companies: Le Village, Canal+
Producer: Charles Petit
Director: **Gaspar Noé**
Teleplay: **Gaspar Noé**
Cinematography: Jean Poisson
Music: Étienne Charry
Cast: Marie-France Garcia, Alain Ganas
28 minutes / Color

LE LÂCHER D'ANIMAUX [*The Release of Animals*] (1995)
Production companies: Rassemblement des Opposants à la Chasse, Gédéon
Director: **Gaspar Noé**
Cast: Alain Delon (voice)
45 seconds / Color

CINÉMATON: "NO. 1,749" (1995)
Production company: Les Amis de Cinématon
Director: Gérard Courant
Cast: **Gaspar Noé**
4 minutes / Color

JE N'AI PAS [*I Don't Have*] (1996)
Music video for the song by Les Frères Misère from the album *Frères misère*
(1996)
Production company: East West France
Director: **Gaspar Noé**
Music: Les Frères Misère
Cast: Mano Solo, François Matuszenski, Vlatcheslav Beriaguine, Blé
Léon Kouame, Napo Romero, Jean-Marc Labbe, Pierre Gauthé, Jean-Luc
Degioanni
3 minutes / Color

LA BOUCHE DE JEAN-PIERRE [*The Mouth of Jean-Pierre*] (1996)
Production companies: Les Cinémas de la Zone, Full Moon, Société des
Producteurs de Cinéma et de Télévision (PROCIREP)
Director: Lucile Hadžihalilović
Screenplay: Lucile Hadžihalilović
Cinematography: **Gaspar Noé**, Dominique Colin
Editor: Lucile Hadžihalilović
Cast: Sandra Sammartino (Mimi), Denise Aron-Schropfer Denise (Solange),
Michel Trillot (Jean-Pierre), Delphine Allange (The Mother), Jacques Gallo
(The Mother's Lover), Françoise Pironneau (The Neighbor), Lois Da Silva (The
Neighbor), John Milko (The Guitarist), Mustafa Hadžihalilović (The Doctor)
52 minutes / Color

INSANELY CHEERFUL (1998)
Music video for the song by Bone Fiction from the album *Charlie the Symbolic
Dog* (1995)
Production companies: Le Village, BMG France, Ariola International
Producer: Charles Petit
Director: **Gaspar Noé**
Cinematography: Dominique Colin
Music: Bone Fiction
4 minutes / Color

SODOMITES (1998)
Production companies: Ce Qui Me Meut, Canal+
Director: **Gaspar Noé**
Screenplay: **Gaspar Noé**
Cinematographer: Dominique Colin
Cast: Marc Barrow, Coralie Trinh Thi, Mano Solo, Philippe Nahon, Pamella Castel
Love, Monsieur Etienne, Steve Derr, Brice Guy, Scott Rider
7 minutes / Color

GOOD BOYS USE CONDOMS (1998)
Production companies: Ce Qui Me Meut, Canal+
Director: Lucile Hadžihalilović
Cinematography: **Gaspar Noé**, Dominique Colin
Cast: Mariana Kiss (Vivienne), Timeo Kiss (Sophyen), Francesco Malcom (Young
Man)
6 minutes / Color

SEUL CONTRE TOUS [*I Stand Alone*] (1998)
Production companies: Canal+, Les Cinémas de la Zone, Love Streams Productions, PROCIREP
Producers: Lucile Hadžihalilović, **Gaspar Noé**
Director: **Gaspar Noé**
Screenplay: **Gaspar Noé**
Editors: Lucile Hadžihalilović, **Gaspar Noé**
Cinematography: Dominique Colin
Cast: Philippe Nahon (The Butcher), Blandine Lenoir (Cynthia), Frankye Pain (The Butcher's Mistress), Martine Audrain (The Butcher's Mother-in-Law), Roland Guéridon (The Butcher's Old Friend), Aïssa Djabri (Dr. Choukroun), Gérard Ortega (The Bar Owner), Alain Pierre (The Owner's Son), Zaven (The Man with Morality)
92 minutes / Color

INTOXICATION (1998)
Production company: Les Cinémas de la Zone
Director: **Gaspar Noé**
Cast: Stéphane Drouot
5 minutes / Color

JE SUIS SI MINCE [*I'm So Thin*] (1999)
Music video for a song by Arielle
Production company: Le Village
Producers: Claudie Ossard, Charles Petit
Director: **Gaspar Noé**
Music: Arielle
Cast: Arielle Burgelin
5 minutes / Color

IRRÉVERSIBLE [*Irreversible*] (2002)
Production companies: Les Cinémas de la Zone, StudioCanal
Producers: Brahim Chioua, Vincent Cassel
Director: **Gaspar Noé**
Screenplay: **Gaspar Noé**
Cinematography: Benoît Debie, **Gaspar Noé**
Editor: **Gaspar Noé**
Music: Thomas Bangalter
Cast: Monica Bellucci (Alex), Vincent Cassel (Marcus), Albert Dupontel (Pierre), Jo Prestia (Le Tenia), Fatima Adoum (Fatima), Mourad Khima (Mourad), Hellal

(Layde), Jaramillo (Concha), Michel Gondoin (Mick), Jean-Louis Costes (Fistman), Philippe Nahon (The Butcher), Stéphane Drouot (The Butcher's Friend)
97 minutes / Color

STRESS (2002)
Music video for the song by Thomas Bangalter
Production company: StudioCanal
Director: **Gaspar Noé**
Music: Thomas Bangalter
4 minutes / Color

OUTRAGE (2002)
Music video for the song by Thomas Bangalter
Production company: StudioCanal
Director: **Gaspar Noé**
Music: Thomas Bangalter
4 minutes / Color

PROTÈGE-MOI [*Protect Me*] (2004)
Production company: Les Cinémas de la Zone
Music video for the song by Placebo from the album *Once More with Feeling: Singles 1996–2004* (2004)
Director: **Gaspar Noé**
Music: Placebo
Cast: Tony Carrera, Axelle Mugler, Ian Scott, Titof
3 minutes / Color

SPOTS CONTRE LE SIDA [*TV Spots Against AIDS*] (2004)
Production companies: L'Institution National de Prévention et d'Éducation pour la Santé (INPES), Euro RSCG
Director: Robert Keller [**Gaspar Noé**]
Music: Thomas Bangalter
Cast: David Tomaszewski, Raphaël
38 seconds / Color

EVA 1 (2005)
Production company: Canal+
Producer: Renaud Le Van Kim
Director: **Gaspar Noé**
Music: Camille Saint-Saëns

Cast: Eva Herzigova
2 minutes / Color

EVA 2 (2005)
Production company: Canal+
Producer: Renaud Le Van Kim
Director: **Gaspar Noé**
Music: Goblin
Cast: Eva Herzigova
2 minutes / Color

EVA 3 (2005)
Production company: Canal+
Producer: Renaud Le Van Kim
Director: **Gaspar Noé**
Music: A Silver Mt. Zion
Cast: Eva Herzigova
2 minutes / Color

WE FUCK ALONE (2006)
Short film for the omnibus *Destricted*
Production company: OffHollywood Pictures
Producers: Neville Wakefield, Mel Agace, Andrew Hale
Director: **Gaspar Noé**
Cast: Katsuni, Manuel Ferrara, Shirin Barthel, Richard Blondel
26 minutes / Color

SIDA [*AIDS*] (2006)
Short film for the omnibus *8*
Production company: LDM Productions
Producers: Marc Oberon and Lissandra Haulica
Director: **Gaspar Noé**
Cinematography: **Gaspar Noé**
Editors: **Gaspar Noé**, Marc Boucrot
Cast: Dieudonné Ilboudo
19 minutes / Color

ENTER THE VOID (2009)
Productions companies: Fidélité Films, Wild Bunch, Les Cinémas de la Zone,
BUF Compagnie, Essential Filmproduktion, BIM Distribuzione

Producers: Brahim Chioua, Vincent Maraval, Olivier Delbosc, Marc Missonnier, Shin Yamaguchi
Director: **Gaspar Noé**
Screenplay: **Gaspar Noé**, Lucile Hadžihalilović
Cinematography: Benoît Debie
Editors: **Gaspar Noé**, Marc Boucrot, Jérôme Pesnel
Cast: Nathaniel Brown (Oscar), Paz de la Huerta (Linda), Cyril Roy (Alex), Emily Alyn Lind (Little Linda), Jesse Kuhn (Little Oscar), Olly Alexander (Victor), Ed Spear (Bruno), Masato Tanno (Mario)
161 minutes / Color

RITUAL (2011)
Short film for the omnibus *7 Days in Havana*
Production companies: Full House, Morena Films, Wild Bunch
Producers: Alvaro Longoria, Lauren Baudens, Didar Dohmeri, Gaël Nouaille, Fabien Pisani
Director: **Gaspar Noé**
Cinematographer: **Gaspar Noé**
Editors: **Gaspar Noé**, Thomas Fernandez
Cast: Othello Rensoli, Cristela Herrera, Dunia Matos
12 minutes / Color

LOVE IN MOTION (2012)
Music video for the song by SebastiAn from the album *Total* (2011)
Production company: Greyshack Films
Producer: Mike Ryan
Director: **Gaspar Noé**
Cinematography: Gaspar Noé
Choreographer: Celia Rowlson-Hall
Music: SebastiAn
Cast: Lente Tresor
4 minutes / Color

WE NO WHO U R (2013)
Music video for the song by Nick Cave & the Bad Seeds from the album *Push the Sky Away* (2013)
Production company: Bad Seed, Ltd.
Director: **Gaspar Noé**
Music: Nick Cave & the Bad Seeds
4 minutes / Color

APPLESAUCE (2013)
Music video for the song by Animal Collective from the album *Centipede Hz* (2012)
Production company: Pitchfork
Producer: R. J. Betler
Director: **Gaspar Noé**
Music: Animal Collective
Cast: Lindsay Wixson
3 minutes / Color

SHOOT (2014)
Short film for the omnibus *Short Plays*
Production company: Arte Mecánica Producciones
Producer: Daniel Guener
Director: **Gaspar Noé**
Editor: Thomas Fernandez
Cinematography: Emmanuel Trousse
4 minutes / Color

LOVE (2015)
Production companies: Les Cinémas de la Zone, Rectangle Productions, Wild Bunch, RT Features
Producer: Vincent Maraval
Director: **Gaspar Noé**
Screenplay: **Gaspar Noé**
Cinematography: Benoît Debie
Editors: **Gaspar Noé**, Denis Bedlow
Cast: Karl Glusman (Murphy), Aomi Muyock (Electra), Klara Kristin (Omi), Ugo Fox (Gaspar), Juan Saavedra (Julio), **Gaspar Noé** (Noé), Isabelle Nicou (Nora), Vincent Maraval (Lieutenant Castel), Deborah Revy (Paula), Stella Rocha (Mama), Xamira Zuloaga (Lucile), Benoît Debie (Yuyo), Omaima S. (Victoire)
135 minutes / Color

CLIMAX (2018)
Production companies: Rectangle Productions, Wild Bunch
Producers: Edouard Weil, Vincent Maraval, Richard Grandpierre
Director: **Gaspar Noé**
Screenplay: **Gaspar Noé**
Cinematography: Benoît Debie
Editors: **Gaspar Noé**, Denis Bedlow

Production design: Jean Rabasse
Music: Thomas Bangalter
Cast: Sofia Boutella (Selva), Romain Guillermic (David), Souheila Yacoub (Lou), Kiddy Smile (Daddy), Claude Gajan Maull (Emmanuelle), Giselle Palmer (Gazelle), Taylor Kastle (Taylor), Thea Carla Schøtt (Psyché), Sharleen Temple (Ivana), Léa Vlamos (Eva), Alaïa Alsafir (Alaïa), Kendall Mugler (Rocket), Lakdhar Dridi (Riley), Adrien Sissoko (Omar), Mamadou Bathily (Bart), Alou Sidibe (Kyrra), Ashley Biscette (Shirley), Mounia Nassangar (Dom), Tiphanie Au (Sila), Sarah Belala (Jennifer), Alexandre Moreau (Cyborg), Naab (Rocco), Strauss Serpent (Strauss), Vince Galliot Cumant (Tito)
96 minutes / Color

SANGRIA (2018)
Production company: Wild Bunch
Music video for the song by Thomas Bangalter
Director: **Gaspar Noé**
Music: Thomas Bangalter
3 minutes / Color

LUX ÆTERNA (2019)
Production companies: Yves Saint Laurent, Vixens, Les Cinémas de la Zone
Producers: Anthony Vaccarello, Gary Farkas, Lucile Hadžihalilović, Clément Lepoutre, Olivier Muller, **Gaspar Noé**
Director: **Gaspar Noé**
Screenplay: **Gaspar Noé**
Cinematography: Benoît Debie
Editor: Jérôme Pesnel
Production design: Samantha Benne
Cast: Charlotte Gainsbourg, Béatrice Dalle, Abbey Lee, Clara 3000, Claude-Emmanuelle Gajan-Maull, Félix Maritaud, Fred Cambier, Karl Glusman, Lola Pillu Perier, Loup Brankovic, Luka Isaac, Maxime Ruiz, Mica Argañaraz, Paul Hameline, Stefania Cristian, Tom Kan, Yannick Bono
51 minutes / Color

THIRST (2019)
Music video for the song by SebastiAn
Production company: Phantasm
Producer: Gary Farkas
Director: **Gaspar Noé**
Cinematography: Benoît Debie

Editor: Anthony Jagu
Music: SebastiAn
3 minutes / Color

THE ART OF FILMMAKING (2020)
Short film screened alongside *Lux Æterna*, drawn from archival footage
Production company: Les Cinémas de la Zone
Director: **Gaspar Noé**
Editor: Denis Bedlow
10 minutes / Color

SAINT LAURENT: SUMMER OF '21 (2020)
Promotional video for Yves Saint Laurent
Production company: Yves Saint Laurent, Phantasm
Producer: Anthony Vaccarello
Director: **Gaspar Noé**
Music: SebastiAn
Cast: Anok Yai, Antonia Przedpelski, Assa Baradji, Aylah Mae Peterson, Charlotte Rampling, Clara Deshayes, Grace Hartzel, Kim Schell, Mica Arganaraz, Miriam Sanchez, Sora Choi, Stefania Cristian
8 minutes / Color

VORTEX (2021)
Production companies: Rectangle Productions, Wild Bunch International, Les Cinémas de la Zone, KNM, Artémis Productions, Srab Films, Les Films Velvet, Kallouche Cinéma, Shelter Prod
Producers: Edouard Weil, Vincent Maraval, Brahim Chioua
Director: **Gaspar Noé**
Screenplay: **Gaspar Noé**
Cinematography: Benoît Debie
Editors: **Gaspar Noé**, Denis Bedlow
Production design: Jean Rabasse
Cast: Dario Argento (The Father), Françoise Lebrun (The Mother), Alex Lutz (Stéphane), Kylian Dheret (Kiki), Corinne Bruand (Claire)
142 minutes / Color

TRES EN LA DERIVA DEL ACTO CREATIVO [*Three in the Drift of the Creative Act*] (2022)
Production companies: Cinesur SA
Producers: Fernando Solanas, Carolina Alvarez, Victoria Solanas

Director: Fernando Solanas
Screenplay: Fernando Solanas
Editors: Nicolás Sulcic and Luca Zampini
Cinematography: Nicolás Sulcic, Fernando Solanas
Camera operators: Nicolás Sulcic, Fernando Solanas, **Gaspar Noé**, Juan Solanas, Luca Zampini
Music: Mauro Lázzaro
Cast: Luis Felipe Noé, Eduardo Pavlovsky, Fernando E. Solanas, Ângela Correa, Susy Evans, Nora Murphy, Paula Noé Murphy, **Gaspar Noé**, Martín Pavlovsky, Juan Solanas, Victoria Solanas
96 minutes / Color

SAINT LAURENT: MEN'S WINTER '23 (2023)
Three short promotional videos for Yves Saint Laurent
Production company: Yves Saint Laurent, Phantasm
Producer: Anthony Vaccarello
Director: **Gaspar Noé**
15 seconds [45 seconds total] / Color

Gaspar Noé: Interviews

Living Is a Selfish Act: An Interview with Gaspar Noé

Mitch Davis / 1998

The interview by Mitch Davis with Gaspar Noé originally appeared in *Post Script: Essays in Film and the Humanities* 21, no. 3 (Summer 2002). Reprinted by permission.

The following interview was conducted in Montreal on September 2, 1998, during the World Film Festival, where *Seul contre tous* [US title: *I Stand Alone*] had its North American premiere. For the record, I chose to transcribe this piece, complete with the odd moment of grammatical awkwardness, in the interest of conveying the flavor of conversation. Gaspar speaks excellent English, but we were talking fairly fast, and it soon became a question of the intent taking precedence over the word. Also, as this piece is now close to four years old, much has gone on in Gaspar's life since the time it transpired. He has recently completed postproduction work on his second full-length feature, *Irreversible*, starring Monica Bellucci and Vincent Cassel (last seen together in Christophe Gans's *Le pacte des loups* [*Brotherhood of the Wolf*, 2001]). *Irreversible* is slated to have its world premiere at the 2002 edition of the Cannes Film Festival.

Mitch Davis: When did you first realize that you wanted to make movies?

Gaspar Noé: When I was seventeen, I had just finished secondary school, high school. I wanted to do comic books . . . as a comic book artist, as an illustrator. But I'm not very good, so I thought I should do something else! So I went to a film school when I was seventeen and came out when I was nineteen. I enjoyed doing a first short there, as a director. And you know, once you start something—when a kid starts drawing something and the parents like him for what he has done, he becomes a painter later—well, I went to this film school, and I did this movie which was quite successful, so I said, "Well, maybe I could become a director." Then I did a second short, and then I worked a bit as assistant director. And then I started writing other scripts, and between them, there was this script of *Carne* and I shot it.

It took me a long time to shoot *Carne*. And once it was released [in 1991], it was a huge success for a movie which was just forty minutes long. It was shown at Cannes and got prizes there. It was even shown in Sundance as a feature film and was received everywhere as a feature, even if it was just forty minutes long. So I decided to do a sequel which would permit *Carne* to really become a feature-length movie. And in fact, when I tried to raise financing for the feature-length version of *Carne*, I couldn't get any money from France because they said, "Well. No. You did this short. Now we know you can be subversive. Now, why don't you calm down and do a normal movie with a normal producer and normal actors." And in fact, I was rejected by Canal+, which pretends to be the most modern-thinking TV channel. The woman in charge of feature film acquisition for this TV channel threw me like a bump. And I thought, "So that's it? Okay, lady. Don't worry. I'll be back. But let's now figure how can I do this movie without that money." And maybe because the movie was rejected, it made me really angry, and I said I really have to do it, and I just got some money from my friends in charge of the short films program of Canal+ to do the sequel as a separate short called *Seul contre tous*. And in fact, I started this movie with that money. Later on, when I was in the middle of the shooting, I really ran out of money and was full of debts. And Agnès B., who had seen *Carne* and was a big fan of the movie, she helped me. She said, "Do you need money to finish the movie?" I said, "Yeah, of course." And she gave me money. So I finished the shooting.

And just after that, *Carne* was released in Japan. I had sold them the movie, and with the small money I got from that sale, I thought I could pay to begin the editing. It took me a long time to do this movie. It took me four years. In between, I started another movie as a producer, directed by my girlfriend [Lucile Hadžihalilović], which was called *La bouche de Jean Pierre* [aka *Parental Guidance*, 1996], and almost all the money I had for my movie went on hers. So, it was a big headache. Maybe there have been some very bad experiences, but that was good for the movie. Now that the movie is finished, I think I was so angry, I was so lacking in money that you can see it on the screen that I really identified in some moments with the butcher. You know, looking for money and thinking of killing people. But I know my weapon is not a gun as it is for him. My weapon is just a movie. But you know, there are some people I really hate in this business, and with this movie, I can tell them, "Get it up your ass."

MD: So, is that it? Do you see filmmaking as a form of terrorism? Filmmaking literally as a weapon?

GN: It's just a very luxurious and efficient way of expressing yourself. In life, some people just know that they have the power of their money. They can sign checks, contracts, and things like that. And they think they are bright just because they can sign these things because someone gave them the possibility to have this economic power over you. And they behave as censors. In France now, there's no problem with official censorship. Once your movie is finished, you always are R-rated. My movie is just R-rated in France. But when you meet French producers with a script like mine, they behave like the most fragile chickens in the world. They just tell you, "Oh, no. You should cut this. You should cut that." And at the end, you have been totally censored on the synopsis and then on the script.

MD: So, it all happens at the treatment stage.

GN: Yes, and they try to push you to rewrite the script as long as it doesn't look like a prime-time movie. There are some movies I love, like *Eraserhead* [1977], like *Angst* [Austria, 1983], and I say, "Well, those movies, I don't care how long it took them to produce them, but . . ."

MD: Yes, *Eraserhead* took something like eight years!

GN: And it's his best movie, you know? And Buñuel, maybe he did *An Andalusian Dog* [1929] and then *The Golden Age* [1930], and he didn't do any other movies. . . . No, he did this documentary *Land without Bread* [1932], but then for ten years he didn't do any movies. I say, "Well, if I had to go through a tunnel ten years without making any movies like Buñuel, I don't mind, as long as I did one good movie.

MD: And make it pure.

GN: Yes. Make a movie that you can be proud of. Like Stanley Kubrick. After doing *2001* [1968], he could die proud of himself. He had done a huge masterpiece.

MD: Going back to *Carne*, it played the festival circuit, sold in Japan. . . . What did it cost, and did it ever make its financing back?

GN: The real cost—no one was paid on *Carne*—the real cost was like sixty thousand dollars.

MD: For 35mm scope?

GN: In the end, it was, but it was shot in 16mm scope because I didn't have the money to shoot on 35mm scope. And even this one, *Seul contre tous*, was shot on 16mm scope. In fact, you just shoot with a normal camera—a 16mm camera—and you put an anamorphic lens in front of the normal lens. And you have to do the focus twice, but in the end, you have an anamorphic 16mm that you blow up to anamorphic 35mm, and then you have a CinemaScope movie. And later, when you transfer it to video, and you show it on TV, or you show it on video, people think it is a 35mm movie. When people are switching channels, they think this is a big-budget movie because, you know, scope movies shown on TV letterboxed are always the big-budget movies.

MD: The grandeur gives it a supposed legitimacy.

GN: Yes. People sometimes, they just stop because they see this scope movie. They say, "Oh, this is a real movie, this is not a TV movie."

MD: When you blow up from 16 scope to 35 scope, is it considerably more expensive or more complicated than just doing a flat 16 to 35 blowup?

GN: Yeah, it is. For negative editing reasons. The negative has to be done on an A and B [roll] so you don't see the cuts, the splices on the frameline.

MD: The fact that you sold it to video anywhere is downright bizarre because there's usually no real market for short films, especially ones with such unwieldy length. When it's forty minutes, it's in that netherland between being a short and a feature. How did you promote it to actually get it sold?

GN: In fact, *Carne* was a big critical success and was also like a big festival success. It was in every festival in the world. But then when we had to sell it, either it was too violent, or it was just a short, and so it couldn't get onto the video market because it was not a feature . . . it was not *Henry: Portrait of a Serial Killer* [1990], it was not *Tetsuo* [Japan, 1988]. I'm good friends with Tsukamoto—*Tetsuo* was a big hit also because it was a feature.

MD: It's so strange how that works. If you're three minutes over an hour, you're a feature. Like *Nekromantik* [West Germany, 1987]. But if you're clocking at forty, then you're just a short.

GN: Yes. And that's why I started this movie [*Seul contre tous*], because I saw that if I could add thirty minutes to *Carne*, it would become a feature, and then I could release it in a much more normal way. But in fact, when I started doing the sequel, I got excited during the shooting, and I wanted to reshoot scenes and add scenes, and I said, "Sometimes you have the chance to do one movie, make it the best you can, put everything in it," so I added scenes every time. Every time I would shoot a scene, I would add scenes, and at the end, the sequel was ninety minutes long and not thirty as it was supposed to be. I said, "Well, I should just add an opening scene like in *Angst*, which would explain what happened in *Carne*, and I have a totally new movie!" And now, no one cares about *Carne*. This is the movie.

MD: You used ninety percent the same cast as *Carne*—was it difficult to get those people back after so long?

GN: No, no. I had some problems. Not to get the people back, but because when you start a movie . . . when it's a short, people don't care . . . but when it's a feature, they want money. They think you are getting into the industry when, in fact, I had much less money to do this one then I had to do *Carne*. But the butcher [Phillipe Nahon] was great during the whole movie. During the whole picture, he was really involved. He didn't care about if he would be paid or not; he really wanted to do the movie as much I wanted to do it.

MD: Was he a professional actor? Where did you find him?

GN: Of course, but because of his age . . . you know, you can become a star when you're thirty or forty, but he's like fifty, and for reasons that I cannot understand, he didn't become a star when he was forty or thirty. Maybe he didn't have enough money to promote himself, or maybe he got into some fights with people in the past, I don't know. But he's a great, great guy. He's the most lovely guy in the world and even if he's scary in the movie, he's the sweetest father that you can think of. I really enjoy working with him. I proposed to him not to . . . he accepted not to read the script . . . he just read the synopsis of the movie—and he would come every day. If I said, "You have to be shooting tomorrow at eight in the morning," he would be there at seven-thirty, you know, waiting for us with the coffee ready. He was really amused by the fact that he would kind of improvise every single scene during the shooting. That's why people look natural [in the film] too, because I said, "Well, I don't want to give any lines to anybody because otherwise, they come out like bricks from their mouths. The important thing is the meaning of the scene, not the words you use, and I prefer that you find your own words to express the scene."

MD: That approach makes sense here because you had the relative freedom of knowing that you would add voiceover for so much of the film, so during the shoot, you could really zero in on spur-of-the-moment emotions and body language. The structure of the film really lends itself to this sort of approach.

GN: In fact, there was much more voiceover in the original text I wrote because I thought that maybe one sentence out of four that he would read wouldn't sound great. I added so I could cut and still have this oppressive voiceover all the time. So I said, "Well, how much?"—I have like sixty minutes of voiceover that I can use in the movie. I could have had two hours of voiceover, but in the end, they're just sixty minutes long. I think if you really count them, in over ninety minutes of movie, you have sixty minutes of voiceover. And you know, the actor was a bit scared of the voiceover. He said, "People are going to kill me!" I said, "Yeah, they'll kill you, but they'll kill me first so you can run!"

MD: What was Nahon's background before working with you?

GN: He worked on a [Jean-Pierre] Melville movie called *Le doulos* [*The Finger Man*, 1961]. He was very young, he was twenty-five years old, I think.

MD: Has he ever had any major exposure?

GN: No, no, no. He's had small parts in many different movies, including *La haine* [Hate, 1995].

MD: So he's Joe Spinell?

GN: [*Laughs*] But now he's coming out. Since this movie, he is very well respected amongst young directors and everyone. He came a bit late in his own career but he's very glad that now he's recognized.

MD: Were there any things in the script that he just didn't want to do?

GN: No . . . no.

MD: Let's talk about the intertitles. Both films feature moments where you throw text across the screen that directly addresses the audience in the first person. Would it be fair to think that with these words, you're addressing the audience directly—as yourself—or are you just keeping the film in tone with its protagonist?

GN: You have "death opens no door," and "survival is a genetic law," and "man is a moral being." That's my point of view, when you see the title cards, that's my own point of view. When I write in the movie, "death opens no door," I really think it. I think it's funny because people always talk about astral projections and things like that and everybody wants to lie to himself, pretending that there's something else besides only the normal life you're living in. Because sometimes life is so heavy and they prefer . . . even myself . . . but I think that it's much brighter just to assume that you're an animal in the jungle and you have to survive.

MD: Both films, *Carne* and *Seul contre tous*, between all the intertitles and voiceover play very much like manifestos. Is there any one thing that you'd like the audience to be thinking when they leave the theater?

GN: I don't know. I think you direct a movie just to express your own self. There are some things . . . some girls tell me I'm a sex maniac, or people I don't know think that I'm a fascist, but I don't feel like one. I really think I'm not communist either, because I don't belong to any political group. But maybe I should. I am left-wing. I am a humanist. But because I was attacked as a fascist when I was showing *Carne* . . .

MD: You were attacked as a fascist?

GN: Yeah, because some people said, "Well, why did this guy stab this Arab?" And I said, "Well, because workers in France are Arabs." They said, "Well, because if you show a man stabbing an Arab in France, it's because you're a fascist, you belong to the National Front," and they started talking about morals. That if you direct a movie, you have to behave morally, and this is it. It was too much for me. I said, "Well, if you want to talk about morals, in the next movie, we'll talk about morals." If you just open your dictionary, "morality" is the sense that separates good from evil. And if you really want to see what evil is, it just says that "evil is the opposite of good." And if you ask, "Then what is good?" it says that it's the opposite of evil. You can put whatever you want inside evil and good in morality. I think in life, people know what they want. They want to survive; they want to have a family. They want to procreate because it's in the genetic law. And in this case [*Seul contre tous*], you have this man who has problems feeding himself—maybe he's too animalistic to behave in a clever way—so he doesn't find a clever way to survive and fulfill his own needs, and at the end of the movie, well, at least there's the one need he can fulfill. It's his need of love . . . in a very twisted way. There is an ending because you identify with the character, and when he comes to this end—not you, because you're very open-minded—but a lot of people are totally fucked up by the end of the movie. Because they say, "It's like a happy end, but it shouldn't be," and "Where did you bring us to?!"

MD: Well, what's your take on incest? Do you actually feel that for some people in certain situations, it could actually make family relationships better?

GN: I think there can be incestuous love. In most cases, I don't know how much. I cannot say if it's ninety-nine percent or eighty percent, but the problem with incestuous relationships is that they often come from frustration. And from need of power. Sometimes, people who feel powerless, they come to bother their own kids, or they come to bother children. In pedophilia, in general, there is this really disturbing thing, which is like the abuse of your power. In the most disturbing way. But I think that people can fall in love with someone who is not of their own generation. In this case, well, this man, the character of my movie, I'm not sure. Because I think the character of my movie is not clever enough. He is too stupid. And when he pretends that he is in love with his daughter, in fact, he just wants to love someone to survive. And the only person that he can pretend to love is his own daughter. The relationship that he can have with her is going to be a really cheap thing, and he pretends that it is going to be a big love. But I don't think it is going to be a big love. Because of the circumstances, it is going to be like a very pathetic love.

MD: How do you feel about the people who say that if you make a film about a pedophile, you're a pedophile, a Nazi, you're a Nazi, a rapist, you're a rapist—unless you openly condemn the act in the narrative, which can usually be stupid? What do you say to people who identify you that wholly with a movie that you make?

GN: Most people feel aggressed by anything that is different from them. I think that in the American film industry—or even in the European cinema—movies are made not to disturb any kind of class or any kind of minority. And in fact, this is an aggressive movie but it's not aggressive towards any particular minority. It's aggressive to the whole world. And that's why the movie in French is called *Seul contre tous*. It means "alone against the world." And in fact, it was translated as *I Stand Alone* because it's a much more common expression in English. In French, you say, "I'm alone against the world," and that means, "I hate everybody and everybody's against me."

MD: You know, I wanted to ask you about horsemeat. Up until I saw *Carne*, I didn't realize that it was illegal in most of the world except France. In that film, when it explains this, it's implied that this is an almost demeaning thing. Is there anything you'd like to say about that?

GN: It's because when I shot *Carne*, I wanted the character to be a butcher, and at the last minute, I said, "Well, this thing in France, that people eat horses"—and

I ate horsemeat too—but it's banned in the rest of the world. It's like these things are accepted here, and they're forbidden somewhere else, and it was funny because this butcher has incestuous thoughts or very passionate feelings about his daughter, if you show him as a horsemeat butcher, he will look much more vicious. And much more male at the same time because horsemeat is the most male meat you can think of. That's why workers in France like horsemeat because it's like a male thing that makes you strong. Cow meat is a much more female meat.

MD: Because of its tenderness?

GN: Yes, it's a much more passive meat.

MD: Was it difficult to get permission to shoot the slaughterhouse footage?

GN: I shot it myself. It was very hard. I had this assistant who was a girl who was twenty, we would call nineteen slaughterhouses, and they would all refuse us to shoot there. The girl who was assistant director, she called the twentieth and said [*putting on a mock-feminine voice*], "We're doing this documentary for a film school; it's the story of this young horse, he gets older and he gets killed, and we want some soft images of this horse getting killed, we won't show the. . . ." And the guy, I think he got excited by the voice of the young girl, and he said, "Okay, come tomorrow, seven in the morning!"

MD: And you shot *La sang des bêtes* [*Blood of the Beasts*, 1949]!

GN: Yeah! And he was there the next day when we came with the camera, and he said, "Where's the girl? Where's the girl I talked to??" [*Bursting into laughter*] And finally, he allowed us to shoot, but we were not supposed to shoot such gory scenes. I think that there was a kind of note between all the slaughterhouses in France that they should never accept any shooting, which this man betrayed. And he asked, "Please do not put my name on your credits." And then we told him, "But don't worry, this movie, I don't even know if we're going to finish it or if it's going to be shown anywhere."

MD: I want to ask you about your technical style—the camera cutting and sound. Not to draw French New Wave connections, but your style is very revisionist. I was wondering, seeing *Seul contre tous* as an extension of *Carne*—the intertitles, pixelated zooms, and voice-over are congruent to the first, but when you make another, altogether different movie, will you use these devices again?

GN: I wanted to keep the same aesthetic. The next project I have will have nothing to do with the subject or the style. I'm going to change totally the aesthetics of the movie. Maybe in a certain movie, I could come back to the title cards and these weird effects, but for the moment, I'm going to go for another thing. I was just thinking that if one day both movies were to be shown together on a tape, it would be better if they had the same ratio and the same kind of effects and everything. It could be like the direct sequel.

MD: Which countries have bought the film so far?

GN: For the moment, I have this sales agent who's going to take care of it, but I received proposals from England, Scandinavia, Japan, and the USA.

MD: England's going to be a rough one for this film.

GN: But they can show it as long as they don't show it in normal theaters. They can show it in clubs where you have a membership card and also at the NFT or the Institute of Contemporary Arts. They can show it as long as it belongs to the state. Otherwise, if it's at a theater owned by someone who doesn't work for the state, they could be attacked for obscenity. It's funny; the only people who can really exploit the movie theatrically are the government! So I received a proposal from the ICA, from the NFT. And there are some theaters in Edinburgh that could show it too because they are associative. So you don't have to go through censorship because it is like a kind of museum and you can show everything. I don't think I could release it with this editing on video. I think in England, I'll go for a scandal; if they ban the movie, I'll go to every single newspaper and say, "You should be ashamed of your country; you are retarded compared to the rest of Europe." [*Laughs*]

MD: Both films in places have a strange sense of patriotism. In general, do you love France?

GN: When I thought of the movie, it was during a very right-wing period, run by [Charles] Pasqua as the Ministry of Interior [Security], and there were all these xenophobic laws that were voted. It was just before the socialists came back to power. The state had become so racist that you could start some kind of racism against France. Because the government was voting racist laws, you could become anti-French. I think that the image of France that is given by this movie is very bleak. The French movies that are promoted abroad are the ones that give a trendy, cultural, petit-bourgeois, upper-class image of France, but it's true that people who are poor in France are the same in New York or in India. People who are poor, they suffer a lot. And people drink a lot, and people take a lot of downers, and there's a lot of unemployment.

MD: But are people less prone to helping each other out in France? In general, is it a much colder atmosphere on a social level? How are people towards their neighbors when they need help?

GN: I think British people, for example, can handle better their own poorness. The image of their poorness. But in France, people don't handle it very well. Either you are normal or . . . if you are poor, you better not show it. Movies dealing with social subjects in France become very paternalist. They want to teach lessons. They don't show poorness like a normal situation. I think in my movie, at one point, I didn't identify with the character in many aspects but considering his poorness, I saw that being poor is a normal thing. I don't think this guy is less of a person because he is poor than if he had one million dollars in his account. He would be exactly the same. For me, in my level of perception, both of them are humans, and they deserve the same respect. But in France, like in most countries, the respect you receive also depends on your class. Sometimes, I have better relationships with my barber then with people who are into cinema from an upper class. I belong to the petit bourgeoisie somehow because of my parents. I'm not from a lower social level, but I think I relate more to lower levels then to people who've got money. And France is a very paternalistic society where people have to be introduced. It's funny . . . in North America, someone who doesn't know anybody, he can go . . . you can be respected for your own identity. It pushes your personality to become stronger. In France, it's just . . . if you're the son of someone, you can be sure that you will have a good life. Because you're the son of this guy or the daughter of that guy you will be introduced to this person who will give you a job even if you're totally incompetent. America, in some ways, is much more of a democracy then France. It is, and it's not. The power that a president has in France is like the power of a king. In America, you know that his power is limited. Maybe because there used to be a king for centuries, and now they're still behaving like they need a king. In England, they need a king. In Spain, they need a king. In France, there is no more king. But they consider the president as if he was a king.

MD: How would you describe the political climate of French youth right now?

GN: It's just another liberal democracy. But it pretends to be a calm left. Not an angry left.

MD: How do *Carne* and *Seul contre tous* reflect the current reality of the French working class?

GN: They don't really, because he doesn't work. He is unemployed. He would like to belong to the working class. [*Laughs*] He is like a lumpen. He is a person who belonged to the working class who became a lumpen. It's funny because the movie was shown in Sarajevo and it got the main prize . . . almost everyone identified with this character! They all went through this thing of not having money to feed themselves. There was no more food in Sarajevo during the war, and they all had guns with a number of bullets they could use. So it's funny that it was a big hit. Someone said, "I've been through that, I've already felt like the butcher for *years*." I think when you are really in deep shit, you can come to have these racist ideas or any kind of "against the other" ideas. You know, anything that's not you. I'm sure if you were a Bosnian during the war, you would wish to kill Serbs. Just because it is the opposite of you and because they're aggressors. And also, it happens to me when I get attacked. I almost added a title card in the movie, which says, "VENGEANCE IS A HUMAN RIGHT." I'm very much into vengeance, in the way that if someone attacks you, you have to attack him twice if you want to survive.

MD: Then, how do you feel about capital punishment? I mean, I don't trust any government enough to give them the right to kill. If anything, it should be left to the individuals involved, if at all. But in extreme cases, how do you feel about death for a person who can only live his life hurting others, for someone who has proven this again and again?

GN: I met this guy in France who is a specialist on serial killers, and he told me that at the beginning, he was against the death penalty, but he said that, "Since I've met some serial killers for interviews, I'm really for the death penalty because these guys really enjoyed killing and killing again." I never really thought about it, but I know that sometimes, in my own life, I really felt like killing people. Because if someone disturbs you . . . they didn't kill you, but you really feel like, "I wish this guy was dead" . . . you know that you will not kill him yourself, but if he gets struck by a truck or by a train, you would really be happy. The good thing about forbidding the death penalty is that society won't be able to kill people who are not guilty, but at the same time, there are some people that are just such a mental mess that, you know, they will never get out of their obsessions, and they can keep them forever. And if among their obsessions there is one that says they're not scared of killing other people . . . I know that in my own personal life, if someone, for example . . . if I had a kid, and someone had touched my kid like in *Carne*, I am sure that if I had a gun or a knife, I would go and stab the person who I supposed touched my kid.

MD: Rather than call the police?

GN: Oh yeah, yeah. I am not a police fan at all. It's not that I dislike the police, but I would never go to the police for anything. It's just that I prefer not . . . not calling them. And sometimes, even when . . . you know . . . your neighbors, for any reason they want to call the police . . . the only reason I would call the police is if someone is getting aggressed in the street and I'm behind a window. But for myself, I would have to take some kind of revenge if my girlfriend had been aggressed, my mother had been aggressed, or my kids had been aggressed. I think I would go for personal revenge. I talked about this with my father. He's much more into forgetting and forgiving, but I'm much more into revenge.

MD: Also, when you bring the government in, it's almost an act of submission. You're giving them even more power. You're giving them that power to decide if what this person did was really all that bad after all and what form of punishment it calls for.

GN: And it usually gets lost because your anger gets lost over time. If you sue somebody, it takes two years, three years, and your anger just gets lost in between. And even if you win or lose the trial, it takes such a long time. If you want to really take a personal revenge, you'd better do it by yourself and at the right time.

MD: Would you consider yourself to be a pacifist?

GN: I prefer periods of peace and love. Societies have progressed much more during times of peace than during wars. But war, sometimes you have to go for it, you know? For example, if you're a Bosnian and suddenly you get attacked by the Serbs, there's just one way of getting rid of your opponents. It's taking revenge and trying to fight as hard as you can. If the Nazis have been destroyed, it's because America got into the war. They went for it, and they got into the fight. I think that wars will never stop, it's just that there are sides. You have to choose your side. And there are more progressive sides.

MD: Is there a particular country where *Seul contre tous* has had bigger success then others?

GN: I think if there is one country where the movie had more problems than in other countries, it was in Belgium because they've had these problems, so I think they were a bit shocked because the whole country decided that they wanted to fight against pedophilia and in fact, my movie is not propedophiliac at all, it's just about the pathetic story of a man that only finds the solution to survive. It doesn't rave about him, it doesn't condemn him either, it just shows how this guy comes to this, but because of the general mood in Belgium now, the movie had some very good responses but very bad responses, too. It was shown at the Cinematheque in Belgium, and it was a big scandal there. I was surprised. People called the Cinematheque and said that they would never go there again. It's weird, but I can understand. Public enemy number one, this Mark Detroux, he could just run away from prison and get caught by a civilian. It was too much!

MD: It was also the direct ties to the government with this case that must have made everyone very uncomfortable.

GN: And also, there was another case because they found there were some other people selling tapes, porno tapes with kids like two months later, and it was too much, so now they're.... [*Laughs*]

MD: Looking at *Carne* and *Seul contre tous*, was there any one incident in your life that inspired you to do the story, let alone to do it twice?

GN: Maybe it was the fact of being rejected. I felt attacked because people rejected me. They didn't say, "We can give you money to do something else if you want," they just said, "No, this movie cannot be done." And I said, "Okay, so I'll do it!" Well, *Carne* was inspired by *The Honeymoon Killers* [1970], and this one was more inspired by *Angst*. It's just like movies that you want to do. Because there are other movies that you liked before, and you want to do better than the original. I don't know if I did better than the originals, but I knew which originals I liked.

Gaspar Noé: A Playful Mise-en-scène

Philippe Rouyer / 1998

From *Positif,* March 1999. Reprinted by permission. Translated by Geoffrey Lokke.

Positif: What did you do before you moved behind the camera?

Gaspar Noé: I was born in 1963 in Buenos Aires. When I was twelve, my parents had to leave Argentina for political reasons, so we settled in France. That's where I went to school. When I was seventeen, I joined the École Louis-Lumière; I graduated after two years, but I stayed on for a third to finish work on my thesis film, *Tintarella di luna* (1985). When I watch it now, I find the film a little naïve in terms of its staging. I'd wanted to follow a storyboard, but I had no idea how to draw perspective. So it only had flat and frontal images, and the film clearly suffers for it—I won't ever storyboard again. But the film did really well on the festival circuit, and it made me want to keep going. I then outlined several projects, including an early version of *Carne*, while I took a few philosophy courses at the Tolbiac Center. In 1986, I made *Pulpe amère*, my second short, thanks to a friend who'd provided me with a 16mm camera, some abandoned film stock, and a photo studio with a bedroom set up in it. I shot the film in one day, but it took me six months to edit. That's when I discovered the pleasures of intertitles and narration. There was no dialogue, just an uninterrupted voiceover of a man trying to justify his behavior as he raped his maid. The psychopathology of this character has a lot in common with the butcher in *Carne*.

P: Where did you get the idea for *Carne*?

GN: The title, borrowed from an Argentinian erotic film, comes from the Spanish word *carne*, which means both "meat" and "flesh." At first, I'd wanted to make a film about a butcher whose sexuality is affected by what he reads in the newspaper. It would've had the same comic distance as *The Honeymoon Killers*. There are other films about seemingly unconnected events that I love, like *From the Life of the Marionettes*, but I didn't want my film to feel so cold. For reference, I drew upon a couple of magazines I was into: *Harakiri*, for its corrosive humor, and *Détective*, which details the cruelty of the crimes but also tries to comprehend the psychology of the killers.

P: How did you finance a "medium-length" film?

GN: I self-produced it through Les Cinémas de la Zone, the company I started in 1986 with Lucile Hadžihalilović. We both hate being producers, but it's the only way we've managed get some of our weirder projects made. For *Carne*, which was first conceived as a twenty-minute short, only Canal+ would offer me an advance (about thirty thousand francs). It was barely anything, really, but it was enough to buy some film stock, start casting, and do some location scouting. The shooting itself didn't take long, but more than two years passed from the moment I shot the first scenes, and when it was screened at Cannes in '91. I had to stop shooting whenever I ran out of money to buy more film or pay my bills at the lab. In order to survive, I took jobs as an assistant on music videos and commercials, but all my thoughts remained with the film, how I could finish it, how to pay off my debts. After seeing some of the early footage, Canal+ gave me a little more money, and I also got a small grant from the CNC. So, the film slowly expanded over time. It runs forty minutes, but remains pretty close to the original script.

P: Did *Carne* winning so many awards inspire you to make a sequel?

GN: Yes, I think so. I thought that after winning all these awards, people would be eager to help me make a sequel, a second midlength film that, screened alongside *Carne*, would approximate the length of a feature. So, I made the rounds of television channels and other companies. But no one wanted to get involved. My film didn't seem very "prime time," and the topic frightened people who would've preferred to have me shoot a thriller or some other genre film. Despite all the awards I got for *Carne*, every door was closed on me one after the other. These days, finance people generally make their decisions based on the script and the cast without seeing the director's short films. To convince them, it's probably better to be a screenwriter or an actor—to have real contacts in the industry—and line up some big names on the poster than to be a good director of shorts. Once again, only Alain de Greef and the people in charge of short programming at Canal+ offered me an advance for a new short film. When I started down this path, I didn't know if I'd be able to make it to the end. I took the risk that the film would only exist in fragments, like some unrealized films by Orson Welles. But I figured that once the machine was up and running, maybe people would come to help me along the way. Then Agnès B. made a huge contribution out of nowhere just as the production had come to a halt. She had apparently loved *Carne* and had heard about everything I was going through.

P: So these financial problems explain the seven years between the two films?

GN: More or less. After *Carne*, I wrote the sequel and a script for another experimental film. I then shot the first part of *Seul contre tous* in 1994, but it was just a foot in the door, a way of forcing me to come back to it later. In the meantime, Lucile wrote the screenplay for *La bouche de Jean-Pierre* and had found some money to get it made. Les Cinémas de la Zone couldn't handle two projects at once, so we decided to start with Lucile's film, which I shot, produced, and edited. Only after I finished *La bouche de Jean-Pierre* did I get back to my film. So it gestated for about four years, but I only worked on it for two and a half.

P: How did these constraints shape how the project evolved?

GN: If I only was allowed to operate on the fringes, then at least I could be formally extreme. If all of the films came out through Les Cinémas de la Zone, at least I'd be satisfied on that level. I mean, if you don't make the movies you want to make when you're young, then you'll never make them. I got along with my actor, Philippe Nahon, and he wanted to keep going. So we just went for it. But making *Seul contre tous* was way more complicated than making *Carne*. I had to organize the production around my personal income, as well as the availability of locations, people on the crew. Anytime someone got offered a better-paid gig, they'd take it. When Philippe had another project or was on tour with a play, I had to wait. In terms of the locations, it was the same, I had to be flexible. Since I couldn't rent them at full price, I could only use them under special conditions. There were places I could only enter after hours. Other times, I had to deal with their clientele. At some of the bars, the situation escalated because real people, a little drunk and overexcited by the presence of the camera, wanted to participate—but on their terms. The simplest thing actually was to just give them a tiny role, hoping they would play ball and not insist on staring directly into the camera. A few times, though, the crew had to pack up in a rush to avoid a fight. . . . Anyways, because of my lack of resources, locations would often fall through at the last moment. I'd find myself with a crew and equipment at my disposal but no set. So, I had to improvise new scenes on the fly. Like the scene between the butcher and the junkie in the hotel. I'd originally imagined it in an apartment that one of my assistants had secured. The film changed in response to all these accidents. Ultimately, it got its body and texture from integrating very structured narration with aspects caught on the fly that are almost documentary in nature. The cast includes both professionals and amateurs.

P: Where did you find these people?

GN: In the street, bars, from friends of friends. They are part of everyday life in Paris. Actors generally belong to a particular social class; they are often petite bourgeoisie, pretty girls, or people who like to show off. But I also found myself with sad, struggling people, the kind you only see in documentaries. They were very happy to be in the film and didn't pose for the camera. If you ask a professional actor to play an alcoholic at a bar, he'll probably overact. If you take someone who has never been in a film, they'll speak normally. Over three or four takes, there'd always be a moment when he or she suddenly got used to the camera. On the other hand, for an important role like the butcher, it's in your interest to hire someone who can handle it. I needed someone whose job—vocation—is to cry in the arms of his daughter. Otherwise I wouldn't have captured what Philippe Nahon gave me, as he was clearly self-assured and could give himself over to that scene.

P: Was all of the dialogue improvised?

GN: I'd written some dialogue, but none of it is left in the film. Before filming, only Philippe Nahon had access to the script. Subsequently, I would read him his lines in the morning, or I'd just describe the action to him, letting him bring in his own words. With the other actors, professional or not, I was the same. And to keep it feeling alive, after shooting ten or so takes, I'd ask them for new variations, to change at least one word each time. So I ended up with a lot of material. But now I'm so used to improvising on set that even if I had a real producer and a real budget, I'd have trouble sticking to a script.

P: Was the voiceover written beforehand?

GN: Yes, but I had only written part of it before shooting. I wrote everything else after I was done editing, over two or three days, while I was sorting out some money problems. My guiding principle was to overlay with voiceover all the moments of silence, most of which I had timed meticulously. I'd also recorded additional voiceover to overdub lines that Philippe had stumbled over, as well as other silences and the sounds of his breathing. That's what gives the film its frenetic flow. In general, I am all for screening movies in their original language with subtitles, but here, I think a foreign viewer would lose a lot if he had to read the subtitles. The text imposes distance, but the voiceover generates a sense of proximity with the butcher. Even if the viewer condemns his views, he is forced to share in his emotions throughout and to follow him through his most terrifying excesses.

P: During the screening of *Seul contre tous* at Cannes, the butcher's incessant voiceover led a few critics to cite Céline. Was he a point of reference for you?

GN: Yes, I've been told a lot about *Journey to the End of the Night*. I still haven't read it. The writers I idolize most are Dostoevsky and Diderot. Diderot is very clearly having fun with his narration, and I'd love one day to make a film as dazzling in form as *Jacques the Fatalist*. Like Diderot, I get inspired sitting in bars during cocktail hour. Apart from that, I had two conscious cinematic influences: *Straw Dogs* for the intensity of the violence and *Angst* [an Austrian film distributed in France on video under the title *Schizophrenia*], whose pervasive, hypnotic voiceover forces you to feel a kind of intimacy with the killer. Both of these films set the bar very high in terms of audience resistance, and I wanted to do the same. With *Carne*, there was a lot of violence, but it was of a different nature. *Carne* was more of a camp, "videophile" film, with its silly Catholic characters and the masked wrestler. The world of *Seul contre tous* is much more naturalistic. Everyone has experienced depression at least once in their life, and some of the butcher's remarks repeat what we all say to ourselves in those moments. Everything depends on the spectator's state of mind at the time of the screening: some people came out laughing; at other screenings, the film induced a depressive atmosphere clearly marked by buried anxieties. The humor in *Seul contre tous* is not always clear to people. In a Machiavellian way, the film plunges the butcher into despair, while the mise-en-scène remains, on the other hand, sort of playful. It's a bit like *The Young and the Damned*, which is my favorite comedy. Buñuel pushes cruelty so far that one has to laugh. There's a real joy in breaking the rules. Strictures are found everywhere in life, but few people try to break past them, or if they do, they try to do it in too polite a way. For me, I wanted to focus on a disturbed character without telegraphing an explicit moral point of view. Which is fairly unusual, I think. Most filmmakers pose the notions of "good" and "evil" and excuse themselves morally before they've even presented their subject or their characters.

P: Wasn't the film almost called *Morale* [*Morality*]?

GN: Yes, because the question of morality, mentioned in the opening sequence, is at the heart of the film. When something is said to be amoral or immoral, it's often in relation to an official morality. According to a dictionary I read once, morality is a science that's meant to distinguish good from evil. But what is good, what is evil? There are plenty of times when the distinction is not so clear. It's up to each person to find their own way, to find their own morality. Throughout the film, the butcher acts by following his instinct and seeks out moral justifications. He always feels the need to validate his instincts through his intellect. While looking for a title, I'd also thought about using *Rance* [*Rancid*]. It's an anagram of *Carne*, and it corresponded well to the atmosphere and the world in which the butcher finds himself. France has changed a lot in recent years, but five years ago, when all the anti-immigration laws were passed, it was suffocating. If I'd kept this title, I would have placed a French logo in the credits to allow the association of ideas. I even thought of naming my film *Pénis* or *Le pénis* in reference to the scene where the butcher compares himself to a cock. *Le pénis* has a virile element but it's also a piece of flesh disconnected from the rest of the body. By phonetic association, the title would have also referred to the National Front and some of the butcher's more paranoid tendencies. Xenophobia, however, is just one of his character traits; he is, above all, a hater of whatever is not him, whether it is the rich, the old, women, homosexuals, foreigners, etc. Although it sounds a bit like a western, in the end *Seul contre tous* was the title that most closely resembles the final film.

P: In addition to the voiceover, you also took control of all of *Carne*'s formal elements: scope, color, the intertitles . . .

GN: I prefer scope to all other formats. It corresponds to human vision better than 1.66. In terms of money, shooting with 16mm scope is not very expensive because the biggest costs have to do with printing, and only the best takes are retained. But onscreen, it immediately gives the impression of being an expensive film; it looks like *cinema*, whereas with my subject and the social environment the characters come out of, one could've expected a TV movie treatment. Also, scope allows me to underscore how stifling the enclosures that surround the butcher are. He's affected by his surroundings: he finds himself crushed against different materials, the walls, the meat. . . . At the same time, when I was considering the formal aspects of *Carne*, I wanted to radicalize them. I was interested in black and white (because of *The Honeymoon Killers*), but I went with color in the end. I decided to have fun with it by removing the greens and blues from the sets and costumes in favor of yellows and reds. After talking with Dominique Colin, my director of photography, we decided we wouldn't subject the image to any further treatment. Although, we added a little gold to the color grading and printed it on high-contrast film so we could get those purplish hues reminiscent of *Détective*'s monochrome pages. Yellow and red are colors associated with fascism, communism—forms of violent politics. By comparison, in *Seul contre tous*, I favored gray, brown, and other dull colors that felt more in line with the misery of the story. To emphasize the feeling of claustrophobia, we only shot on location and when it was overcast, without framing the sky, except for the last scene. We kept the interiors as dark as possible, we avoided using projectors and the usual electrical setup you find on movie sets. We also replaced the sixty-watt bulbs that were already in place at the sets with supercharged bulbs—two hundred watts. So, the direction of light was very realistic. The intertitles are divided into two categories: those that are purely informative and have no other function than to make a completely contrived story feel more real, and those that offer some kind of commentary. "Death opens no door" is one example. It sums up the content of the scene but is also meant to shock the viewer. My love for intertitles comes out of my passion for comics. I discovered cinema at the age of three with *Jason and the Argonauts* before seeing *2001: A Space Odyssey* at age six (which I still watch at least once a year). But when I was a kid, I filled my life with comic books. For a time, I thought about making it my profession. I finally chose to be a filmmaker, but I kept a keen interest in lettering, which is reflected in the choice of typefaces for the titles and credits.

P: Could you tell us about sequences that are accompanied by the sound of an explosion or a cymbal strike?

GN: The cymbal strikes accompany black screens, and the "detonations" underscore a number of editing effects. I put together some of these effects using a second camera and then went through the footage frame by frame. The others came together in postproduction, doing a kind of zoom down into the image. Originally, I had planned to do exponentially more of them, but sometimes they'd ruin the atmosphere of the scene, so I had to rip a lot of them out in the edit.

P: You handled the editing and the production with Lucile Hadžihalilović. How does your collaboration work?

GN: We have been collaborating more or less constantly since 1986. It works in both directions—I help her with her films as she helps me with mine. I believe that a director always needs an ally on set. This might as well be another filmmaker—see [Marc] Caro and [Jean-Pierre] Jeunet—rather than an actor, cinematographer, or a producer. I get along well with Dominique Colin and Stéphane Derdérian, my assistant director who gives me a lot of great advice during editing. But the gestation of *Carne* and *Seul contre tous* lasted for so long that I can't imagine having had anyone other than Lucile as that person. From writing the script all the way to working in the editing room, she was able to warn me against any number of mistakes or wrong turns. We also have similar tastes, both in cinema and other things, we know each other's palette and imagination. Which is obviously necessary for doing this type of work together.

P: What are you working on next?

GN: Nothing is decided, but I have several projects in progress, starting with *Enter the Void*, a screenplay I wrote years ago. I was asked to adapt *The Story of the Eye* by [Georges] Bataille. I'm very interested, but there's a funding problem because the film would need to be as pornographic as the novel, with some violent sequences as well. If neither of those projects come through, I could make an experimental erotic film. The love scenes would be explicit, but the film would be about pleasure and the playful side of sexuality.

"The Rape Had to Be Disgusting to Be Useful"

Geoffrey Macnab / 2002

Irreversible, which will receive its British premiere at the Edinburgh festival, comes billed as "a violent trip—from hell to paradise." Formally, it is ingenious. Like Martin Amis's *Time's Arrow* (a book which Gaspar Noé admits to owning but not to having read), it begins at the end and works forward. Like the Buenos Aires–born director's arresting debut feature, *Seul contre tous* (1998), it is shot in 16mm and blown up to 35mm. Much of the film is improvised. Sequences are held for a small eternity. Sound editing is hyperbolic in the extreme. (When somebody is having his head mashed to a pulp with a fire extinguisher, we hear what sound like thunderclaps.) At times, especially when we're stuck deep in the slimy, dimly lit bowels of the Rectum club (the gay S&M parlor that is the site of much of the film's most explosive violence), it is like being cast back into an expressionist horror movie of the 1920s. ("There is something in the architecture of this movie that is close to *Metropolis*," Noé acknowledges, a trifle pompously.)

He is a deceptive filmmaker, part polemicist, part aesthete. As critic Tony Rayns once remarked of him: "Scratch a punk, and you'll find an art college wannabe inside." *Seul contre tous* superficially resembled one of Fassbinder's morality tales about the little man ground down by the system. Its protagonist, Jean Chevalier (brilliantly played by Philippe Nahon), was a woebegone butcher, just out of jail, without work or money, who vows revenge against the "n----r faggots" and "faggots in suits" responsible for his predicament. Although the film paid lip service to the conventions of social realism, Noé's interest was less in unemployment, racism, and the rise of the right than in making an outrageously skewed psycho-drama about a Travis Bickle-like outsider—and in upsetting as many groups as possible by doing so. "Noé claims to have wanted his film banned . . . to prove its confrontational power," the film magazine Sight and Sound noted at the time. "Instead, a film he had expected to alienate ninety percent of its audience and draw flak from feminist groups, gay groups, antiracist campaigners, and conservatives has been lavishly praised by the press, communist and conservative alike."

Gaspar Noé likes to describe himself as "a straight kind of guy and a bit of a wimp." When he was a teenager, he was too squeamish to sit through Sam Peckinpah's *Straw Dogs*: "I thought it was too heavy to handle. During the rape scene, I had to walk out," he confides in his softly spoken voice. Discussing a favorite book, J. W. Dunne's *An Experiment with Time*—a 1927 study by an English aeronautical engineer who developed his own pet theories about dreams, perception, and reality—he sounds like an earnest young philosophy student. Nonetheless, this seemingly placid thirty-eight-year-old has now made a movie so extreme that it provoked mass walk-outs and prolonged catcalls—as well as wild applause—during its press screening in Cannes.

The tone is set right from the outset, as we hear a martial-sounding drum roll over the credits (which, perversely, are projected back to front.) "I liked the drums because it gave me the idea of execution, like when people are being hanged or walking to the scaffold . . . you feel that something tragic is going to happen and that somebody is going to die. Also, it's so elementary. It reminds you of the perception of time—the boom, boom, boom is almost like a watch that you're listening to," says Noé.

Noé himself operated the camera, even at the most chaotic moments. "I was behind, just shaking the camera in every single direction. You get excited also by the violence of the actors. All their energy gives you energy, and when they start beating and punching, you do the same thing with your camera. The result may look preconceived, but it's totally instinctive."

The central conceit, he argues, isn't so different from that of classical tragedy. The elements are rape and revenge. Once the furies have been unleashed, there is nothing that can be done to stop them. As his director's statement puts it: "Time destroys everything . . . all history is written in sperm and blood . . . premonitions do not alter the course of events."

What so polarized the audiences in Cannes wasn't so much the subject matter or structure as the graphic and prolonged way in which the rape itself was depicted. Three-quarters of an hour into the film, Alex (Monica Bellucci) is attacked and viciously assaulted by a pimp in the subway. There are no cutaways or rhetorical tricks. What we're presented with is an uninterrupted, nine-minute sequence clearly intended to shock and to disgust.

"Because the subject of the movie was a rape, I said it has to be as powerful as it can be, to be disgusting enough, to be useful," says Noé. "If you do a movie with a rape and don't show it, you hide the point . . . the thing is that if you show it in a disgusting way, you help people to avoid that kind of situation. Like in

Clockwork Orange, when they show images of terror to Malcolm McDowell to stop him doing those kind of things, it is useful that it is shown."

The scene was shot six times over two days. Noé says he had no idea how long it was going to last. That was in the hands of Bellucci and the actor playing her assailant. "The results were great the first day but even more perfect on the second . . . they [the actors] were more and more confident with each other, and so they could go further and further. I didn't know if it would last for six minutes, ten minutes, twelve minutes, or whatever. The whole scene was in her hands, and even the guy who was playing the rapist was at her service. If she didn't want to do the scene like that, she would have said it. I really admire her for having taken that scene so far."

Bellucci's performance is indeed courageous. She and her husband Vincent Cassel (who plays her boyfriend in the film) are a national obsession in France: a celebrity couple along the lines of Burton and Taylor or Tom Cruise and Nicole Kidman (hence Noé's remarks about *Irreversible* being the film Cruise and Kidman should have made with Kubrick instead of *Eyes Wide Shut*). Noé describes Bellucci (shortly to be seen in the *Matrix* sequel) as "a mix of Brigitte Bardot and Claudia Cardinale at the same time." She had little obvious to gain by appearing as a rape victim in a lowish budget, arthouse film that—in its detractors' eyes—comes perilously close to exploitation.

Noé is clearly riled by the attacks made on the movie following its Cannes premiere. "People are mad about the movie, but accusing it of misogyny is a stupidity, as is accusing it of homophobia," he complains. "It's not because you have characters that depict aspects of humankind that you agree with them. I think that Paul Schrader said that about *Taxi Driver*—just because you give a portrait of a criminal, that doesn't mean you are a criminal yourself."

On one level, Irreversible is a companion piece to "bad girl" road movie *Baise-moi*, which also featured a brutal rape sequence and the kind of stomach-churning violence that makes Jacobean Revenge drama seem understated. Both films were financed by the same company—Studio Canal offshoot The Wild Bunch. Noé is friendly with the makers of *Baise-moi* (the codirector, porn actress Coralie Trinh Thi, appeared in *Sodomites*, the hardcore safe-sex promo that he made for French TV in the late 1990s). He describes it as "a bomb of energy" and claims that the changes it brought about in French censorship laws enabled him to make *Irreversible* with complete freedom. When asked about the way distinctions between arthouse and exploitation have begun to blur, he says: "Maybe the audiences are more mature than they used to be."

It's a moot point whether he is really saying anything very profound about violence or rape in *Irreversible* or whether he's still driven by an adolescent desire to shock. Some of his explanations sound glib. For instance, in describing his two male protagonists, he suggests that the extrovert Marcus (Vincent Cassel's character) is "the guts," while his much quieter friend Pierre (Albert Dupontel) stands for the brain. Disconcertingly, it's Pierre who's behind the most violent act of all. ("The brain takes control of the guts but, at the end, the brain just follows the guts.")

Whatever else, *Irreversible* is already a *succes de scandale*. Noé's claims that it is a "feminist" movie sound farfetched, but he certainly offers an extraordinarily pessimistic view of male sexuality. What's unsettling about the film is not just the bloodletting of the first half but the way that the characters behave in the moments leading up to it. For instance, Cassel, in the long, seemingly idyllic scene in which he lounges about in bed with Bellucci, uses language that echoes that of the rapist.

It is apt that *Irreversible* is surfacing in Britain just as *Straw Dogs* is rereleased. The arguments that Peckinpah made in 1971 (namely that he wanted to make audiences "very, very uncomfortable about their potential for violence") are similar to those that Noé advances when I speak to him. Noé, however, argues that he has gone one step further than the old western maestro by making a film that ends—albeit with heavy irony—on an optimistic note.

"Peckinpah was always saying his next movie would be a life-affirming movie. But they never were," Noé notes. "He'd do another revenge movie or another movie about man's inhumanity to man. In this movie, I achieved a goal which he didn't really achieve. The last scenes are life-affirming. I cry sometimes when I see my own movie . . . you have at the end of the movie a scene that represents something that happened before the drama—a great moment that can never be reproduced again. In that sense, it's life-affirming."

"Time Destroys All Things": An Interview with Gaspar Noé

David Sterritt / 2002

From *Quarterly Review of Film and Video* 24, no. 4 (2007). Reprinted by permission of David Sterritt, editor-in-chief, *Quarterly Review of Film and Video*.

Gaspar Noé was born in Argentina in 1963 but has lived in France since the midseventies. He studied filmmaking in his teens, then turned to philosophy, although he recalls being a far-from-conscientious student. He entered the French film industry as an assistant director of shorts, then made his directorial debut in 1991 with the forty-minute *Carne*, about a misanthropic butcher who takes revenge on the wrong man for molesting his autistic daughter and goes to prison for it. Noé further explored these characters in his 1998 feature *Seul contre tous* [*I Stand Alone*], in which the butcher opens up a new shop in the suburbs with his mistress, then reunites with his daughter and contemplates the prospect of ending their lives in a murder-suicide.

Both films raised a critical ruckus, but the 2002 debut of *Irréversible* went farther still, reportedly inducing physical illness at the Cannes Film Festival and leading a normally unshockable *Village Voice* reviewer to denounce it for aiming to inflict "nausea [and] moral indignation" on its viewers. Especially controversial were the film's frequent uses of expletives directed at homosexuals and women and a several-minute scene in which the character played by Italian actress Monica Bellucci is anally raped.

Irréversible, which tells its story in reverse chronology, consists of about thirteen long, apparently unbroken shots. The first is a brief prologue featuring the butcher who appears in both of Noé's previous films, rehashing his sordid past. The camera convulsively swoops and gyrates throughout the scene, providing only fleeting moments of clarity.

The camera then plunges into the bowels of an underground gay nightclub called The Rectum, where two men—Marcus and Pierre, played by Vincent Cassel and Albert Dupontel—are determined to find and kill a male prostitute known as Le Ténia—The Tapeworm—who has raped and tortured Alex, the current girlfriend of Marcus and former lover of Pierre. Thinking they've found their quarry, Pierre smashes his skull with a fire extinguisher—only it isn't Le Ténia at all, but a hapless bystander. The camera's constant movement mirrors the chaos and violence of the situation.

Moving back in time, we next see Marcus harassing a taxi driver and a transvestite hooker as he searches for The Rectum, while Pierre pleads with him not to be so violent. Moving back in time again, we see Alex walking into the dark subway underpass, where she is raped and beaten. We then see the situation preceding the rape—a party at which Marcus plays around with other girls, leading Alex to walk home by herself.

Eventually, a less obtrusive directorial style comes into play, and we see Marcus and Pierre as pleasant young men who joke around with Alex as the three of them head for the party. Then comes a romantic sequence in which Marcus and Alex indulge in love-play and play-fights. The film ends with Alex, newly pregnant, surrounded by children and families as she relaxes in a park. Here, the camera soars free of its moorings in a different way, flying into a gyroscopic spin that turns the scene into a swirling hallucination of dizzying, delirious intensity. This gives way to a stroboscopic barrage of black-and-white frames and a printed repetition of the film's motto, first articulated by the butcher in the opening sequence: "Time destroys all things." This was the film's working title, gleaned from Ovid's *Metamorphoses*.

Critics, in general, dismissed the film at Cannes, and many despised it, although it was better received at the Toronto International Film Festival a few months later. I interviewed Noé at the Toronto festival in 2002, using questions provided by Mikita Brottman in addition to my own.

David Sterritt: In Cannes, I spoke with a lot of people who were very shocked and upset by *Irréversible*. But here in Toronto, the people I'm talking with mostly seem to like the film very much.

Gaspar Noé: Have you found anybody who actually hated the movie in Cannes and likes the movie now?

DS: No, I don't think so, although there probably are such people. My first question is about the J. W. Dunne book, *An Experiment with Time*, that we see in the film.

GN: I don't remember much about his series [of books]. I read three books by him years ago. . . . The main thing I remember is that he would note his dreams every morning.

DS: Yes.

GN: And then he would find out that there were a lot of things he'd note from his dreams of the previous night that would happen during the day. The whole series said the future is already kind of written by yourself and all the elements around you. And you have a precognition of important things that you are in contact with in your own brain, a few hours later, or a few days later—big events in your life, like deaths, accidents, and so on.

DS: And is that central to the concept of the film? That idea of precognition?

GN: Yes. For example, I wanted to add many more symbols to the movie on the way to this tragedy. I thought I would put more elements that would, like, announce things that would happen later because you know what is going to happen later. Then you would see a symbol on a wall, or in the paper, or just people saying something. Then you would see these things happen. Because you know what's going to happen, and then you say, well, people don't even read the signs around them. That would make the whole movie much more paranoid. But on the set, finally, we didn't put in many elements of that kind. Specifically, for example, at the end of the movie, when she's waking up after having sex with her boyfriend, she says, "Oh, I had this weird dream. I was in a red tunnel, and the tunnel broke," but she doesn't pay too much attention to what she had been dreaming.

DS: And her boyfriend Marcus can't feel his arm.

GN: Yes, he can't feel his arm. Also, some [elements in the film] were not done purposely. For example, Marcus says [to Alex in the bedroom] at one point, "I want to fuck you in the ass," and because I shot the rape scene [quite a while] after that scene, I didn't know [yet] that she would be sodomized. But just the day before the [bedroom] shot, I said, do you mind if he says, "I want to fuck you in the ass," and you say, "No, no"? Now when you see the movie and he says that at the end . . . it suddenly brings you back to the scene of the rape and makes you think that also Marcus is a potential rapist, maybe. There are many elements that have resonances at other points in the movie.

DS: Yes, absolutely. Would it be true to say that the film itself is an experiment in time, in that the reverse chronology is not just a trick but an essential element in terms of what you're saying about cause and effect?

GN: Yes. Someone asked me recently, "What's the difference between a drama and a tragedy?" It's that in a drama, dramatic things happen, and in a tragedy, they unfold. In a tragedy, you cannot change the events. In the way [*Irréversible*] is told, the characters cannot change their future because you've already seen what's going to happen next. So all you can ask is, "What happened before?" But yes, there is something that is close in its structure to the writings of Dunne.

DS: So you feel that what happens to the *Irréversible* characters, in terms of cause and effect, is fixed? Are things simply fated to happen, or is there some way out?

GN: I think they could have escaped it. But . . . the way it's told, it seems that they cannot escape it because you already know where they're going to. If you [told] the same story in a normal way, you would feel like their power of will could bring them somewhere else than where they go. But if you tell it backwards, you know where they will go.

DS: What's your idea of fate and destiny? Do you feel we actually have freedom to control our lives?

GN: I think we have present freedom. But you're not free from your genes. You have a genetic code that brings you to things above anything your brain can tell you. So, in a very general way, no, you're not free. You're drawn by your guts. You're not free from fighting for your survival, and the survival of the species, all the time. And seen from a softer point of view–questions like, "Should I take coffee, should I take tea? Should I take this one or should I take the other one?"—yes, you can choose, but your freedom is very limited.

DS: Why did you then choose to tell the story in this way—backwards?

GN: Because I thought it would be more melodramatic. And maybe because my two previous movies were very linear. When I've seen nonlinear narratives—for example, [in] Tarantino or Christopher Nolan's *Memento* [2000], or other movies—I thought they were more amazing than linear narratives. Also, you experience things in a linear way, but when you reconstruct them with your mind, they're not linear anymore. Your remembrance of your own past is not linear. It's just emotions, and moments, and they're in a chronological disorder. If you want to write a diary of what you did, like, three years ago, it will take you a long time to remember in which order the events took place. You just remember faces, moments, doors, rooms.

DS: In a way, *Irréversible* is linear, though, because it's directly backwards.

GN: Yes. It's more conceptual, you see. It's linear, and it's not linear. There was an article in France where they said it was a Rubik's Cube. You could take it to pieces and put it together the other way. In that sense, it's a bit childish because it would have been more ambitious if it could have been made not only backwards but more going back and forth.

DS: Maybe that would have been too much for an audience to take in?

GN: Yes. Because it's like a game. I think after the third scene, people understand the rules of the game, and they want to play with you and try to understand it. You could do something more complex, but it's true that it would get people lost. *Mulholland Drive* [David Lynch, 2001] is more complex than my movie from a structural point of view.

DS: Your three films are *Carne*, *Seul contre tous*, and this one. I'm a big admirer of *Carne*, especially. I think it's a wonderful film. And they're all very, very dark. Are you very, very dark?

GN: I don't think they're dark. They're very visceral but not dark.

DS: They are visceral, and visceral things can be joyful, but these are not joyful films, right?

GN: They're joyful. For me, *Los Olvidados* [Luis Buñuel, 1950] is a funny movie dealing with visceral subjects. It's a joyful movie. You can tell that the movie's joyful when there is energy on the screen. I think bitterness doesn't bring you too much energy.

DS: Bitterness?

GN: Yes. I have problems, for example, with Ingmar Bergman. There is something very dry and bitter in his movies that is not joyful. And I think my movies, even if they're much more violent, graphically, are much more life-affirming than Bergman's movies. There are some movies by Bergman that make me want to commit suicide. [Michael] Haneke is not that funny either. They are very sentimental. Some people are very sadistic and sentimental at the same time. They're not sadistic in real life, but when it comes to directing movies, maybe it brings out their sadistic, sentimental part. Be mean, but be gentle at the same time.

DS: Very interesting, because when I think of *Seul contre tous*, for example, I certainly think of the main character as a very bitter man, but I guess at the end of the film, he kind of chooses life. Is that accurate?

GN: He's more of a lost dog. You know, those dogs in the street, they don't have anybody to take care of them, so you don't know if they'll end up being killed or whatever; they're just lost. And for me, the character in *Seul contre tous*, he's just a lost dog.

DS: How do you relate to this lost dog? How does that affect how you view the character?

GN: I could be like him, but I have many friends to take care of. I'm a dog, but I am not lost!

DS: Back to *Irréversible*, would you agree that this is an apocalyptic film? Do these characters represent "the way things are"—in society, in France, maybe in human life itself? Is this film a metaphor for the human condition?

GN: The movie's not that ambitious. It's not *2001: A Space Odyssey* [Stanley Kubrick, 1968]. It's more obsessing about someone you love, losing someone you love, and reproducing yourself with someone you love. It's much more unpretentious than that. All the structure is funny, the camerawork is full of energy, but it's more about losing someone you love. And that was already the subject of *Carne*. I mean, in *Carne*, the father thinks that his daughter gets raped by someone, and then [seeking revenge] he stabs the wrong person. So, it's quite close to this movie, but the structure is just the opposite. I am very sentimental, and you can see that.

DS: So you see this, then, as a very personal, intimate kind of film?

GN: Yes. It's an intimate film.

DS: How did you shoot the movie in terms of chronology?

GN: I shot it in chronological order. Not completely—for example, we didn't shoot the park scene at the very beginning of the movie. We shot the apartment scene first, then the park scene, then the next Monday, we shot the subway scene, then the party scene. But we shot them in chronological order apart from one or two scenes. The last week was the gay bar, and the opening scenes were shot at the beginning.

DS: And was the film very tightly scripted or storyboarded?

GN: No, no, no storyboard. I did the camera, so we were improvising with the camera. We improvised with everything—the dialogue, the camerawork, all that on the set. The whole script when we started shooting the movie was three or four pages long.

DS: How did the movie come about?

GN: It was financed on the names of Monica Bellucci, Vincent Cassell, and mine. We all had six weeks to prepare the shooting, and then we were shooting, and I knew I wouldn't have time to write the dialogue, so we just did the best lines that came on the set. I don't know if they're the best lines, but they're very realistic. They make sense, not because they're deep, but because they come out in a natural way. We would shoot a scene two times, three times, up to twenty times, and usually, we would keep one of the last takes because the first ones were a lot shorter, and the best ideas came when we were shooting. People would make comments–the assistant director, the camera assistant, the actors—like, "Oh yeah, that part was good; you should do that again." We had two or three days for each scene. There is nothing really interesting that is said, but the way things unfold is interesting. It's not a very verbal movie. *Seul contre tous* was a very verbal movie. You could cut the images and just listen to the soundtrack, like a radio show, and you'd get the whole movie. In this case, it's the opposite. You could turn off the sound and just watch the images.

DS: How many scenes are there?

GN: I think the whole movie has maybe thirteen scenes.

DS: It was a fairly quick shoot, then. You didn't take a long time.

GN: Five weeks and a half.

DS: And in terms of editing, once all the scenes were shot? Was it just a question of splicing them?

GN: Yes, it was a question of choosing the best take. Also, we did a lot of digital postproduction. Some takes are actually made of two takes, and we made a morphing in the middle to go from one take to another. For example, the scene in the gay club—that looks like one take, but it's made of maybe thirty different pieces. There's a lot of dark, and you can cut in the dark, and make a match with another take.

DS: Was this how you did the head being broken?

GN: Yes, that was a lot of work. The guy who was responsible for it took care personally of that special effect. He was working with that for something like three months. It was a mix of many things—many different takes, some with a dummy, some with a real actor . . . it's a mix of many different techniques.

DS: It's extraordinarily successful.

GN: We had as a reference a documentary of a guy who was executed in Lebanon. They shoot the guy, and the rifle destroys just half of his face, and the other part of his face keeps screaming for something like a minute. So he's a person with half of his head missing and still screaming. And when I saw it, I was really . . . I felt like vomiting because, you know, in movies, people get killed very quickly. But here you see so much suffering, for a whole minute, and he's screaming, and he knows he's going to die, and he cannot die because his brains keep on working. And that really shook me, so I said, "Well, if we show these crimes in this movie, let's do it in a way that would be closer to that documentary and not to what we usually see in a fiction movie."

DS: I assume the rape scene was one continuous take?

GN: No, there is one cut. When she comes out from the party, we follow her, and she goes into the tunnel, and there is one cut there. It's when the camera goes to the [sign over the tunnel reading] "passage" and comes back. It's like in the beginning of *Snake Eyes* by Brian De Palma [1998], where there are many invisible cuts. There's one invisible cut there, and then we go to another take, where she gets raped.

DS: And the rape itself is all one continuous take.

GS: But still, there are some special effects in that scene. For example, when the rapist comes out, you can see for five seconds his erect penis. That was added in postproduction because [the actor's] zipper was closed. We added the penis with some blood. So it looks much more realistic, and people were thinking when they saw the movie, maybe they were having sex during the whole scene, and how could Monica take it? But no, we added that and also we added some blood on her face at the end of the scene.

DS: It's all completely convincing. But it gets us back to the darkness of the film. I'm curious about two things that are related—your motivation in making the scene so incredibly difficult to watch and whether you were concerned that this might simply send people out of the theater.

GN: I didn't think it was bound to send people out of the theater. In fact, in France, one person out of ten did walk out, and still the movie was a commercial success. Word of mouth was very positive–even from people who were coming out saying, "I can't take it; it was too violent," because that would excite other people to see it. But no, you don't do a movie to make people walk out. You just say, "I want to do the violent scenes really violent." That's the only useful way to do it. I walked out when I saw *Straw Dogs* [Sam Peckinpah, 1971] when I was seventeen, and still, I think it's a great movie. I saw it again on DVD later on, but I know that the day I first saw it, I walked out during the rape scene. And I almost walked out the first time I saw *The Texas Chain Saw Massacre* [Tobe Hooper, 1974]. It's just that you get scared. If you see people walking out—some people even fainted in Cannes at my movie, in the film festival—I don't think it's bad that they feel this way. As long as people know what they're going to see, they get prepared.

DS: I'd still like to hear more about why you made the rape scene that incredibly brutal—so long, so close, so anal. It's a painful scene!

GN: That's the thing. I could not think of doing a rape scene that would not be painful. Otherwise, you're not [thinking about] what you're shooting, what you're representing. The thing is, you really are emotionally linked to the victim and not the rapist. In many movies, you get linked to the rapist because it's shot from a subjective point of view, the guy coming at the girl with a knife, and so on. But in this case, it's evident that you are linked to the victim and not for one second to the aggressor.

DS: Let's move to a different subject. You're from Argentina originally?

GN: I was born there, yes.

DS: And when did you come to France?

GN: When I was twelve. Because my father had to run away from the country for political reasons.

DS: How did you get involved with filmmaking?

GN: When I was seventeen, I went to a film school, which was a very good one. I finished there when I was nineteen. I was supposed to start working, but I was too young. So, just to avoid working, I started studying philosophy, but I was not a very serious student, so I would never go to the lectures or anything like that. Then I started working as assistant director on some shorts and things like that.

DS: Why did you want to become a filmmaker? Had you always wanted to be an artist?

GN: No, no, no, no. I don't think if you're making things, you're doing art. If you're making, you're making. If you enjoy doing it, it's a lot of fun. It's a lot of pressure; it's a lot of suffering if you don't get the financing and you get lots of debts. But still, you're working with a team of people, and you can choose the people you work with, and it's very exciting. It can be art as many things are–as creating furniture is doing art, and even politics is doing art. You're inventing, or reinventing, a lot of things. But sometimes the word "art" is very pretentious. When people claim they are artists, usually it's because they are not.

DS: But you did want to do some kind of creative work?

GN: Yes. But many things are creative. Maybe the scientist is much more creative in what he's making.

DS: It doesn't have to be a contest. [Laughs]

GN: [Laughs] But I don't like the word "artist" because people say, "Oh, I'm a poet," like people say, "I'm crazy." If someone comes to you and says, "I'm a crazy guy," don't believe him. He may be just the most square person in the world pretending to be crazy.

DS: Well, your own films to date are obviously from a very distinctive personality—that is, they're not the kinds of films other people make.

GN: I saw one movie this year that I really thought—well, it was not close to mine, but there was some energy in it, so I really feel sort of linked to it. That is City of God [Fernando Meirelles, 2002], a Brazilian movie. It's so well shot. When I saw it, I thought, "This is a movie and a script that I would have liked to shoot myself." Maybe there would be some differences—for example, there was a rape scene that he shot, and then he cut it and so there was not any reason to really show that rape. In my case, I would say no. If you shoot the rape, you show it. But still, it's maybe the movie this year that I come the closest to. Some people complain that it was a bit of a pop video, and I don't think so at all. It's full of visual ideas, but it's not a pop video. . . . I think there are a lot of people who hate things that are too visual. Also, in my case, some people say, "The filmmaking is pretentious because you move your camera and use cranes." Why not? Should you always put the camera on the same level and shoot flat?

DS: How did you do the camerawork for Irréversible, by the way?

GN: Hand-held camera.

DS: Do you go to the movies a lot?

GN: Not when I'm shooting. The rest of the time, yes, I will see a lot of movies. But when you're shooting a movie, you just sort of forget about it.

DS: When you go to films, what do you like to see?

GN: I liked Mulholland Drive. I liked City of God. There's one movie I discovered lately that I love. It's an old movie called The Thief [Russell Rouse, 1952], with Ray Milland paying a Russian spy who's stealing documents for the Russian government. It's made in the fifties, and the whole movie's silent. There's not one sentence in the whole movie.

DS: Oh, I have seen that, yes. There's sound but no dialogue.

GN: Yes. And it's great, it's really scary. It's one of the best suspense films I've ever seen. From time to time, you discover these old movies you haven't seen. Like I Am Cuba [Soy Cuba/Ya Kuba, Mikheil Kalatozishvili, 1964], that's another.

DS: Yes, I agree.

GN: Maybe that was my main inspiration for this film.

DS: Really? *I Am Cuba*?

GN: Yes.

DS: It is a very visual film. And in ways, a very nonlinear film.

GN: Yes. I mean, dialogues don't come that much. It's more how the face is represented, and so on . . .

DS: And yet you said earlier that *Seul contre tous* is a film which is very verbal. It has a visual element, but . . .

GN: It's a sort of radiophonic movie.

DS: Yes, yes. So do you see yourself moving much more in a visual direction now, or . . .

GN: Not so much. I just didn't want to try the same movie. As soon as you go far one way, you say, "Let's go another way." Still, there are a lot of similarities between *Irréversible* and *Seul contre tous*. But I suppose the next movie is going to be even less talkative than this one.

DS: Can you tell me a bit about that?

GN: I'll just say that it's experimental and hallucinogenic.

DS: Does it have a title?

GN: Yes, but I'd rather not speak about a movie that might come out in two years.

DS: Okay. Can you see yourself making a comedy?

GN: Sure. But I think I would rather do a black-humored comedy. Still, I think *Irréversible* is funny.

DS: There's some funny stuff in it.

GN: I think *Seul contre tous* is funny. It's black humor. I was thinking one day of doing a kids' movie.

DS: Really?

GN: An Andersen tale or something.

DS: Why?

GN: Because I think there's a big audience in it. You're much less rational when you're a kid, and I think if you respect kids for what they are—future adults—sometimes I think they're more intelligent than adult people. Your vision of life might be much more square when you're forty, fifty than when you're six because [young people are] just drinking, drinking, drinking all this energy. For example, *2001: A Space Odyssey* was much more popular with kids than with older people. I remember I saw it when I was six, and it was just like, it was giving me an ecstasy trip. I felt like, "Well, bloody hell, what is all this? What does it represent? I don't understand!" But I noticed that I liked the movie much more than my parents, although I was six years old. I think I will go at least once in my life for a general-audience movie.

DS: You've mentioned filmmakers like Kubrick and David Lynch and Buñuel. Do your tastes tend to run toward art films, toward more serious kinds of personal cinema, or do you enjoy Hollywood movies as well?

GN: *2001* is a Hollywood movie.

DS: Yes, but a very peculiar one.

GN: Yes, yes. [I like] those kinds of movies. But Hollywood scripts are getting worse and worse. *The Matrix* [Lana Wachowski, Lilly Wachowski, 1999] is an ambitious script inside the Hollywood system. But besides *The Matrix* . . .

DS: Do you tend to think a lot in visual terms? I know you said you studied philosophy for a while, even though it wasn't seriously. Do you think of yourself as a verbally oriented person as well, or do you think that your imagination works in pictures?

GN: Well, I think I'm much more visual than verbal. . . . I'm not a drug addict, but I'm addicted to rushes. I feel like every two weeks, I have to be afraid of something, to motivate me.

DS: To be afraid of something?

GN: Yes. I like it when things get out of control, when I'm out of control, when I don't control things. For example, doing a movie, when you're shooting, and you say, "Well, improvise the dialogue," you're not controlling things. You've put yourself in a position where you're just guiding people; you're not controlling them. Some people are control freaks. I'm not a control freak at all. I like to put my brains in a closet and see what happens in front of my eyes. I love going on roller coasters and things like this, with people screaming. From time to time, you just need to have a big rush of fear, like jumping with a parachute. . . . I like the idea of putting yourself in a position where you might die. When you're dead, your fear of death is over, so you start laughing.

DS: You said earlier that *Irréversible* did well in French theaters.

GN: It did very well.

DS: Was it well received by critics?

GN: Not so much the critics. But it's weird because it was shown in competition at Cannes, and the president of the Cannes Film Festival didn't want us to show it to the daily press before we had shown it to some big magazines. And so a lot of journalists were hating the movie because they were not invited to see it. And when it came to their turn that they should talk about the movie, I had one hundred percent of the daily press against it. It's weird because a lot of cheap, popular magazines were raving about it. So the people [whose reviews] came out [just as it opened] were hating it because they were not invited to the party before. It was funny because when the movie opened—the day following the official screening—all the newspapers were saying, "Oh, this is a piece of crap," and you could not take them seriously. It was not a real point of view on the movie.

DS: That's an embarrassing thing about some film reviewers. But have you read articles about any of your movies that you've felt were smart and that maybe you've been interested in?

GN: Sometimes. The review can be good or bad, but sometimes, they put their finger on things that are really interesting. It's funny; there was one good review of the movie, and the guy was saying it was a Christian movie. I never had any religious background in my life. I never went to church, whatever. I couldn't take it as a positive thing . . . to say it's a Christian movie. I said, "No, no, it's not a Christian movie!"

DS: That reminds me of another question. I mentioned the other day [after a screening of *Irréversible* at Toronto] that when I saw your movie at Cannes, it ended with the words "Time Destroys All Things" on the screen. The words weren't there at the end of the print shown here, and you seemed surprised that they had been removed.

GN: I just found out that [the words] hadn't been removed, but the projectionist just stopped the movie. The screen is black for eight seconds, and then you have this title afterwards. Maybe he just saw a black screen and thought the movie was over, so he stopped it. But at the beginning [of the production], the first title I had for the movie was *Le temps détruit tous*, which is a famous sentence of Ovidius, this Latin author, from the *Metamorphoses*. I thought it would be a good title for the movie, but then I found *Irréversible*, which sounded better. Still, at the beginning, the butcher from *Seul contre tous* [who appears as a character in *Irréversible*] says, "Time destroys all things." So I'm not really sure you need it again. So yesterday, when they cut the film before the title card came up, I thought, "Well, it's okay without it."

DS: "Time destroys all things" sounds like a very negative statement, a very pessimistic statement. Still, what happens in your film is that we start with all this horror, but at the end of the movie's running time, in the last scene, everything's light and pleasant and happy. So, in a way, time has destroyed the ugliness we see at the beginning of the film. It reminded me of Dante. *The Divine Comedy* starts off in hell but ends up in heaven.

GN: Also, you have an architecture in *Metropolis* [Fritz Lang, 1927] kind of close to the one in my movie. There you have the gutters of the city with the poor people fighting in an underground world [against privileged people living above]. And the people in [*Irréversible*] live in the top of a building, and they seem quite rich, or maybe they have money from a rich family. Alex seems to be living a little bit on her money. Also, the rapist is a bit of a visionary—he says, "Who do you think you are, you rich bitch, because you're rich, you have everything." So there's a little bit of rich and poor, up and down, light and dark.

DS: Like *Metropolis* and other films. So, in a way, it is a film that has social commentary built into it.

GN: Not really, because it's so binary that I couldn't say it's a commentary. It's just that there's joy and there's danger. If you value something, you have to protect it because things can happen to you. Unless you have a bodyguard!

DS: And then you have to worry about the bodyguard. Do you feel that way? You say you like to let control go, but you don't seem to be a fearful person.

GN: No, no, I'm not fearful, but there are some situations that I wouldn't put myself into. . . . I don't do illegal things, although I appreciate it when other people do them!

Is Gaspar Noé's *Irréversible* Inexcusable?

Gerald Peary / 2003

From the *Boston Phoenix*, March 13, 2003. Reprinted by permission.

French filmmaker Gaspar Noé was in a sweat in March at the Miami International Film Festival. He told me that someone anonymous had threatened to kill him because of his transgressive film, *Irréversible*. He'd been looking over his shoulder, anticipating an attack. Earlier, he and his leads—Monica Bellucci, Vincent Cassel—were greeted with jeers and boos (and also applause) when they appeared for the press conference following *Irréversible*'s premiere at the 2002 Cannes Film Festival.

At Cannes, Noé couldn't have been surprised that some journalists were jolted by *Irréversible*'s most incendiary scenes: a guy being pummeled to death by a fire extinguisher in the bowels of a Paris gay bar, Rectum, and a seemingly endless, no-escape brutal rape in the corridors of a Paris metro station. He's asked: why trap an audience to watch?

"There are days you don't want to see such things," Noé conceded. "As for trapping people: when there are aggressions on the street, including rape, people come up to see. There's a visual fascination. On television, such things are on all the time. I saw something recently at 8:30 of people killing each other with machetes. In movies, you have killings without emotions. But rape? It's almost taboo in the cinema.

"I wanted to make a film I like. When I see Buñuel films, I like them. People talk about the scandal of *Irréversible*! A few people left the press screening, but there was no scandal. I can understand this movie can shock some American distributors, who are more and more politically correct, because of the multiplexes. This film will be R-rated or NC-17. Maybe in the 1970s, it would have just passed by."

Actor Cassel: "Why does a filmmaker have to justify his film? If everyone liked *Irréversible*, it would be strange. People I really love, I told them not to go. That's the best advice I can give them."

Actress Bellucci, the rape victim: "I have friends who say they didn't like it, but we were on the phone talking for hours. I said, 'Are you sure you didn't like it?' A lot of people detest the film, but some love it. There's a reason to make it: it's an important, deep film."

Noé explained the rape scene: "My idea was to use Jo Prestia, who had been a rapist in an Eric Zonca movie. He was perfect. He used to be a boxer, a world champion of Thai kickboxing. He's very, very nice. I introduced him to Monica, and she was scared not of the rape but that he would hit her. That wouldn't happen. He knew how to box, to control himself.

"It's a totally artificial rape. Everything is simulated. Although it seems a continuous shot, actually, sixty little bits were put together from twenty-minute continuous shots. There were nine months of postproduction, many sleepless nights, putting the scenes together. Now the rape scene is credible, it wasn't originally. The rapist's penis wasn't there originally, or blood on her face. Special effects technology allowed us to add all that."

Bellucci: "How did we prepare? I looked at various films concerning rape in the day, like *Deliverance* and *The Accused*. Gaspar only asked me to be strong and truthful. I did my best. The first day, we shot my love scene with Vincent. The rape scene in the metro, we shot four times, and then we chose the good version. It's true; when I see the rape scene now, it hurts. But as Gaspar said, 'The film is not a crime. It's a film about a crime.'"

Noé: "Compare it to real revenge movies like *Mad Max* and *Death Wish*. *Irreversible* isn't a revenge movie. The guy seeks revenge on the rapist-killer, but I don't believe in that. We need to see the beast within us and then refuse it."

Gaspar Noé Meets Hubert Sauper

Hubert Sauper and Jan-Willem Dikkers / 2006

From *ISSUE* magazine, 2006. Reprinted by permission of Jan-Willem Dikkers / *ISSUE* magazine.

Born in 1963 in Argentina, Gaspar Noé spent his childhood between Buenos Aires and New York. At age twelve, he moved to France. After studying philosophy and cinema at L'École Louis Lumière de Paris, he released his first short films in the 1980s: *Tintarella di luna* and *Pulpe amère*. In 1991, he made a short film, *Carne*, introducing the character of the Butcher, played by Philippe Nahon. An angry man, the Butcher seeks revenge on whoever hurt his disabled daughter. After working as an actor, cinematographer, writer, and director on some other projects with the backing of Agnès B., Noé made his first feature film, *I Stand Alone*, continuing the story of the Butcher after he does time in jail and abandons his daughter. In 2002, Noé received major public notice and outrage with the controversial *Irréversible*.

Hubert Sauper was born in the village of Tyrol in the Austrian Alps. He lived in Great Britain, Italy, the USA, and since then ten years in France. He studied film directing in Vienna (University of Performing Arts) and in Paris (Université de Paris VIII) and graduated with a BA (Mag. art). Hubert teaches film classes in Europe and in the USA. The last two documentaries he wrote and directed (*Darwin's Nightmare* and *Alone with Our Stories*) were awarded twelve international film prizes.

Gaspar Noé: You have been to Africa several times? Even before going there to film, right?

Hubert Sauper: Yes, *Kisangani Diary* was made at the end of a long stay, actually my first. Aside from that, I lived briefly in Tanzania in '97, working with a friend that had opened a production company. This was the first such business in Tanzania's history. I helped out in making TV commercials for the national Tanzanian soap, known as the Findi or Winner, a sort of long yellow baguette that you cut pieces off of. This soap was used to wash yourself, for laundry, cars, boats, airplanes. . . . It was during the shooting of an airplane washing scene that I met these Russian pilots that later played a role in *Darwin's Nightmare*.

GN: But that wasn't actually the town where you filmed *Darwin's Nightmare*? Why did you go there initially?

HS: The first trip was for the soap.

GN: Why this town and not another?

HS: It just worked out that way; I don't quite remember. My friend had landed a bunch of contracts and had asked me to help out in making these ads, as he was overwhelmed. We spent a whole month crossing Tanzania. I already had a project in mind dealing with the refugees in the Congo, as the airlifts had been removed from Tanzania. I had already been in touch with the UN. Then, after meeting the Russians, I went back to see the UN [and said], "So there, I know a few pilots. Can you take me along in the planes?" And I was off to the east of the Congo with my partner Suzanna.

GN: And what the heck was she doing there?

HS: Suzanna? She played the accordion. No, she actually did a bunch of things. She took care of the children. We were discovering Africa. We were meeting a lot of people, and I was preparing this documentary. And the only way to get into the Congo was via the UN transport planes. So, the end of my six-to-seven-month stay in Africa was a month and a half in the Congo.

GN: Did you use a professional film camera?

HS: No, it was this crappy Hi8.

GN: The thing is that the sound is surprisingly clear.

HS: It's clear since the people I am filming are relatively close, and there are no highways nearby.

GN: Because I remember, you have this shot with a bunch of kids and this guy getting up, and the image is rough looking with really big grain, but the sound is super clear.

HS: It's just the mike from the camera, it's because there is no noise. That's the advantage of filming in the jungle: everything is very present.

GN: When making documentary films these days, it no longer crosses your mind to do it in 16mm? The whole process of putting the reel in the camera, changing it, knowing that you need to stop in ten minutes, develop the negative . . . a lot more complicated than using a camera like the Panasonic DVX100 . . .

HS: I guess it all depends on your level of concentration. Sometimes, when you need to film a lot, it is hard to keep up.

GN: Getting back to Africa, in comparison to the West, death is dealt with on a daily basis. Everyone is telling you that they have lost half their children, that their brother is dead . . . You say it is a sort of general *hécatombe* [carnage], but surprisingly, I don't have the impression that they themselves feel they are punished. I mean for them, the hardships they endure, having lost a child, or the wife that has lost an eye . . . they've taken so many blows for such a long time.

HS: Yes, I think this is more so just a part of their life, but the mourning associated with the loss of a child is the same. One hundred years ago in Europe, it was just as common to watch your child die.

GN: Have you seen the film *Children Underground* [Edet Belzberg, 2000]? It's about these kids that live in the subway in Romania. These kids that have been abandoned by their families. This little girl gets raped, yet when you see her hideous stepfather threatening her, who's a meter taller than her, you can understand why she would prefer to live in the subway surrounded by all these other kids that hit her. When it comes to human cruelty, documentaries can go so much further than films.

HS: Documentary can play a better role of representation if it is used as cinema. Documentary is too often thought of as a news report, a sort of illustrated text in our minds. I just try to see the firemen when they arrive and to hear their voices when they arrive. When one does that, who does he think I am? Does he think that I can't see the firemen arrive? Am I considered an idiot? If considered an idiot, the mind will go to sleep after three times. We don't just lose our attention span, but also all sense of responsibility because this voice is explaining everything we see. If you want to fly an airplane, you need a license or even a car, you need a license. If you spread idiotic images throughout the world, you don't need anything. Anyone is free to do so. It's quite strange, as there ought to be responsibility associated with the making of images and sound without the know-how required.

GN: I'm in the process of looking for special effects for my next film, which has led me to watch all the *Armageddon*, *Apollo 13* . . . science fiction films . . . I've watched about sixty films. In conclusion, you realize that it's all propaganda filmmaking. It's all the self-confident Americans, sympathetically sending their people to go fight Martians or the destruction of the world. It's always the Americans going off and saving everything. This doesn't exist in Italian cinema or French cinema.

HS: Well, it's all part of a much longer conversation related to the Second World War because you have the British and the Americans that let Hitler go a long way before reacting till things had gone much too far. So, in a sense, just as they saved the world, they also let it sink.

GN: And then they took part in sectioning Europe, which led to many more problems, and the same with the Middle East. Actually, they came to share the cake. There's a fabulous three-hour documentary on Saudi Arabia, *House of Saud*, and how the Americans infiltrated. In the past, wars were over politics or religion; now, it's nothing but economic wars for taking over markets.

HS: I think that if you were to make a film about the state of our times, it would be about nothing more than economics. Before, it was more about the ideas, Marxism, etc. Now, the bottom line is always the dollar. All human relations have been reduced to this sort of game, "I give to you, you give to me."

Jan-Willem Dikkers: There are people that seem to believe there is a conflict when creating a documentary or news report if you already have a premeditated outcome to your work.

HS: For *Darwin*, the film existed in my head well before I even began filming.

JWD: I think this is probably the first time I have seen something that has been put together in such a way, a documentary film where there isn't any sort of narration guiding you throughout, like a new form in cinema.

HS: It's hard to say. In a sense, it is classic narration, where you give certain elements. Well, I knew one thing: the mind does not like to receive orders but rather elements from which it can draw its own conclusions. If you get the impression that you start to be aware of something that I already know, you get this sort of intellectual satisfaction. This way you will really learn something. This is what makes the art of it; it's been this way since the beginning of time: giving clues from which you create your own internal film or story, where the unspoken can be so much greater than what actually is said. *Darwin* was a reflection. I wanted to go back to this part of the earth. I wanted to get a better understanding of what was going on, wanted to make it better understood and share what I had learned. For quite some time, I had been wanting to make a film on the foolishness of global exchanges that really don't lead anywhere, but I hadn't found which angle to attack from. I had found the core and place for the story. There are all sorts of theories about form and body, but I also just did a lot based on pure instinct. The thesis often comes later.

GN: Have you seen the film *Mémoire d'un saccage* [Fernando Solanas, 2004]? It's a lesson in economics about the stock market crash in Argentina. It's really complex and really educational. I think that the lesson learnt in *Darwin* is pretty simple. Documentaries contain many more useful elements for the human mind than do fiction films.

HS: You also have educational fiction films. I prefer to speak of cinema or noncinema. Cinema is typically a sort of poetic product, intelligent and artistic, in contrast to fast-food images void of meaning. I will be making a fiction film in the Congo. A fiction film with so-called actors, a script, yet it will still be pretty heavy as well. It will be a film that will emotionally and intellectually strike the same chords.

GN: In Africa, in particular, you have so many existential plots. I had interviewed this guy that had quite recently discovered that he had AIDS, and he still hadn't told his wife or kids. He didn't know if he should tell them. He'd think to himself, "If I tell my wife, she will leave running, and I'll find myself alone with my three kids." He had no money, no electricity, nothing. It had been four months, and he would no longer make love to his wife. When we filmed in his house, the kids were so excited to see an electric lightbulb for the first time, yet his wife would just keep asking him why he was being filmed—a very strange situation. You very rarely run into such existential cases in rich countries. In Africa, you can make a real tearjerker from just about anyone's life.

HS: In a way, this is a good point. Could you imagine making a film on global capitalism in New York? You just can't find things on the surface like that: You have computer screens, people on the phones, everything is very indirect. In Africa, things are much closer to their true nature.

GN: Will you be using documentary elements in your next film?

HS: I may use certain images.

GN: You can also make fiction with people that are actually close to the subject. A lot of films are made this way. I notice this in this film *Lilya 4-ever* [Lukas Moodysson, 2002], which was shot in part in Russia and in Sweden. It's the story of this Russian girl whose mother disappears, abandoning her. This guy offers her work, and she ends up at age sixteen hooking in the streets of Sweden.

HS: This film had a political impact in Sweden.

GN: Actually, a little everywhere. It was used trying to stop sex traffic. There is a poetic sequence that I found quite poignant in the film when you see this young prostitute's subjective view of all the guys she's had. It is a two-to-three-minute sequence where you see about fifty faces that come and go. Some guys that are not too unpleasant forty-five-year-olds or young, athletic twenty-year-olds. You see all these faces run by one after another. It becomes really suffocating. You think to yourself, "This is what work is for a prostitute." Prostitutes must have between thirty to forty guys a day. And when you ask them if they take pleasure, they answer, "Yeah, twice a week, there are some guys that I like." But when you do the math, two guys out of two hundred, what's that? Films that present prostitution as assembly line work are quite rare.

Did you have moments during the making of your film where you felt the urge to cry? During my filming in Africa, I had moments of deep sadness.

HS: I cried at the editing table. Alone with two hundred hours of footage, I was faced with seeing it all and hearing the voices. Seeing Elizabeth, that had been killed. I watched her speak, knowing that she was dead. When I was there, I was with my friend, who was assisting me. Often, we would find ourselves in our small room at night, and we would ask ourselves, what was this day all about? Sometimes, you just don't find what you are looking for anymore. And then all of a sudden, there is like an explosion of new elements that start working together.

GN: And don't you feel that when you are faced up close to people's true sadness that it strengthens you, not from sadism, but that your life by comparison seems magnificent, your little narcissistic problems are stunted by comparison to their true sadness, linked to genocide and sickness.

HS: Yes, but then it's the big question as to the definition of sadness, and I think that sadness is pretty equally dispersed throughout the world. Having nothing to eat, that is sadness, but being alone in an apartment at ninety years old, not being loved, or for a child to see his father go off to work, that is another form of sadness. Here, our sort of glaciation of society is as collective a sadness as hunger in Sudan.

GN: In *Kisangani Diary*, you have lots of moments that are really disturbing. Like when you see that child born dead. But one of the worst: The little child that is all alone, that is put on the ground, that is picked up, then put down again, he is dead, he is not dead, and you see this photographer pass him by with his huge lens. The man is well-fed; he has clean pants. He looks and asks himself, "What do we do with this baby?" And then, all of a sudden, it is as if he himself no longer perceives this as a human life. It's useful or not useful: it's something quite simple when you see the baby, you just want to take him in your arms and take him away, yet you know you can't because when you are sitting there, watching the scene, there is nothing can be done, that baby has already died.

HS: On film, the scene is unbearable, but in real life, it is quite banal. It's strange how film isolates this view. It is just part of rows of children all in the same state, and when you live within this, you can't be at the battle of Stalingrad and cry when you see someone die; no, in reality, everyone around is dying. Here, it was the same, and I don't recall this particular moment as being particularly unbearable, just another moment among others. Sometimes, the camera can see better than our own eye. It's almost a miracle.

GN: The goal is to try to create more consciousness so that people make the effort to think their own way, to take part in change, or rather to be able to create something that will exist long term, to create continuity and balance in regard to what is happening?

HS: Hard to say. My reflex is not to make a film for the good of the world. I think I do have the desire, as do many other authors, to reveal myself, to bring my perspective, and to say clearly, here, this is what I think, this is what I see, and I have personally experienced this story and I would like to tell it to you.

GN: In your film, you don't have the bad guys on one side and the good guys on the other. That's talent.

HS: I know that not everything I film is new. I am not the missionary that tells you that Africa is in deep shit and that children are dying. Yet I do feel that we are missing different image treatments, put together in a different kind of way. I think it specifically works on the form, the rhythm, and the editing, that can make a difference in bringing more complexity to this reality: the polarity of the white man, with his large lens camera, and at the same time not trying to denounce him, or make him out to be some kind of living asshole. I wanted to show this because it was important, but without saying: Here, this is the ass, because he was there, just like I was. I was there, too.

GN: In *Darwin* there isn't any music and sound effects. Yet in *Kisangani Diary*, you use this effect that I like, which is quite artificial and usually used in horror films, it's the use of infrabass sound. There are lots of sequences where, aside from the music, you have this infrabass going, "*ououou.*" It creates this feeling of fear, which is presumably the true feeling you would have in such a place because the military forces are not far because you have people being eaten away by sickness, and then you feel this sort of uneasiness, and it's this artifice, almost fictional, but it works really well. In the same way, you can do things in color or black and white; black and white tends to be more dramatic, but with this sound thing, it is as if you were underlining parts, as if you were saying these are the parts where you should feel scared.

HS: The use of black and white was not about dramatization. It was rather a technical issue: the tapes were so fucked that I need to take the color out. Yet the use of bass and music in the film, when I see it today, I think it is a bit much. A lot of people have criticized me for this, but I do understand. I was looking for a very direct way to express this extremely deep sense of anxiety, so I looked to push the form really far. In this regard, I take responsibility for my choice. To transfer what is lived, or the anxiety, the state of being, is also an essential element of documentary filmmaking. It might be this as well that separates this sort of film from other documentaries because their goal is to represent a true reality, a story as truly as possible. I can show the reality of an airport by showing the flies on the windowpanes since the flies represent this sort of strange, unspoken element. Actually, they are much more truthful than some kind of numbers showing the time it takes the Kalashnikovs to be transferred within the airport. I have been criticized at times for not showing certain things, it had not been understood. Too bad.

GN: With an aggressive film, you will get aggressive reactions. *Darwin* is extremely aggressive, and frankly, I am very pleased that it is able to do so well commercially.

JWD: It seems that whether it is about truth or lies, the need to manipulate, choose, cut, or reformat still exists.

HS: There are two kinds of lies when it comes to documentaries: the real lie and the poetic lie. In *Kisangani*, for instance, there is a poetic lie, it is at the beginning of the film when we go through the forest by train. This really did happen, except that I was unable to film as the military had confiscated my equipment. I filmed the return journey of the train and inversed it: in the film, it is the arrival. I can handle this. The jungle is the same. It would be a real lie if I said, "Here, these are the Indians," when they are not. In a film, at an emotional moment, you can say anything, and everyone will believe you. These are little manipulations that all documentary makers have a tendency to do. I can film the head of a company in Rwanda and want to put a plastic fish in his office to make it a funny scene. But if I do that, I am lying.

GN: There are a lot of documentaries where you see people walking, and you have the feeling that there are so many angles like the camera had been moved, and that they must have asked the guy, "Look, now you walk forward, now back." Then you have had this guy repeat the move several times to get this kind of cinematographic cutting. In the end, it works, but it's a little strange because you have these notions of directing, as you can see that the guy must have repeated his steps four or five times, such that it feels normal and the entire sequence is covered. Is this cheating or not? You play with the guy and he becomes an actor?

HS: That's something that I do not do, yet it is a sort of setup that is not cheating since the guy actually is walking in reality. Just usually, it is poorly set up. The guy isn't completely at ease walking anymore. Here I was with the man in his office, and I say to him, "It is a nice fish; what do you think of turning it on?" That's what I said to him. And it is not luck that the fish worked. In the part with all the skeletons, there's a guy with a skeleton on his T-shirt. If I came there with this skeleton T-shirt and asked him to put it on, I would be a liar. No one aside from me would have known, but in doing that, I would have taken energy out of the film, that's for sure. Yet if I capture the scene, then I have captured a particularly strong absurd moment, and this gives me the energy to aim for that. There's also the prostitute singing with the Russian: it was not by accident that I was there filming them when they were singing together. I knew the Russian, I knew the prostitute, we would drink together, I would buy them beers, and I knew that this girl could sing, so I asked if she might want to sing something for us, and then the situation created itself, and it was authentic. I don't pretend not to be there, invisible. You hear my voice, and you see how the camera is moving as if I were drunk, too. It was a little blurry. It became authentic as well because of this. If you begin to lie to yourself, whether it be in film or in real life, all is lost; you betray yourself.

GN: Do you know the film *Isle of Flowers* [Jorge Furtado, 1989]? It is this Brazilian short film, very arty, funny, and very mean. A film about garbage, a garbage island in Brazil, with these kids from the shanty towns that come to eat the leftovers that the pigs have not eaten. Because you can sell pigs, and unfortunately, you cannot sell kids. Then afterwards, there is this whole lecture on the fact that the pigs get to eat first because you can sell them, yet you can't do this trade with children. In regard to the cynicism of commerciality, there are common points with *Darwin*. Except it is more condensed. This film had made it all around the world.

HS: One last thing. People often ask me if the people in the film have had a chance to see the film. This is something that I started in late 2005. I went to Tanzania earlier this year to meet them again and show them the film. I will go to the Ukraine as well in this little plane that I fly myself, sitting on the outside. I will be landing on the runway where you can find these big guys from the film. It will be another film to confront these Russians with their image to see how it all goes. It is a necessary continuation, as I want to know the reactions of people who play a role in the film. Also, to gain a better understanding of this type of work for the future. I am not waiting for anything that's necessarily romantic or consensual. It would be nice if the Russians saw this as a work of art and that they would like to participate in something important like this, yet they could very well become angry. I hope for the first option.

GN: When you make a fiction film, and you are paying people like this, and they don't really know the storyline of the film. . . . On *Irreversible*, some of them assumed that the film was too violent, and they wished to remove their image from the film when it was already too late. Then, it depends on what the people around them are saying. And when it is a documentary, and the guy is actually exposing himself because he is saying things that maybe he shouldn't be saying, in effect, it could be a bit of a problem showing it to them.

HS: But it is a true adventure, not the Camel Trophy [an off-road driving competition].

Les enfants terribles: Gaspar Noé versus Harmony Korine

Harmony Korine and Nick Bradshaw / 2010

From *Sight and Sound*, September 7, 2010. Reprinted by permission of *Sight and Sound*.

We're not sure why, but when we noticed that Gaspar Noé's *Enter the Void* was due for UK cinema release in the same week as the DVD debut of Harmony Korine's *Trash Humpers*, we wondered what would happen if you put the two indie *wunder*-bad boys together in a room. (Both films are, in their different ways, envelope- and button-pushing experiments with cinematic form and content, bravura if not infantile back-alley portraits of lowlife dereliction and excess. But we should refrain from over-rationalizing the idea.)

It turned out that not only were the two already familiar, but that Korine was then visiting an art show in Noé's Paris—and no sooner had we wished it than the pair had met up and delivered us the following audio recording.

As you'll hear, the quality is on the guerrilla side: we're not quite sure where in Paris they convened against a very audible backdrop of howling dogs, baying crows, and what sound like steel sawmills, but perhaps best not to ask.

Question: Inspiration—where do you find it?

Harmony Korine: So Gaspar, do you come up with stories while you're walking down the street?

Gaspar Noé: I don't have so many thoughts; usually, it's a newspaper or something that sticks in your mind for a long time.

HK: For me, it's usually, I'll be walking down the street and I'll see some woman with rollers in her hair, and she has boxing gloves, and she's punching herself. And then I'll start thinking it would make an amazing film to follow her. Maybe she has a really incredible home life. That's usually how my films come about. So, do you clip the newspapers?

GN: Yes, but usually, I then lose the clips. I put them in boxes and then can't find the boxes. Last time, there was a story in the newspapers about a guy in Japan who goes to a cliff to stop people committing suicide, telling them that life is good. I thought that's a good idea . . .

HK: That would be amazing, actually.

GN: I guess for *Enter the Void*, the idea was some drug experiences that you haven't seen portrayed.

HK: That definitely seems like *Enter the Void*. But then a lot comes from people we know, right?

GN: Mainly girls!

HK: Remember you told me something a long time ago that's stuck with me, that you knew this guy here in Paris, and one of his favorite things to do was pretend that he was a chair?

GN: No, no, no, no, no, no, no! I met him accidentally—I went to a nightclub. I was kind of wasted and wanted to sit down. And the sofa was kind of weird, kind of moving, so I put my hands on it, and it was a guy pretending to be a sofa. He'd put on something like a velvet curtain, and when I stood up, I noticed that there were some feet coming out. But yeah, that's a good story, huh?

HK: How comfortable was he?

GN: Er, kind of shaky for a sofa.

HK: Do you remember one guy we went to see, this guy who's a bodyguard for prostitutes? From time to time, he would introduce me to prostitutes, and the prostitutes would say, "Well, there's things I always refuse to do." And I'd ask them what, and they'd say, "Well, they want to buy the used condoms and swallow them in front of me." Can you imagine doing a movie about a guy's perversions?

GN: I remember that guy; he had a motor scooter, and he was reading Primo Levi books.

HK: Yeah, and although he was not Jewish, he had tattooed the number of Primo Levi on his body.

GN: He was a real fan, and a film buff, and a great pimp. One of the world's greatest pimps.

Q: Both *Trash Humpers* and *Enter the Void* rely on first-person camerawork. Do you like the camera to be an active participant in your films?

GN: How personal is *Trash Humpers*? How much does it talk about your own life?

HK: No, no, the camera's viewpoint.

GN: In my case, it's more evident than in yours, a subjective perception of your own life.

HK: Yeah, I think your films always have that, right? The camera's always almost in human form. Even in *Irreversible*, the camera seems to be stalking; it's like a physical presence in motion.

GN: Have you ever thought of doing a movie in 3D? Because if you do a POV in 3D it could be great, and with a voiceover and some Sensurround effects . . .

HK: You should remake the film in 3D! For me, it just made sense because *Trash Humpers* was more like a diary or document of these characters. If the camera didn't have that presence, it wouldn't make any sense.

GN: Mostly, each scene is one long shot.

HK: Yeah, there are no cuts in each scene, there's no coverage, it's like a home movie.

GN: But that's the thing I like doing. When you do a master shot, things happen in front of the camera. But when you start precutting the scene, you're killing the energy. It's better to do many different master shots and then pick the best.

Q: Realism—what is important to show? Do you consciously depict the margins or extremes of society?

GN: I depict the center. I'm the most centered man I know!

HK: You're a centrist filmmaker?

GN: I don't know why people think that's the margin. That's the center.

HK: You mean there's something more underground than what you're showing?

GN: No! That's the center. I think that having fun, I think your mind is in the center of life.

HK: Oh right, yeah, that makes sense. I also think in the end, you just gravitate towards what you find interesting, and you film or photograph what you find compelling or desirable. That's the kind of thing I almost feel is best not to think about. You have to jump off a bridge if you think about that too much.

GN: I think in your case what people can see are margins.

HK: Exactly! Most of the time, what people find really disturbing, I always mean it to be just like a comedy.

Q: Pushing the envelope—are you aware of social taboos when making your films? Is your work set in dialogue with or opposition to prevailing norms of cinema and society, or do you work in blissful isolation? Is there an element of social critique in the films?

HK: If there is, I think it probably just comes through accident. I don't know, do you go into a movie to critique or with any agenda?

GN: No, no. To critique, you have to have a clear point of view on reality; I'm lost all the time. I just know sometimes you feel safer repeating things you don't like to make sure you dislike them.

HK: Exactly. And I guess that would imply that you know where you're going. I think most of the time, you have no idea. You just end up there in a certain place, right?

GN: But also, I think most people who do social critique are bare[faced] liars, trying to make money pretending they're lefties.

HK: Yeah, yeah, yeah. Most people who are social critics, I think are getting paid off by the politicians. I think they're working for Martha Stewart.

Q: Death—are you scared of dying?

GN: Are we scared of dying? Harm?

HK: I mean, it's not something I look forward to . . . [*Giggles*]

GN: I [thought] you liked all kinds of experiences?

HK: It's not anything that when I think about I get excited about. It's also something I don't think about that often. I don't live in fear of it, but I'm not looking forward to it.

GN: Have you ever thought of committing suicide? Seriously—have you ever thought the only issue like next week would be to commit suicide?

HK: I don't think I've ever gotten to a point where it was a serious thought, but you know, you think about everything in life. What about you?

GN: I'd rather go for murder. Killing's funner than getting killed.

HK: Yeah, you seem like the type to murder, I have to admit that.

GN: The worst thing is that knowing that [one day] you'll be dead can help you to work during the daytime.

HK: That's true, I agree. You try and do as much as you can.

NB: Are your films sentimental?

GN: My films are hypersentimental.

HK: Yeah, I think there is something sentimental about your movies.

GN: And yours, too?

HK: Yeah, they're like memories; dreams, maybe, that you wished you'd had.

GN: They're mostly about a man losing a woman . . .

HK: Yeah, they're one step away from romantic comedies.

GN: Could you do a movie for kids?

HK: I did a movie called *Kids*.

GN: No, *for* kids.

HK: Oh. Er . . . that was for kids!

GN: No, not for teenagers.

HK: Oh, for little children? I thought that movie *Babe* was terrific, with the pig that talked. Remember that one?

GN: Yeah, I haven't seen it. But I saw lately *Toy Story 3*, and cried at the end. It's in 3D, and the toys are almost getting burned; they cry all together . . .

HK: Yeah, I heard that was a good one.

GN: That's the thing my parents ask me, "Are you ever going to do a movie for kids?"

HK: If the money was right, I'd be open to it.

Q: Filmic narrative—reform, revolution, or destruction?

HK: I think all of the above and then some. I just think that you make movies the way you see things and the way you want to see things. When you tell a story you tell it in a certain way, with a certain style.

GN: I think it's not about reinventing the language. It's just that you get bored of the usual language, the close-up of an actress talking, another close-up of another actor talking, then another close-up of the actress reading her dialogue, and then after a while, all movies will be TV movies.

HK: That's a really good way to put it, I think: there's just a boredom that goes with making films in a traditional narrative. It's just the same thing over and over again.

GN: Does it happen too that you get more and more bored by movies?

HK: Of course!

GN: When I was a kid, I'd watch a movie every day; now, I can barely watch a movie every two weeks, and at the end of the year, I have two or three movies in mind that were worth watching.

HK: I think that's terrible, too, but I don't know what that is. Is it the movies being made, or is it me?

GN: It's you: you've seen it, and then you don't believe the tricks anymore. You believe the magic tricks as long as you're not a magician, but once you understand how they're done you don't buy the acting, you don't buy the makeup, the lighting, the story . . .

HK: That's true. Except the movies I used to love, I still love, and they're still kind of exciting. Like I know you could watch *2001* over and over again. I could watch Pam and Tommy's sex tape . . .

GN: What's your favorite porn movie?

HK: My favorite porn movie? I don't really have one.

GN: Have you ever seen one called *Defiance of Good*? It's the only porn movie where I thought the narrative was really strong.

HK: But you can always watch Chaplin movies over and over again, and they're going to be funny. You can always watch Buster Keaton. But I understand what you're saying.

Q: Taking the money and running—what would tempt you to Hollywood?

GN: Not the drugs, not the cocaine, not the swimming pools . . .

HK: I don't think that exists there in the same way.

GN: What scares me about Hollywood is not so much the producers or the agents or the actors; what scares me are the guilds, that you have to work inside a guild system. I don't think you can have as much fun working inside the Hollywood film industry as you can as an outsider in the European way or in the independent way as an American.

HK: Right. For me, honestly, it's never even been an issue. It hasn't been a huge factor in my life; the movies generally are pretty far away from that. I just think you take everything on a case-by-case basis.

GN: Do you have an agent who sends you scripts?

HK: I have an agent, but he doesn't send me scripts!

GN: I receive scripts from time to time, but then they tell you who's already going to be the director. The worst story was Cronenberg: after he did *The Fly*, or just before, they asked him to make *Beverly Hills Cop II*.

HK: See, I would actually jump at the chance to make *Beverly Hills Cop II*. That's actually like a fantasy for me. But it's never going to happen.

GN: But also—have you lived in LA?

HK: Never.

GN: I don't like it; it's too sleazy.

HK: It's too sleazy for you?

GN: No, sleazy in that they're all obsessed with money and celebrity. It's not a sexy city . . .

HK: It's mostly accountants and pencil-pushers.

GN: Yeah, and people trying to be on TV.

HK: Yeah, pickpockets, accountants, and pencil-pushers. None of them are sexy; all of them have forked tongues.

"I Never Get Killed in Dreams, but I Often Kill in Dreams": An Interview with Gaspar Noé

Philip Concannon / 2010

From *Phil on Film*, September 20, 2010. Reprinted by permission.

Gaspar Noé is one of the most daring and controversial filmmakers working in contemporary cinema. His three feature films to date—*Seul contre tous, Irreversible*, and now *Enter the Void*—have each offered an unforgettable cinematic experience marked by the director's stunning technical ability and his willingness to explore the very depths of human nature. In every film he makes, Noé seems determined to see how far he can push both himself and his audience, and *Enter the Void* is his most audacious work yet, depicting death as the ultimate trip. I met the director when he was in London recently to talk about his extraordinary new film.

Philip Concannon: This has been a dream project of yours for so many years. Why has this film been such an obsession for you?

Gaspar Noé: I would say it's because my favorite movie ever is *2001: A Space Odyssey*. I saw it when I was seven years old, and that was my first drug trip. I was with my parents, and when I came out of the movie, I was totally stoned. What was that tunnel of light? What was that weird baby with the big head at the end? They told me that the fetus is a baby before it is born, and I was told by my mother that before I was a baby, I was a fetus inside her belly, and that was because my father put his penis inside her vagina, so maybe I associate that movie with me learning about my origins. My whole life, I was trying to reproduce the shock I had with *2001: A Space Odyssey*, so when I started smoking marijuana at the age of thirteen and taking acid at fifteen, it was because I wanted to go through the tunnel again, but you never get those images again. When I went to film school, I said I wanted to do a trippy movie that could reproduce the vision and perception you have when you are stoned. The whole dream was to make another movie like the one I saw as a kid and to put people in an altered state like I was put in when I watched *2001*. You have been in the world of Oz, and you want to become the Wizard of Oz years later.

PC: And at what point did you make the decision to shoot the film from the main character's point of view?

GN: Accidentally, one day when I was twenty, I was on mushrooms, and I went home and saw *The Lady in the Lake*. I thought it would be great if the trippy project I had could be seen through the eyes of the main character so all of the distortion would be linked to his perception, and then I was reading books about out-of-body experiences. At that time, I didn't know what the movie was going to be about, but I started taking notes, and I was obsessed with movies that were dealing with hallucinogenic things, like *Easy Rider* and *Flatliners*, and when I put all the pieces together, I realized I should make a movie about someone who gets shot, and then you follow his dream of coming out of his body. I thought I should also apply the structure of *The Tibetan Book of the Dead* so the trippy part of the movie with him outside of his body could be much longer. I had been doing lots of breathing exercises, inhaling every three minutes, because I read that it could lead to out-of-body experiences, but it never happened to me. I studied hypnosis and tried lots of chemicals to come out of my body, but it never happened, so I came to the conclusion that you cannot separate the soul from the flesh, and the only way of coming out of my body is by making a movie. I can put a camera on a crane and film that, and that can be my only out-of-body experience ever. So it's a long process, and I was also buying experimental music and watching experimental videos, and while I was working on other projects I kept on working on this one. It is like a collective dream. Maybe there's something you believe in, and you want to procreate that collective dream. I don't know if Steven Spielberg believed that aliens and flying saucers existed when he made *Close Encounters*, but there's a collective dream that you want to portray.

PC: What were the technical challenges that you faced as you set up those long tracking shots?

GN: We had to rebuild all of the locations that were shown in the flashbacks. They were real locations, but we had to rebuild them in the Toho studios in Tokyo. We were shooting from above on a crane; each crane scene took a whole day, and we were doing many different shots because we knew we could not cut those scenes. Thankfully, working in Japan is very different from working in the States. The people are so passionate; they can work twelve to thirteen hours a day, six days a week. At the point where they get their salary, they are not counting the minutes like they did in Montreal because there are so many guilds, or whatever. So you pay the same salary in Japan, but you don't have all of the extras that you would have in many other countries. The thing I liked in Japan was that the team was very perfectionist, and for a perfectionist director to have such a team is the ultimate dream.

PC: The Japanese setting is hugely important for the film as well. Tokyo looks incredible on screen.

GN: Originally the movie was to be set in France. I decided it would be better to film in English because it could be shown in most countries without subtitles, so I came to London and New York, but then somebody said the best country to move this story to would be Japan. It's far trippier, and it looks like Las Vegas with the lights, and it has this psychedelic feeling.

PC: Was it a challenge to get such an ambitious and experimental film financed?

GN: It was hard convincing people to put money into the movie. I knew from the beginning that there would be a few explicit sex scenes, that I didn't want to use famous actors, that I wanted to shoot in Tokyo, and that it would be very experimental—how can you convince people to put big money on that? What helped me was that *Irreversible*, which was a very violent movie, was commercially very successful, so the same people who sold that movie abroad ended up financing this movie. I don't know if they're going to get their money back. I'm sure in the long term they will, but in the short term, I think the film is too anguishing to be a hit. The script didn't show that it was an anguishing movie; it looked far more sentimental, but once you put the drums on the soundtrack and the effects of the bad trip, I was conscious that the film would be more anguishing than I ever told them. You don't tell your financers that, though. You always tell them, "Oh, it's going to be like *Trainspotting* mixed with *Mulholland Drive*, and those movies made great money." [*Laughs*]

PC: I was interested in the different versions of the film because I saw the cut that was presented at last year's London Film Festival, and I watched it again in a shorter version that was screened to the press recently.

GN: When we first watched it in Cannes, the movie was not completed. The very final cut of the movie was shown in Sundance in January of this year on a 35mm print, and there are just two versions of this movie. The official version, which was shown in France and some other countries, that is the two hours and thirty-five minutes version, and I had to sign a contract that said if it goes over two hours and twenty minutes, I would do a shorter version. Instead of reediting the movie to make it shorter for other countries, I decided to recut the reels, so you could just pull reel number seven out and you can show the movie with either eight reels or nine reels. I guess the version you've seen during the press screenings is the shorter version, where seventeen minutes are missing, just a whole segment. During the London Film Festival, they were showing the long version, but now they're going to be mostly releasing the shorter version and then they'll put both on DVD. I like them both. Maybe the people who really enjoyed the shorter version will see the longer one. They said they would show it at the Curzon Soho in the opening week, the last screening of Friday night and Saturday night, they would show the longer version.

PC: How did you make the decision to lose that particular reel?

GN: The scenes that are missing are mostly some astral visions and the moment in which the guy wakes up at the morgue and thinks he has come back to life, but people say, "No, you didn't come back to life, you are just a zombie, you can't even talk" or whatever. But I think both versions work, and weirdly, it is not a censored version because the reel that is missing doesn't contain any explicit sex or anything that is shocking, so it's not because of censorship. It's mostly because they saw that the shorter version could be more comprehensible and more commercial, that's all. Maybe if someone liked the shorter version, they will make sure the second time that they see the seventeen minutes that were missing, like now they are rereleasing *Avatar* with nine more minutes, so why not? [*Laughs*]

PC: You seem drawn to melodramatic narratives . . .

GN: Life is melodramatic. I cry very often. If I just think for one second of my parents' death, I start crying, and just by saying the words, my eyes fill with tears. The moment you fall in love with someone, you are already afraid of losing that person, so you have these obsessions. There are aspects of the brain that are very universal, so if you put two kids in the movie who are losing their parents, that talks to everybody. I was watching *Toy Story 3*, and the moment you see all of the toys close to getting burned and they hold hands, I started crying, and I couldn't believe I was crying at a 3D cartoon, but anyway. Even if you want to make a movie that's as trippy as can be or as cool as can be, the thing that makes it closer to life is the fact that there is some melodrama inside.

PC: You also enjoy challenging your audience and provoking extreme reactions from them.

GN: We all enjoy playing spectators with our fears, and when you go to see a movie, it's like a shamanic trance. You want to be scared by seeing things that you don't want to happen in your real life. It's like in a dream, I never get killed in dreams, but I often kill in dreams, and I want to wake up because I'm so scared that I will be going to prison, but then I'm back in the safe world. When you see a movie that's a bad trip, you come out, and your life seems so much sweeter compared to the bad trip. People say the movie is pessimistic, but you can say it has an optimistic secondary effect of people coming out and saying, "Whoa, my life is so sweet and I'm so lucky." Even with Pasolini's *Salò, or the 120 Days of Sodom* that happens, seeing what torture is and what fascism is can turn into, "I'm so lucky we're living in a safe country and not living in wartime."

PC: Now that you've finally completed this dream project, what are you planning on doing next?

GN: There is one thing I was thinking of for many years, I have never seen the ultimate love movie. I suppose it would be a love story, a melodrama, and a porn movie. When I fall in love, I have sex, and when you have sex in real life, it's hardcore, so why can't you mix love and sex in a movie? In most erotic movies, there are no feelings, and in life, there are feelings, but since the beginning of the history of cinema, nobody ever came close to what your everyday sexual life is. Sometimes an arty movie will include an orgy scene or a gay sex scene, or they will show a blowjob in the movie, but the point is not about showing the thing. The point is, why can you not portray a loving sexual encounter between a man and woman on the screen without there being a scandal?

Gaspar Noé Interview: *Enter the Void*, Illegal Substances, and Life after Death

Ryan Lambie / 2010

From *Den of Geek*, September 21, 2010. Reprinted by permission.

It's unsurprising, given the assaultive, powerful, and often disturbing nature of Gaspar Noé's movies, which have included the controversial *I Stand Alone* and *Irreversible*, that an interview with the director himself should prove to be so unusual and meandering.

Speaking enthusiastically and at breakneck speed, Noé discussed the making of his latest film, *Enter the Void*, an extraordinarily hypnotic, individual meditation on life, drugs, sex and death . . .

Ryan Lambie: The film is astonishingly ambitious, both technically and philosophically. There can't be many directors attempting to show what it's like to die in the first person and then be reincarnated. What set you on the path to such a film?

Gaspar Noé: I read books on reincarnation and many books about out-of-body experiences. Actually, the movie is not so much about reincarnation. It's more about someone who gets shot while on acid and DMT [dimethyltryptamine], and trips out about his own death and dreams about his soul escaping from his flesh because he wants to keep this promise to his sister that he'll never leave her, even after death.

I don't believe in life after death. But I still enjoyed the idea of doing a movie that would portray that collective dream, that collective need. Like flying saucers are a collective need for people who need to believe in flying saucers. You don't need to believe in flying saucers to do a movie about Martians or flying saucers.

You just say, "Well, it's in literature and books, and people need to believe there's something after [death] because otherwise life is too short." It's better to tell people that, "Don't worry, life is short, but you get to have a second chance. You can survive and always rearrange things that happened in your lifetime."

That's what all religions rely on. They say you'll be rewarded somewhere up there in the sky, or if you misbehave, you'll go to hell. But those are brainwashing tools to make people take their money and bring it to the churches.

Buddhists are not as hardcore as Catholics and other religions, but they're still, I think, part of such a huge lie that it's scary. I didn't want to promote that lie, and at the end, when you see the baby coming out from the mother's belly, you don't see the face of [the central character's] sister; you see the face of the mother, so you don't know if you're seeing his original birth. He's recreating a false memory of that traumatic moment that was his birth when he discovered light and oxygen. Or is he just getting into a loop, and your perception of time is only likened to how your brain is built?

You don't know if the character dies at the start of the movie or if he's going to wake up in a morgue or in a hospital or in prison. You don't really know what happened after he got shot. The only part that is really specific is the beginning.

Then, technically, the movie is very complex, and I was happy that this project was delayed and delayed and delayed for many reasons. I was not financially bankable because I had not made a commercial success before *Irreversible*, so the movie could finally happen after *Irreversible*, and would never have happened before.

And also, the fact that it was delayed meant the beautiful aesthetic I got for this movie is far, far better than anything I could have dreamt of eight years ago.

Towards the end, the weird trip turns into a bad trip, like sometimes mushroom trips or acid trips turn into bad trips. But a bad trip can be very rewarding because when you come out of one, it's like coming out of a bad dream where you get killed or something, and the moment you wake up, you still feel the presence of that reality and the dream, or the nightmare, is always real. But you feel so safe coming back to the real world, and some people said when they came out of this movie that they were still scared.

Kubrick said something about *2001*, that it's an acid religious movie. I did another acid movie pretending to be religious or Buddhist, but, at the end, it's dysfunctional enough to see that it's not all it seems.

RL: You mentioned the trip that turns bad at the beginning. It's almost like its own separate film. How much input did you have in that sequence?

GN: Actually, I drank a few times ayahuasca, which is a drink full of DMT that is only legal in the Amazonian jungle, so you have to go there to take it. And when you drink it, you have visions that are far scarier or far more futuristic than any visions in altered states you can get from any other means.

You forget that you have a human form and that you're on a planet. It's a really hardcore experience that I absolutely do not regret, as when I went there, I was already thinking about this project, and I was thinking about images. It was almost like professional research.

So you always have this excuse that you're not just going there for some existential means; you're going there for professional reasons.

Sorry, what was the question?

RL: Did someone help you with the psychedelic . . .

GN: No, no, I came back, and one day I was in a city where a guy told me about smokeable DMT, and I said I know, there's another version of DMT that you smoke that lasts as fine and strong. And I said that when I smoked DMT once, it's like an ayahuasca trip, with the promise that ayahuasca lasts four or five hours, and that seems like a whole day.

Sometimes it's like a crazy journey, but when you smoke DMT, you say, "Oh, I had a great trigger for a four-hour movie or a one-day-long movie, and then I did a second time, and once again, the trip was very intense, but it just does it for five minutes, and then the moment was gone."

I said, "Well, instead of having the guy being on acid at the beginning, I should do a DMT trip that would last five minutes on screen like it lasts in real life," but the point then is how to portray those visions that are very graphic and very geometrical.

Very many people say that they look like the movie *Tron*, that they are just bright neon lights, and so, of course, they were going to be done with computer graphics, and hopefully, I was working with this company who accepted not only to do the visual effects but also to coproduce the movie.

BUF are the best in France, and Pierre Buffin, visual effects provider and coproducer of the movie, put me in contact with the best graphic designer since but worried that his best graphic designers were doing DMT visions or that they had never even experienced mushrooms, so I had to have all these visual references. I want the shapes of the underwater forms of life. I want them to be made of neon lights, and I want the background to be black. It has to be scary.

And they came up with many different visuals that were really amazing, that allowed them to make this five-minute film. At the end, some people who were DMT smokers, they came up to me and said it's close.

Sometimes, when you're on ayahuasca, you have visions that are almost too simple, too silly, to be spiritual images. You feel that you're going through a tunnel. It's like in dreams, where you never know if you're going to have a nightmare or a sweet dream. I read that maybe the molecule that makes you have dreams is the DMT that you have inside your brain.

So actually, if you smoke it or you drink it, you have very long and colorful dreams that you would have any night, but only in a small amount. The DMT's inside your brain already.

And there's another theory that when people have these final trips where they're dying or near death, it's because of the amount of DMT. Because of a car crash, because of fear, because of this or that.

RL: The film's psychedelic use of color, it reminded me of Japanese videogames and Japanese anime. Is that why you set *Enter the Void* in that country, because of its colorful culture and the neon signs, and so on?

GN: Tokyo's like a huge pinball machine. The first time you're there, and you don't understand what's going on, it's like "ding ding ding ding ding" everywhere. The lights are changing; the neon lights are moving.

In Hong Kong, you also have that, but I'd been to Hong Kong just once, and I'd been to Tokyo fifteen times. I love their cinema, I love their nightclubs, I love being there. I thought Tokyo would be the very best place to shoot this movie.

And, of course, if you get busted with any drugs in Japan, it's very bad news. Not only if you're arrested with a small piece of a joint, if you get arrested with cocaine, speed, or marijuana in your pee, they make you do a pee test, they can make you go to prison for six months, and you're never allowed to go back to Japan after your sentence.

So, I thought, if you want to have a young, cool drug dealer being in danger, Tokyo is perfect because if he's taking twenty pills to a friend and he's arrested, that could mean four years of jail. So, the tension's much higher.

If you got arrested in England with twenty pills of ecstasy, nothing much is going to happen to you. I didn't want the guy to be a big drug dealer. I just wanted him to try to survive on the small money he can take from his friends and his friend's mother. At a point in the script, it was said that he was a DJ, so maybe he got a little money from there, but the guy has problems providing for himself.

RL: A lot's been talked about the visual aspect of the film, but the audio side is also fascinating. It reminds me—and I know you used Coil on the soundtrack—of John Balance's *Time Machines* project, in that there's this throbbing, pulsating stereo effect that—

GN: What's that?

RL: You know the band Coil? He [the band's late founding member John Balance] did an album called *Time Machines*—

GN: I don't know that record. I used another one called *ANS*, where he used a Russian synthesizer. And I met him, he came to Paris, and not only did he give me the rights to use that record *ANS*, but he also called his ex-partners in Throbbing Gristle and said, "Gaspar wants to put 'Hamburger Lady' in a scene of his movie." And he convinced the other partners in Throbbing Gristle to let me use the music for my film.

His music for Coil and Throbbing Gristle was trippy. Sometimes, just a drum can put you in a hypnotic state, and there aren't many musicians that play with drums and frequencies that can hypnotize you and put you in a dream state.

RL: How important do you think the audio is in achieving that, with the strobing and pulsating that you have all the way through? It almost creates an altered state in itself.

GN: Whatever helps to make the audience feel stoned was good. [*Laughs*]

In fact, some people, when they came out of a screening because there are no end credits, said it was just like being on a rollercoaster. And it's like *zoom!* And *whoosh!* And people come down shaking from the screening room, and say, "What a trip!" and it takes them five minutes or so before they say anything else!

RL: Gaspar Noé, thank you very much.

Gaspar Noé on 7 *Days in Havana*: Interview

James Mottram / 2012

Interview conducted and article written by James Mottram and first published in 2012 by *The List*, Edinburgh, UK. Reproduced by the kind permission of *The List*.

One of the highlights of this year's Edinburgh International Film Festival, *7 Days in Havana*, is an anthology movie set around the Cuban capital, inspired by the likes of *Paris je t'aime* and *New York, I Love You*. As the title suggests, seven filmmakers called the shots, from actor Benicio del Toro, making his directorial debut, to classy auteurs such as Laurent Cantet and Julio Medem. Straddling Latin America and Europe, however, is Gaspar Noé, the forty-eight-year-old Argentinean-born, French-based provocateur behind such controversial outings as *Irréversible* and *Enter the Void*.

"I really wanted to discover Cuba," he admits, when we meet at Cannes, where *7 Days in Havana* made its world premiere. "My father was obsessed with Cuba. He's Argentinean, and he went there in '73 or '74, and he loved it. It was a mystery for me. I don't know what happened to my father in those two weeks—I'm sure he had a second wife in Cuba!" After *Enter the Void* was invited to the Havana Film Festival, Noé got a taste for the city and decided he wanted to come back for more.

This being Noé, however, there was inevitably trouble. Having written a treatment for his short, he refused to provide a complete script to the producers, saying he was intending to improvise the dialogue with the actors. "They were afraid," says Noé. "The Spanish producer said, 'If Gaspar doesn't deliver a script, then we're going to do a movie called *6 Days in Havana* . . . so fuck him!'" Worse still, the delays meant that Noé was forced to make his short on half the money allotted to all the other directors, who had begun to divvy up his budget between them.

Even with his back against the wall, there's no question Noé's film *Ritual* is the most distinct of the seven with its depiction of an African-Cuban teenager, caught by her parents in bed with her girlfriend, then subjected to a voodoo-style "cleansing" ritual with the local witch doctor. Shot with lashings of style and an ominous drum-beat soundtrack, Noé spent time investigating such local rites. "They're kinda scary. First, you're not really welcome. And even when you're welcome, they're kinda scary. People believe so much in that, at a point, it's contagious."

Noé did make some changes; usually, it would be a female shaman or healer who would perform the ritual. "I thought it would be scarier and more emotional if it was a guy with a big knife," he smirks. If this lends the sequence a phallic energy, the one thing Noé did draw the line at was including an animal sacrifice. "I'm phobic of the animal sacrifices they usually do," he says. "I eat meat, I'm very carnivorous, but killing chickens or lambs for a sacrifice is not part of my way of being."

There was one other cultural difference Noé discovered during the casting process. "Girls are very lesbo-phobic there," he says. "In France, any teenager would kiss her best girlfriend just to impress the boys around. In Cuba, if a girl kissed another girl, she's banned from the community! Many girls came out from the casting so offended!" Gaspar Noé, it seems, can't do anything without a little controversy.

Seul contre tous: Interview with Gaspar Noé

Laurent Aknin / 2014

From *L'avant-scène cinéma*, January 2014. Reprinted by permission of *L'avant-scène cinema*. Translated by Geoffrey Lokke.

Gaspar Noé explained his intentions behind *Seul contre tous* in advance of the film's theatrical run, remarks that were widely quoted in the press and later included as bonus material in home video releases. Fifteen years after the film's debut, it seemed vital for us to sit down with the filmmaker to discuss his first feature as well as *Carne*, the medium-length film that had preceded it. In his recollections, we discovered a very precise, even obsessive director, one who brings up Jacques Becker when we ask him about Dario Argento . . .

Laurent Aknin: How do you view *Seul contre tous* fifteen years after its release? And *Carne*?

Gaspar Noé: They were my first real films. I felt like it was the first time I'd done something that I was actually proud of. This was coming off my first shorts. I'd thought to myself, "Let's do better," keeping in mind the kinds of films that I like. *Carne* was a cinephile film, the film of a guy who loves *Deliverance*, Hershell Gordon Lewis, Godard, and [Georges] Franju. So I mixed together a lot of things. The result resembles my obsessions from that time. *Seul contre tous* was an extension of this. Initially, it was intended to be a second short film to be coupled with *Carne*, thus forming a ninety-minute feature film, kind of like [Patrick] Bouchitey, who had just made a short that was then inserted into his feature *Cold Moon*. But in the end, the film took so long to make that my "sequel" became independent of the first film. Today, I can tell the film clearly resonates with its time. I've been told a lot that it was "Célinesque," but the truth is that I hadn't read any Céline back then. I obviously knew who he was, and I'd tried to read *Journey to the End of the Night*, but I'd failed twice. Above all, I think that the film conveys a very French strain of thought, very "bistro," or what you hear when you go to the hairdresser or in a taxi. It's a film about bars in France. I couldn't have moved the scenario elsewhere.

LA: What was the starting point, the first inspiration? Philippe Nahon told us that when you offered him the film, the pitch was simply "the story of a butcher who raises his daughter alone."

GN: Maybe I didn't want to scare him off. I wasn't going to tell him right away that the father had incestuous desires. I had an urge to paint a degenerate portrait of the country I lived in. It made me happy, for example, that the father was blond; it reminded me of National Front imagery. But at the same time, he had a communist past. This was the period, especially at the time of *Seul contre tous*, when people liked to scare themselves with the National Front, whereas the France of the 1950s and 1960s and after was extremely racist, if not more so. There are films that deal with this subject, like *Dupont Lajoie*. So when France became socialist, we had fun crying wolf. In fact, *Carne* and *Seul contre tous* were also born out of my love for *Harakiri*. When I arrived in France, I devoured *Harakiri*. I said to myself, "Look, in this country, they have this wonderful sense of humor, you have to take advantage of it." So I stepped into the breach.

LA: In addition to Céline, [Emil] Cioran is sometimes cited in regard to this form of pessimism.

GN: After leaving film school, I studied philosophy for two years, mainly to get a student card and the discount rate at the cinema. I loved taking courses on Plato and Nietzsche. But I was skipping all the other classes, so I don't really know anything about Cioran. My mother had given me *The Trouble with Being Born*, but almost as a joke. As a filmmaker, if you don't scratch yourself for a long time, by the time you get around to finally making a film, you end up putting a lot of yourself into it. You'll scratch your racist side, you'll scratch your depressive side, you'll scratch your paranoid side. Maybe all that went into it is things that I would think or say if I'd been poor and in as rough a shape as the butcher. There are manic-depressive people, those with schizophrenic tendencies. . . . I know that I'm an obsessive person. For example, I never question myself, but I always question others. I'm one of those people who, when they go on vacation, walks back two or three times just to check that the door is closed properly. There's no need to go looking for other writers or philosophers. The main source is me and the bullshit I hear at bars and elsewhere.

LA: The beginning of *Seul contre tous*, in addition to summarizing the action of the previous film, offers the complete biography of the butcher. Some of these elements already appear in *Carne*, for example, the fact that he is an orphan. Was this character fully formed in the first film?

GN: I think that his being an orphan comes from the fact that [Jean-Marie] Le Pen had been raised by the DDASS [Department of Housing and Social Affairs]. When I was making *Carne*, I wanted to do something of my own inspired by Franju's *Blood of the Beasts*, among other films, but I also wanted to create a portrait of a Dupont Lajoie figure who had started with good intentions. So I also had in mind Le Pen when he was younger. With a somewhat Strasbourg face—at any rate, someone closer to Germany than to Spain. In *Carne*, the character has no name. It's only in *Seul contre tous* that we see his ID card.

LA: "Philippe Chevalier" . . .

GN: Philippe, because it's Nahon, and Chevalier, because he sells horse meat, and because he's all alone—that made it a bit more romantic, I guess. I regret naming the girl Cynthia. Well, her name is Cynthia in *Carne*. But at one point, I thought about taking *Carne* back and editing the soundtrack; every time he calls her Cynthia in the voiceover, I'd change it to "France." And by combining the two films, the film would have been called *France*. I even had ideas for the title sequence: the "F" and the "N" would start to slide down, and only "RACE" would've remained. Race, FN . . .

LA: In any case, you are very fond of on-screen text, title cards, intertitles. . . . Some are citations. *Carne*'s end card, for example, references Dario Argento . . .

GN: No, that one's from *Le trou* by Jacques Becker. In the film, there was something that stayed with me: a character called Gaspard. He's quoted in the last sentence, "Poor Gaspard . . ." and then it says, "You have seen a film by Jacques Becker." But maybe Argento also stole from *Le trou*? Or maybe I mixed up the two; sometimes, we steal things without realizing it. For example, in *Seul contre tous*, I wasn't really aware that I was lifting from *Taxi Driver*, which I hadn't seen for a long time. Namely when he goes into the cinema and starts thinking to himself. I saw it again afterwards, and well, the connection is pretty obvious. The butcher's scheming, I know a lot of that's taken from *The Honeymoon Killers*.

LA: If we read across your films to date, we see a number of themes in the first two that come up again later . . .

GN: The pregnant woman . . .

LA: Yes, everything related to reproduction . . .

GN: There are people who are repressed fascists, others are repressed homosexuals, maybe I am a repressed father . . .

LA: There are always motifs around fertility: bellies, periods . . .

GN: . . . and always red, wet tunnels! In the next film, there's still this question of fertility. Maybe if I had children, I'd be less obsessed with it. But there's something else. When you make a movie, if you want strong emotions and intensity, the stuff of daily life isn't enough for that emotion to pass through the screen. When someone has to die, he needs to die in the most horrible way possible so that people can experience the fear of death. Likewise, when someone attacks someone else. When someone hits a woman, it can be violent in life, but on the screen, you know they're two actors. But if he hits her in her stomach and she's pregnant, then people will jump. But that's something of a bias. . . . In Haneke's *Amour*, when he slaps his wife, you jump out of your seat, and in *Blue Is the Warmest Color*, when they separate, reunite, and cry, you cry with them. So maybe it's just me. I told myself that when there is violence, it has to be as violent as possible, and when there's a death, it must be horrible, and when a memory is happy, then you have to put on some Bach or *Pachelbel's Canon* . . .

LA: But there's been some evolution, perhaps: in *Seul contre tous*, when the old woman dies in hospice care, you project a card: "Death does not open any door."

GN: Yes, and I still believe that.

LA: Yet *Enter the Void* can be seen as a soulful journey through rebirth or reincarnation, themes treated with derision by the *Carne* preacher.

GN: He does not reincarnate. For *Enter the Void*, the key is that it's all in his head. He does not go beyond. He just took DMT, acid, the same day, and he has a kind of trip or hallucination when he gets shot and falls on the ground. But you don't really know what happened with him. It's all a dream in his head since the more one moves toward the end, the more one sees his mother who died on a plane with a baby; he mixes up his mother, his sister. . . . And the childbirth, we shot it with the woman who played the mother, not his sister. When you see the birth in that subjective shot, the face you see, a little blurry, it is the mother's. It all comes back to memories of his birth. In my head, I was doing all this to bring the film closer to *The Tibetan Book of the Dead* while also allowing people to see how all of this mysticism is completely dysfunctional. There is no reincarnation taking place. Half of the people who see the film realize that it's the mother at the end, not the sister. I think life opens a lot of doors, but when you are dead, you are simply dead. I saw my mother die in the hospital, and it had the same lighting. When it happened, I thought to myself, "It's strange; I feel like I'd already staged this scene in *Seul contre tous*."

LA: Speaking of visions and mindscapes, the television shows in *Carne* are not realistic or believable. Were they a gag, or do they correspond to the mental landscape of the characters, Cynthia in particular?

GN: *Blood Feast* could have been shown on Canal+. . . . But for me, *Carne* wasn't that serious of a film, so there are things in it that relate more to my own taste. . . . Like the Mexican wrestlers, of the Santo type. Unfortunately, these things correspond to my taste and not to the reality that the film's supposed to depict. So, the film is a bit of a hybrid. If I had to do *Carne* again today, I wouldn't include *Blood Feast* or the masked wrestler. But it made me laugh. People consider

Irreversible to be a serious film, but there are a lot of childish things in it, like calling the club "The Rectum" and the rapist "The Tapeworm." It's all sardonic. I don't know if it's always the best move, but in *A Prophet* Jacques Audiard used music that doesn't correspond at all to the world of the prison. When you're a director, you try and stick to reality, but your own taste slips into the mixture. In *Seul contre tous*, the reason I put in the porn sequence is probably because I was watching a lot of porn. When I was depressed, I'd usually go walking at night. I once walked into a sex shop and it made my depression worse. It all depends on the context in which you're watching porn. It can be exciting or a thousand times more depressing than anything you've ever imagined. A depressed person shouldn't watch porn . . .

LA: On that note, what's the porn film that we see in *Seul contre tous*?

GN: I really have no idea! . . . I think my assistant, Stéphane Derdérian, had found a copy or a reel . . .

LA: In terms of *Irreversible*, why did you include this opening (or closing) sequence with Nahon? Was it just a nod or a wink, or did you feel the need to finish something and make a clear transition away from your first films?

GN: It's an important sequence, even if it doesn't make the films an actual trilogy. First, I had promised Nahon that he could be in the film, since he had worked his ass off on *Carne* and *Seul contre tous*. I was happy that he'd asked. But where did he belong? I couldn't see him in the club scene. And he asked me, "Is my scene with Albert and Vincent?" He knew both of them because he had done some work on *La haine*. I thought about having him play a cop. . . . In fact, we shot *Irreversible* in chronological order, not the order of the film (in reverse), but in the order of the story. He called me every day: "Where's my scene?" There was no place for him. He couldn't be in the subway scene, etc. How could I keep him happy? By then he was starting to freak out. Finally, I shot this epilogue. I wanted to use the music from the closing moments of *Seul contre tous*, the military march. And I also had my friend, the director Stéphane Drouot, who was living in a psychiatric hospital, who was so, so brilliant . . . I thought it would be nice to have them both in the scene together: Stéphane Drouot, someone who had missed out on life, who had taken too many amphetamines. His life had been tragic, but he was brilliant. He could be in the scene with Nahon, not with Philippe playing himself, but sitting alongside the kind of person the butcher is meant to represent. It'd be a meeting of the fallen butcher with a kind of fallen intellectual. Still, I didn't really know where I was going to put it. I thought about setting it outside the club, or maybe they would be walking around, and one of them would be holding a gun or something. And then I realized it could be funny to do something reminiscent of Nahon sitting in his cell in *Carne*. Pierre Jamin, who played Gérard, was a very good friend of Stéphane Drouot . . . he was willing to do the same scene but in a more psychotic way. In the end, Stéphane improvised all of his own lines. But I wrote Philippe's dialogue.

LA: Among other things, he finally confesses that he had slept with his daughter . . .

GN: Yes, and Nahon didn't want him to admit it! He already had endured questions about it when we were promoting *Seul contre tous*. He told himself, "No, he's thinking about it, but he won't do it." But in the end, you know, he's playing with her breasts. So he'd say, "But none of that was in the script." Eventually, he told me that we didn't have the same conception of the character. I had always let Philippe say whatever he wanted as the butcher. For him, he's a much nobler character than he is for me. But the scene in *Irreversible* allowed me to make him say the opposite of what he had been saying in interviews! It resonates with one of Drouot's improvised lines: "There is no wrongdoing, there are only facts."

LA: It's interesting that you brought in Drouot because he was probably the first to use 16mm scope for a short film.

GN: Yes, that's right. When I started making shorts, there were only two films that impressed me: Caro and Jeunet's *The Bunker of the Last Gunshots* and Drouot's *Star Suburb*. It's because those two films that I worked so hard making my first short. I thought: "Hey, you can do visual stuff, American style, for three francs in your apartment in Paris." You can have idols who exist far from your reality: Kubrick, Tarkovsky, etc. But you also have people close by. There was Drouot, but also [Jean-Baptiste] Mondino, who had made music videos that I really liked. I lifted stuff from both of them, from Mondino, especially when I made music videos afterwards, from Caro and Jeunet, as well. When I saw *Vibroboy*, too. But I'd also met Alain Cavalier, who meant a lot to me and with whom I became friends, even if that seems a little unlikely.

LA: You all have in common a desire for independence and self-sufficiency.

GN: In any case, something had rubbed off on me and you can see it in *Carne* and later in *Seul contre tous* because we did them with very little money. I was in debt the whole time *Carne* was being made, but then I managed to cover my bills. Afterwards, when I made *Seul contre tous*, we were producing Lucile Hadžihalilović's *La bouche de Jean-Pierre* at the same time. Half the money I had went into her film. After a while, we didn't know where we were. It was like a double Titanic, and you had to decide which ship you were going to save first. Ultimately, we decided to focus on *La bouche de Jean-Pierre*. But that film, in turn, probably influenced *Seul contre tous*. For example, there were very long sequence shots in her film, which were very good, whereas there were none in *Carne*. In *Seul contre tous*, when the father takes the daughter in his arms at the end is almost the counterpoint to the shot between the girl and Jean-Pierre in *La bouche*. It's the exact same situation, with only slight changes . . .

LA: The real difference is that *La bouche de Jean-Pierre* is seen from a feminine point of view, the little girl's, while *Seul contre tous* follows, for good reason, a male point of view.

GN: With the accompanying voiceover, yes. . . . But what's very weird is that these films generate a lot of confessions. I've had a lot of people who come talk to me about *Enter the Void* and their experiences with mushrooms, LSD, etc. A few people came over to tell me that they'd been in a car accident because I was also in an accident when I was a kid. But it's often about drugs, or else people think I'm a Buddhist. (But I never actually believed in any of that for a second.) With *Irreversible*, there were a lot of people, some of them guys, who had been raped who told me that it had made them reexamine things. You'd never have guessed they had been raped or beaten. After *Seul contre tous*, I had a lot of girls and guys who told me stories of incest, which I'd never have suspected. Even a girl whose boyfriend I knew talked to me about it, saying that I shouldn't tell her boyfriend. . . . But in this film, the guy is lost. In most movies that talk about incest, father-daughter, the man is demonized, he is shown as an executioner; it's rare to see a man like that shown as sympathetic in some respects. . . . By the time the film was released, we had blurbs from other directors of my generation about him; there was one from Christophe Gans, which I found really funny: "A vigorous plea for incest that won't leave you unmoved!"

LA: Where are you heading with your cinematic "trip" or hypnosis approach?

GN: We'll see. For the next one . . . that is, for *Enter the Void*, I wanted to use voiceover throughout the entire second half. But I realized that it was very difficult to use voiceover when it's someone whose face you can't see. In the end, we just gave up. For the next one, which I'm going to shoot in France, but in English, I think I'm going to use staccato voiceovers, but there won't be any subjective vision. I like people who play with sound like Godard does. In the latest film by [Nicolas Winding] Refn, there are a lot of people talking, and you can't hear anything. There's an Iranian film, *Manuscripts Don't Burn*, where people talk, then stop talking, but the voices continue. . . . For a film to become hypnotic, you have to keep bludgeoning the audience at every turn. . . . That's why in *Seul contre tous*, at the end, you are immersed in the guy's mind. The most conscious film reference I had was *Angst* [also known as *Schizophrenia*]. The voiceover is very well written; it is coming from the guy who is killing all these people. As he murders them, he talks about his childhood, how much he was victimized. It's as if you had two films moving in parallel. It's really fascinating. For my next film, I will probably go back to a technique closer to *Seul contre tous*, but in Technicolor, with effects and graphic images at every turn.

Matthew Barney and Gaspar Noé

Matthew Barney / 2014

This interview, "Matthew Barney and Gaspar Noé," was commissioned by and first published in *BOMB*, no. 127, Spring 2014. © Bomb Magazine, New Art Publications, and its Contributors. All rights reserved. The BOMB Digital Archive can be viewed at www.bombmagazine.org.

In his latest opus, *River of Fundament,* a nontraditional opera and live performance as film, Barney assembles a grimy and naughty cast from the Osiris myth (loosely based on Norman Mailer's *Ancient Evenings*) to mingle with contemporary New York artists and literati at Mailer's wake, underway on a barge crossing a septic urban river. The automotive industry and reignited steel mills are the backdrop. The nearly six-hour film is a daring and astonishing visual-acoustic ride through ancient Egyptian and current American rituals enacting rebirth and regeneration while dwelling on physical and spiritual labor and gushing with the fluids of life. In homage to both the book that inspired his film and to Barney's own *Cremaster* series, Mailer's character reincarnates through three separate protagonists, all stand-ins for Osiris, while three cars—a Chrysler, a Pontiac, and a Ford—serve as vehicles for metamorphosis. Blaring horns, screeching voices, crushed cars, flaming steel, rushing waters; mud, sewage, slime, feces, blood, sperm, and urine; memories, desires, and power struggles all flow into the roiling pool that is the present, which pharaoh Usermare decries in the film as "little more than the excrement the past leaves behind. It repulses us until that also becomes the past."

On the eve of *River of Fundament*'s world premiere at BAM, Barney spoke over the phone with French filmmaker and long-time friend Gaspar Noé, whose epically psychedelic *Enter the Void* (2009) has a related theme. Departing from *The Tibetan Book of the Dead*, Noé's film follows a departed man's attempt to reincarnate as a spirit and remain present in the lives and bodies of the people he's left behind.

—Sabine Russ

Matthew Barney: I'm curious about what you've been doing since *Enter the Void*. What are you up to right now?

Gaspar Noé: I've been slowly preparing my next movie, which is a very sentimental, erotic film. So I'm meeting kids—girls and boys—and I will continue for quite some time. In the end it will be a very, very naturalistic love story, even if the style is not going to be naturalistic. It will be a love story seen from a sexual point of view.

MB: Is it a coming-of-age story? How young are the kids?

GN: No, I get bored by coming-of-age stories because they make a big deal out of something that is finally not so big. Mostly, the real passion comes after that, when boys and girls are nineteen or twenty and want to try everything and get lost in all the temptations.

MB: Is it a New York–based story?

GN: No, it's based in Paris. But the main character is going to be an American, Canadian, or British film student, so I can see the story from his point of view and then add a voiceover in English to the character. It will be a kind of international movie but shot in France.

MB: Cool. I was really interested in the aerial photography from *Enter the Void* and how one could understand that conceptually as a POV, while, in fact, it's more of an objective view of the city where the story takes place. So, it's an objective and subjective camera at the same time. I know that you're interested in Kubrick. We've talked about that in the past because it's something that you and I have in common—

GN: You're obsessed with Kubrick, too.

MB: Does he still occupy your mind, or was he more of an early influence?

GN: He was more of an early influence. Kubrick has been my idol my whole life, my own "god." I was six or seven years old when I saw *2001: A Space Odyssey*, and I never felt such cinematic ecstasy. Maybe that's what brought me to direct movies, to try to compete with that "wizard of Oz" behind the film. So then, years later, I tried to do something in that direction, like many other directors tried to do their own, you know, homage or remake or parody or whatever of *2001*.

I don't know if you ever had that movie in mind for your own projects. But in my case, I don't think about *2001* anymore now. That film was my first "trip" ever. And then, I tried my best to reproduce on screen what some drug trips are like. But it's very hard. For sure, moving images are a better medium than words, but it's still very far from the real experience. I read that Kubrick said about Lynch's *Eraserhead* that he wished he had made that movie because it was the film he had seen that came closest to the language of nightmares.

MB: Wow, I've never heard that.

GN: There are not many movies that really reproduce the language of dreams and nightmares. Maybe Buñuel's *Un chien Andalou* is another good one. And your movies also represent it quite well. They get very close to that mental language.

In life, sometimes you are going in one direction, you do your best there, and then you go in another direction. My next movie is going to be totally different, in every single point, from the previous one.

MB: As was *Irreversible* from *Enter the Void*. I like the way you change the problem from one project to the next.

GN: Have you ever tried 3D?

MB: I haven't. I remember the last time you and I hung out. You were taking some pictures on the Bowery with a 3D camera. My interest in filmmaking is probably less connected to technology than yours is.

GN: Actually, I don't like technology. But I like working with people who are really good with it. For example, for *Enter the Void*, I did visual effects with this company called BUF directed by Pierre Buffin. It was the only way of reproducing those hallucinatory images that I wanted on a screen. Of course, it was not my desire to be with a postproduction company for months and months, sitting with people in front of a computer. But the results are amazing.

Have you seen *Gravity*?

MB: No, I haven't.

GN: The first two takes are around fifteen minutes each, but you've never seen such a visual rollercoaster inside a movie theater. Those opening takes are incredible, also because the background is all black, and you really have a sense that you're in space. The camera is spinning around the astronauts, and it's all computer-generated imagery. The result is incredibly mind-fucking. Everything is fake, and it all looks so real! I'm sure you'd be amazed by that movie.

MB: This sounds like the type of film that I could never imagine making because my addiction has to do with performance, with creating a very real situation and then dealing with all the physical problems surrounding it. I spend much energy trying to realize situations and occurrences physically before I give in to digital effects. In that way, digital effects, for me, always feel like a compromise, but not unrelated to the kind of compromise that one faces as a sculptor. You know, on the classical level, a figure often needs a third leg to stand. Or the material problem you set up for yourself fails, and you need an additive or an adhesive to make the material survive or stand on its own. Compromise is so much a part of the process of making film—or the process of making sculpture, for that matter.

GN: I would say being an artist or a performer or a director is also being a magician, and very often, you need to use every trick you have in your pocket to make the show stronger.

The problem with all these new digital effects is that they are always being used in the same direction, by the same people, for the same kind of movies. But someone like Kubrick, because of his great technical knowledge of special effects, managed to create the craziest images of what was supposed to be life in space and "beyond the infinite." With all kinds of techniques he developed in the sixties, he succeeded in creating his magnum opus and in bringing spectators to places where they had never ever been. No one in mainstream cinema was going that far in terms of artistic ideals.

MB: Kubrick revolutionized a lot of techniques and technologies that we take for granted now—the Steadicam, for example. My relationship to Kubrick has much more to do with camera motion. In *The Shining*, the camera moves through either a very slow zoom or a tracking shot where the camera does not pan. It is similar to what I was saying about your aerials in *Enter the Void*—it's somewhere between being objective and subjective. In a film like *The Shining*, it makes it possible for the architecture to become a protagonist, which interests me very much. It frames the environment in a way in which doors and windows become completely organic. It isn't just that the elevator starts bleeding; it's the way in which that doorway is framed and the way the camera drifts toward the door. It isn't the perspective of a person, it's a moving perspective—a moving point of view. I love that about Kubrick.

GN: Have you ever seen the movies of Max Ophüls?

MB: No.

GN: He was a German director who moved to France and to the States for a while. Kubrick was obsessed with Ophüls; he was one of his favorite directors. The camera movements in his movies are absolutely incredible. When you watch *Le plaisir*, *La ronde*, or *Lola Montès*, you can see how much they inspired Kubrick. Also, in terms of narrative perspective, there's something very playful in *La ronde*. Its omniscient narrator sometimes appears inside the same long camera movements, inside the story, playing different secondary characters. The narrator's in and out. It's very weird. It's like objective, subjective, everything all at the same time.

MB: Have you ever worked in theater or live performance?

GN: No. Actually, somebody just called me from Poland because they want to commission film directors to direct operas. I have never done anything like that. Have you done opera yourself?

MB: What I've been working on recently is a combination of cinema and live performance, and these live scenes have all of the ingredients of opera. I can't say it's an opera, but it certainly relates. So it's definitely something that's been on my mind, and, in a way, this hybrid approach has resurrected my interest in filmmaking, which I had lost for a while after working in Japan. The film I made there dealt with many of the same problems I had worked with in the *Cremaster* cycle. I felt like I hadn't found a new problem to solve. So, when I began working on *River of Fundament*, I started by setting up these live scenes and filming them. The final film is a combination of documentary and cinematic photography. It's quite different from things I have done in the past, but it has definitely clarified what interests me in live performance and what doesn't. Early on in the project, I presented a preliminary sketch onstage and learned that the stage doesn't interest me. A kind of site-specific situational theater is a more natural fit for me.

GN: You've never done the same play onstage twice?

MB: That sketch I made was part of a festival in Manchester and of the writing process for this piece, and I found the stage problematic. You know, as a moving-image maker, I felt the loss of the close-up and the loss of the macro-view of textural changes and material behavior. I felt like I couldn't exercise those qualities or use those tools from my toolbox. I felt crippled. The fixed perspective of somebody sitting in the theater also seemed very limiting to me. Stage performance is such a different discipline. It's interesting to me that there are so many people who move back and forth between film and theater when they are so utterly different.

GN: But *River of Fundament* is a film?

MB: Yes, it is. It's five and a half hours long. It's being presented in opera houses and proscenium theaters with a couple of intermissions—like an opera. The majority of the work I've been doing over the last seven years has been for the live performances in *River of Fundament*. The cinematic work for it has been done over the last two years. And what I've ended up with is a hybrid between the two. The aspect of filmmaking that I'm most interested in has to do with creating a live condition, where something is actually happening in real time, and then filming in response to that. To a certain extent, I've always done that—the *Cremaster* films were full of situations like that. It's not a very economical way of making a film—to set those situations up, and shoot them in real time, and then edit it all down.

GN: How many cameras did you use for this project?

MB: For some of the live scenes, there were ten or twelve cameras rolling—from hotheads in different positions that were controlled remotely. Trying to make the camera invisible to the live audience is a very difficult way to make a film. You often feel that the camera is not in the position you want it to be in, but you can't adjust and move the camera the way that you would do on a film set. A good example is the scene where the audience group was positioned on a barge pushed by a tugboat out on an industrial river in Detroit, and while underway, they came upon a crime scene. The barge started hovering in the current while the investigators called in a crane barge to pull a submerged car out of the river and land it onto the larger barge in front of the audience. The investigators were ferried from the shore to the barge on a smaller boat, and the investigation continued. From a filming perspective, there were several stacked layers of action which needed to stay in line for the cameras, while the tugboat was struggling with the current and the wind.

GN: What about the music?

MB: It's nearly through—composed with live music, and the singing is often carrying the text of the story. Like I said, it certainly has many elements of opera, but I'm hesitant to call it an opera because I'm not committed to the genre's conventions.

GN: Did you compose the music yourself?

MB: No, I collaborated with Jonathan Bepler, who did a lot of the *Cremaster* music. So we worked on it together from the start and did a lot of the writing together. It's a long project in collaboration with somebody, which is both completely rewarding and challenging at the same time.

I'm curious about how you set up your longer sequences, for example, the rape scene in the tunnel in *Irreversible*. The brutality in that scene is really compounded by its duration. How many takes do you do, and how do you develop a scene that depends so much on duration?

GN: I thought that it would be good to do a movie with only long master shots. Also, I didn't have a full-length script at all. When I shot the movie, I just had a three-page synopsis, which contained each scene in a quarter of a page. And there was one scene in the middle of the script saying that the character portrayed by Monica Bellucci comes out of an apartment and gets into the tunnel, where she meets this guy who's fighting with a transvestite. Then the transvestite runs away, and the guy assaults her verbally, then physically, then he rapes her and beats her up, and then that's the end of the scene. In most movies, at the moment the rape starts, they would cut or go to the next scene, or they would just show the wall or whatever—because those things are quite hard to stand. Everybody is afraid of rape and murder. But murder in movies, it's a *figure imposée*, an imposed figure. No one in the audience believes that someone is killing someone onscreen. It's all fake, like the millionth time that you see that same cheap rabbit coming out from the hat. So I thought for both the murder scene at the beginning and for the rape scene, that making them last without cuts would be more shocking for the viewers. I also let the actors improvise their dialogue and told them to be as extreme as they could be. For example, the rapist was improvising his insults, and we did that scene six times.

But actually, I cheated a lot in the film, too. The master shot looks real, but it's full of tricks inside. When she gets into the tunnel, she watches the panel above, and then the camera tilts up; we see the entrance of the tunnel, and then it comes down. With that quick movement, I could edit the beginning of one take with the rest of another of the six takes of the rape that we did during two nights. It looks like one continuous shot, but it's made out of two. Also, in that scene, a lot of small details were added to make it more real. For example, when the rapist comes out of her, of course, the actor had his zipper closed, and there was no penis there. We digitally added it so when he's finished, you see an erect naked penis, which makes the scene much more shocking.

I was maybe one of the first to introduce that kind of "porn" visual trick inside a commercial movie with famous actors. Lars von Trier did this a lot in *Nymphomaniac Volumes 1 & 2*, his latest film, which contains a lot of fake explicit sex. The actors don't consider it porn because they're not doing anything sexual, but the end result looks pornographic.

When the producers signed with me to make *Irreversible*, they didn't expect the detail of the added penis. Also, because the dialogue was not written yet, they didn't expect the rapist to say such nasty, disgusting things. Because it was not written—that may be why we could make that movie. The whole movie was made with master shots, and the contract I had signed protected me from any forced reediting. Of course, at one point, the producers said, "This has to end, you need to cut it." I said, "No, I cannot cut it. It's a master shot." There was no way to cut; the whole movie is made of master shots leading to each other.

I was very lucky with the actor who played the rapist, and I was very lucky that Monica was ready to go that far in the representation of the scene. As the director, I just created a playground for the actors. The whole scene was in their hands. They made the scene. And then, in postproduction, I added a few elements to make it stronger.

MB: That is quite close to live performance, isn't it?

GN: Yeah, of course. The rape scene was twelve minutes long. I normally do a scene over and over from the beginning to the end because it gives the actors a better energy. And it opens possibilities for improvisation.

MB: It's interesting that there's no proper script for the film. That's fantastic.

GN: Have you ever thought of directing a fiction film, a narrative based on a novel or a personal story?

MB: Well, *River of Fundament* is based on a Norman Mailer novel called *Ancient Evenings*. So, in that way, having the novel as a text to work from, toward a script or a libretto, is completely new to me. And I've enjoyed that very much. You know, I would not say that it's a traditional narrative film by any means, but it has aspects of filmmaking that I haven't worked with in the past. There are scenes with dialogue carried by professional actors, and I worked with an editor who comes from a commercial filmmaking tradition. While it's a step in the direction of traditional narrative film, I still don't know if I could actually do one. Technically I could, but my interest in storytelling relies so much on experimentation with structure—and this is one of the reasons why I like your films so much.

GN: I think there's something very square about how scripts, and movies in general, are written now. You see one or two, and you've seen them all; you can close the whole thing inside your head, like, *Oh, I understood that*, it goes from point A to point B and from point B to point C. There are not many movies that stay in your mind the way dreams stay in your mind. When people ask me what my favorite movie is, I say that the two I can watch the most are *2001: A Space Odyssey* and *Un chien Andalou*. I can watch them over and over and never get bored by them. *2001* is narrative, but at a certain point, it reaches a level that toys with a part of your mind that doesn't read events but reads symbols. What are your favorite movies?

MB: For sure, *The Shining* is up there. I like films that are trapped in one location—*Das Boot* or *Jaws* or the seventies "cabin in the woods" horror genre films—where the location often becomes the main character. I also loved early Cronenberg. *The Brood*, in particular.

GN: If you haven't seen it, you should check out *Wake in Fright*. It's an Australian movie from the seventies. It's very sick.

MB: A lot of my favorite films are actually commercial films. I mean, I love the spirit of experimental films, but I've been influenced much more by commercial films. It has something to do with the fact that my development as a filmmaker has come from a performance background. It started with performing an action by myself and having one person hold the camera and simply document the action. That slowly evolved into storytelling and into something that resembles a filmmaking practice, but my interest was never in cinema from the start. I was a bit of a tourist with cinema, but I had an interest in horror from an early age.

GN: Are you a fan of Lon Chaney?

MB: Definitely.

GN: I think he's the best actor ever. "The Man of a Thousand Faces." And in each movie, he plays another cripple—his face is burned, his legs and arms are missing. For his time, he was the master of transformation.

MB: When I first started working with performers other than myself, I was thinking about something along the lines of Lon Chaney—like how can you, as a director, put a performer into a situation that can overcome their tendency to act? In other words, how do you restrain somebody from acting in a mannered way? It was the kind of thing I was doing to myself as a young artist—I was putting myself into situations where my body was restrained as an attempt to change my behavior, the behavior of my art-making gestures. So, once I began working with other people, I started restraining the actors. And it led to very interesting situations, for sure, like experimenting with prosthetics and costuming in the development of a character—and Lon Chaney was always a model for that.

GN: Do you always work with the same makeup artists?

MB: I've done a lot of work with Gabe Bartalos in California, the makeup artist who did all of the *Cremaster* work. And with Keith Edmier, who is a sculptor based in New York, who worked in the makeup FX industry when he was younger. I just did this last project with him after not working together for almost twenty years, which was really fun. For obvious reasons, I'm very interested in prosthetic makeup artists because their process is so similar to mine as a sculptor—the casting, and the mold-making, and the experimentation with material behavior. The alchemy in that interests me very much.

I've got another question for you. Why do you think so many brutally violent films are being made in France?

GN: In France? Just because they are, or were, easier to finance here, I guess.

MB: Is that all?

GN: The French are not softer or harder than any other country. There's an even stronger tradition of cruelty in Japanese cinema compared to European film. And among the Europeans, the Germans tend to top the French, Spanish, or Nordic countries when it comes to S&M or hardcore gay sex or things like that in real life. But mostly, when you make a movie, you need money. There was a moment in France when it was easier to get money to do extreme movies that were inspired by the Italian horror movies of the seventies, like Dario Argento's, or *Cannibal Holocaust*—but also by *Taxi Driver* and *Deliverance*. So, when the door got closed in America for projects of that kind, maybe at that time it got opened wider here in France. I did *Irreversible*, Virgine Despentes did *Baise-moi*, Catherine Breillat did movies with fake explicit sex scenes; and there are many other directors who also managed to do horror movies that were quite extreme. But that was a few years ago, and now it has gotten bad again. There is one pay-TV channel called Canal+ that was financing a third, or sometimes more, of the budget of all these partly transgressive movies. They still do, but now they have more and more moral considerations about what can be shown or not, and most of the wild projects end up not being made. The last feature film that I saw that is quite extreme when it comes to the reproduction of sex or violence is the second part of *Nymphomaniac*. There are some graphically explicit images in there that are very frontal.

MB: Have you heard of this book called *The Art of Cruelty*?

GN: No.

MB: It's by a woman named Maggie Nelson, and it follows the history of extreme visual culture from Marquis de Sade and Antonin Artaud to the present. And the position the author takes is that, because of our current situation with images of torture in the news and pornography online and reality programming on television, we don't really need extreme images the way that we did in the past. In the 1960s and '70s, there was Viennese Actionism, for example, which functioned as a political provocation. But this may not be true anymore with extreme image-making. I'm curious what your position is on this.

GN: In France, like anywhere else now, when it comes to pornography and images of cruelty, the internet is the gate to the Wild Wild West. You can find everything, even things that I thought were illegal, on the web. Do you remember the story of that Canadian guy who killed a Chinese student a year ago and then escaped to France? He made a short film about himself killing the guy and cutting him to pieces, then he added the music from *American Psycho* and put it on some regular websites. Before it got banned, more than six million people had seen that movie by Googling it, and certainly thousands of very young kids among them. Because it was edited and had music, it looked fake, but all of it was real!

I was raised during a time when there was censorship. But now, any seven- or eight-year-old can just type the name of a porn star into the computer and see the most savage double or triple penetration. It's very different, and I don't know how it's going to affect the minds of the new generation.

MB: So, do you consider yourself more on the cusp of advocating that kind of restriction? Is it different for you than for someone who is younger?

GN: Censorship is when things are being put on hold—by your government or your family—to protect you from the dark sides, or what's supposed to be the dark sides of life. Now, almost all these images of what some call evil are accessible from any iPhone, any computer.

MB: I've been working with some adult film actors and filming some quite explicit scenes for *River of Fundament*. I think my interest in this has nothing at all to do with political provocation. I think it has to do with taking a kind of fundamental, albeit extreme, action and trying to naturalize it into the context of the narrative or into what's happening on screen. And so, in some way, it's about trying to remove its shock value. So I'm very interested in this book, *Art of Cruelty*, and the questions it raises.

GN: Do you know this French artist from the sixties—Michel Journiac?

MB: No, I do not.

GN: He was doing very radical performances in France and was certainly inspired by Otto Muehl and the Viennese Actionists. He did something like . . . he brought a lot of people to a gallery or museum, where the event took place, and he was taking their blood. If you wanted to see the performance, you had to give your blood. After he took the blood from all these people with a syringe and everyone was inside, he closed the doors and put all the blood together and cooked it. Then he made sausage out of it and asked people to eat the sausage.

MB: Wow, excellent!

GN: A friend of my father described that performance to us when I was eleven, and it was the ultimate image of cruelty for me. I don't know if it was Journiac or someone else who did this thing with cats—they were cutting their legs off and putting them on a large white canvas to run and create an abstract painting. I thought, *How the fuck can someone do that?* But that was in the 1970s—and now people do other kinds of cruel things.

MB: Hmm.

GN: Do you like Otto Muehl?

MB: I do like Otto Muehl. Muehl's relationship to sculpture isn't as strong as some of the other Actionists—Rudolf Schwarzkogler, for example—so Muehl isn't my favorite. But I like his films, especially the color films. They are lovely.

GN: When you start playing with the representation of cruelty, sometimes it's easy to lose track because there is a shock value that can excite you without a real need. Pasolini's *Salò*, for example, was really shocking, but it has a very complex vision of humanity, of human cruelty and power. So, the whole project was complex enough to make that cruelty intelligent and bearable. Some people accused me of useless cruelty in *Irreversible*. I guess because parts of that rape scene were closer to a real rape instead of how you see it in most movies.

MB: Absolutely.

GN: There was a retrospective of cruel movies at the French Cinémathèque, among them classics like *Umberto D.* and Fassbinder's *Fox and his Friends*. The Fassbinder film is just about a poor guy winning the lottery. His bourgeois gay friends end up stealing all his money and using him, and then throwing him away. The movie is so cruel that it's really scary. Sometimes cruelty doesn't need to show blood or physical fights—there are also relational behaviors that are as cruel as the worst violence.

MB: Exactly. I'm thinking now again about *Enter the Void* and how there's a level of artificiality in that film—the aerial perspectives over the city, for example, or the sex scene where the people's genitals are lit up, glowing with phosphorescent light. There's an artifice in that film that is so different from *Irreversible*, and I'm curious if your next project is heading deeper into that direction.

GN: It is going to be very artificial but in more of a Godardian direction. It's going to contain a lot of words—maybe because my last film was very visual. The next one is also going to be almost silent as its scenes are being filmed, but during the editing I will add a lot of text-over and voiceover. It's going to be a more brainiac exercise, I guess.

Gaspar Noé

Jessica Piersanti / 2015

Originally published in *Apartamento* magazine, no. 15, 2015. Reprinted by permission.

No other interiors magazine has done it yet. And with good reason: to enter the "inside" of Gaspar Noé is an impossible mission. We are good friends, he's often been around to my place, we've shared some nice memories . . . but he is a little defensive when I ask him to talk about the movie he just shot or reveal the place where he lives. This being said, I have the chance to share my life with the talented Artus de Lavilléon, who, by creating a visual dialogue with his drawings, gave us the opportunity to enter Gaspar's world during a mad working period. At 9 a.m. on a cold Paris morning, he receives us in his editing room, where he will be working day and night for three months on his next film, called *Love*: a sexual melodrama shot entirely in 3D. His eyes framed by a sleepless night, he opens the door on a slightly arid space: three computers, some monitors, a flat-screen TV, cables, and a sofa. Gaspar does not speak easily about personal experience. That's how he is. And he doesn't hide the fact that he is not fond of formalities. Right away, he holds out a pair of 3D glasses to Artus and another pair to me. He is watching us discover the first images of his film. He sees us tumble into his mental space, and he seems to like it. This might be it: to fully understand the work and personality of Gaspar Noé, you must, above all, understand that there is nothing to understand, only to "see." What he seems to want most is to provide his audience with a visual delectation, much like a painter would. The rest doesn't really matter.

Jessica Piersanti: We have known each other for quite some time now, and I know you don't like to invite people to your place. Why?

Gaspar Noé: I feel invaded. Even for dinner parties, I always prefer to dine out rather than in people's homes because I can always show up for coffee at the end or leave in the middle. I like to be able to escape from a place whenever I want. When you're at home, you have the impression that it's your private reading and resting place. My worst nightmare is when you throw a party at home, and people stay and stay and don't want to leave until morning.

JP: You're not the kind of person who shows magazines the interior of his house. Why is that? Do you think it's a bourgeois thing to do, or does it simply not interest you?

GN: It doesn't interest me.

JP: That's why we thought, Artus and I, that it would be easier to do drawings rather than photographs to go with this piece. But you're also a really private person, don't you think?

GN: I'm a private person, but when you suddenly start promoting a film, you become a public figure, and you pass from one extreme to the other. A director's work is very cyclothymic because you're all alone for a long time, and then overnight, you're swamped with people talking to you. And it's the same when you're shooting: you find yourself having to lead sixty people, and the next day, you're all alone again in your editing room. It's a very bipolar way of life.

JP: But, in general, you don't speak very much about yourself?

GN: No, I prefer drinking in bars. [*Laughs*]

JP: You rarely mention where the inspiration for your films comes from.

GN: Let's say that some films speak more than others. I heard an amazing thing the other day; it was a friend who told me he was in a bar and a girl said to him, "Come on, beat me, you're a friend of Gaspar Noé, I can see what kind of guy you must be." That's when I think to myself, damn, my reputation! The image that people have of me is only the image of my films.

JP: Of course, most people think you are just like your films!

GN: At the time of *Irreversible*, a lot of people thought I was hardcore/SM/gay just because the opening scene takes place in one of those clubs, while that's not at all the case.

JP: Or very violent, very dark.

GN: Or very fascist, like the main character in *I Stand Alone*.

JP: When I suggested that we do this interview, you said, "Let's do it in my editing room," and this is where we are now. Do you spend a lot of time here?

GN: Right now, I spend all my nights here. I love editing with my coeditor during the day, then alone until 4 or 5 a.m. Then I fall asleep on the sofa, or I go back to my place. But the best time for me to work, to paint, or to edit has always been between 10 p.m. and 3 a.m.

JP: That's usually the time when you're outside and partying!

GN: Yes, when I'm not editing. When I'm preparing a film, I spend a lot of time outside. But after, when you actually get the big chance to shoot it, you change your habits.

JP: You got this place not so long ago, right?

GN: Yes, but I'll have it for a long time. I think that until I finish the film, I'll spend six to seven nights a week here, glued to the computer.

JP: For almost every new film, you do your editing in a different place. What have you done to personalize this space?

GN: I painted the walls, and I brought in some movie posters that I haven't hung up yet.

JP: What did you choose?

GN: This is an architectural model that appeared at the end of *Enter the Void*. It was made in Japan; I recovered it and decided to reuse it in this film since it's called *Love*. Maybe this film will start with the same model that appeared at the end of the last one.

JP: And what is that poster over there?

GN: It's the biggest star of Argentine erotic cinema, Isabel Sarli. She was Miss Argentina in the fifties, and then she became the Argentine Marilyn Monroe. She had huge tits. Most of her movies were banned, then finally released after one scandal or another.

JP: And what is this one?

GN: This is another Argentine movie poster from the film *Baby Doll* by Elia Kazan.

JP: This is all you need in your workspace?

GN: Yes.

JP: How many months are you going to spend here?

GN: Shooting lasted six weeks, and I think I'll spend at least three months editing.

JP: You were really reluctant to speak about the film before its release. Why?

GN: Together with Wild Bunch, I decided not to provide any information before the film's release date. I don't know when the film will come out, but I'd like to be ready for Cannes. Nowadays, it's very hard to make a film without having people leak details, without finding unwanted images on the internet, without the extras taking pictures or revealing the names of the actors.

JP: How would you describe the evolution of your work in this film?

GN: It's in 3D. It's softer. There is no narrative violence. There is a lot of verbal abuse because it's the story of a couple who love each other but make a complete balls-up of their lives. They don't stop insulting each other and fucking, sometimes with insults that you would never want to hear in a relationship.

JP: So you think that this time, nobody will be able to complain about the violence?

GN: There will always be people who are quick to moan, so if I release a new movie and no one complains, that means I should worry because the movie certainly must have been weak.

JP: Why did you choose to make the film in 3D?

GN: First, because we had some financial help to make the film in 3D, and also because I love to take photos in 3D. I have a Loreo camera, which works with Kodak film. You can see the photos in 3D straight after developing them by using a small viewing box. 3D, to me, looks more like reality. But when you use it for a film, it makes you reconsider every way you shoot. For example, if you want to use a handheld camera, it becomes very nauseous, so suddenly, you're just doing still shots. This film only uses still shots.

JP: 3D is usually found in big, spectacular films. Here, it's more of an auteur film in 3D?

GN: Yes, there's not a single special effect. 3D is usually reserved for movies with monsters, Martians, or children's stuff, but this is an adult film in 3D.

JP: How has 3D changed the way you make a film?

GN: It's much more complicated. 3D cameras are giant ships, and if I want lighter shots, it becomes impossible. As soon as you try to get close to your subject, the camera is so large that it casts a shadow. For example, if you want to do a sequence within a small bathroom, you can do that with a Canon SD or with a small 16mm camera, but here it becomes impossible. You need bases, cranes, stuff like that, even if we're working with the lightest professional system.

JP: Did you give any particular attention to the interiors in this film?

GN: We've used rather colorful decor. Initially, we thought we'd have really featureless stuff, but sometimes, between how you want the film to be and the day of the shoot, you realize you are doing the exact opposite. For this film, I found myself repeatedly contradicting what I had originally proposed. I'd had the idea of making a very pared-back film, almost theatrical. I wanted very plain sets in the style of Jean-Luc Godard, but in the end, I only chose scenery overloaded with detail. We made all the backgrounds blurry, though, because of the depth of focus related to 3D. So even if the sets are full on, it can't really be seen.

JP: Did you work with a set designer?

GN: Yes, I did. But besides the main character's apartment, I mostly worked with existing sets, which we accessorized a little. I brought over a lot of personal items: things that I've bought at flea markets or even things that people have suggested to me.

JP: What kind of personal items have you put in this film? In this sequence, for example. There is a painting above the bed. Is it one of your father's?

GN: No, this is a painting made by a friend. There is one sequence in an art gallery in which I've put some of my father's paintings, but I don't know if I'll keep the scene. But the most personal thing—wait, I'll show you. At one point you can see the very first toy I ever had in my life: a little tiger.

JP: What is the importance of painting in your life?

GN: I love it, but I've kind of put it to one side because I also collect movie posters. I never spend money on records, I already have a fair few books, but movie posters are something eternal. I love painting and posters; when I go to see exhibitions and there's conceptual art or video art, stuff like that, I don't get it. For me, art is a two-dimensional thing that you hang on the wall.

JP: Your movie poster collection is quite big. Do you hang them up in your apartment?

GN: No! I have piles of them. Like any good collector, I stack them.

JP: So, what do you have on your walls?

GN: Nothing. [*Laughs*]

JP: Have you put some of your favorite posters in the film?

GN: Wait, I'll show you another scene. Here, there are posters for Fritz Lang's *M*, Pasolini's *Salò*, *Taxi Driver*. I put a lot of my collection on the bedroom walls of the main character. *Flesh for Frankenstein 3D* and the movie *The Bible*—

JP: Do you feel the need to protect yourself much, seeing that the content of your movies is often controversial?

GN: Not really. I kind of start to feel paranoid when I go to a bar because there are so many people who come to talk to you. Initially, it's nice. They come up to you and say, "Hey, I love your movie." But if you don't say anything more than "thank you," because they are mostly drunk, many people become aggressive. These same guys come and ask me if I can read their short film project or whatever, and if you say you don't have the time, they'll be like, "Who the fuck do you think you are?" That's why you become paranoid: because the same people who approach you can totally change their attitude in the space of fifteen minutes.

JP: Do you feel completely free in what you do, in the choice of your subjects, and in the approach you take?

GN: It depends on who you work with. For example, I've been making films with Vincent Maraval [from Wild Bunch] since *Irreversible*. The guy gives you freedom because he's also getting something out of it. You know, freedom is often the means they give you. If there is no TV channel to invest in your project, and if there is nobody else to put in the money, you only have the freedom that you grant yourself. So, it's often conditioned. I'm lucky to have met the right people. If it weren't for Maraval and two or three other people, I might be doing some other job. Within the American system, for example, I don't think I'd be able to make the same films. If I were in another country, I might be teaching cinema instead.

JP: What did you think about the four million people marching recently in France to defend freedom of expression?

GN: It's good, but it was still surprising to see all the lifelong enemies of *Charlie Hebdo* marching for them. When you looked at the head of the procession, you could see the faces of all those people who were ridiculed every week in the magazine! The whole story is mind-blowing; it also gives the impression that three morons have brought the country to its knees. There might be a surge of national cohesion, but I think we're entering an era now where people are completely desperate to exist. It's almost like these same guys who used to take drugs or drink alcohol shifted overnight into such desperate acts, more to get on TV than anything else. Contrary to what they say, I don't think it's a religious cause or anything like that, but a narcissistic despair that's growing and spreading every day around us.

JP: You love sordid stories, *faits divers*, stories that go wrong, don't you?

GN: I stopped buying the true-crime newspaper *Le nouveau détective* when I was twenty-three, but at the time, I really liked it. People often tell me stories, and some are more significant than others. For example, I hear many stories about people who use drugs, and in this film, drugs have a really negative image. Maybe this time I'm making an antidrug activist film. People go mad because of that stuff. My last film wasn't very clear on the subject. But in this one, the love story is crushed because of drugs and alcohol. My next film should be against religion, one of the very worst drugs around.

JP: You're mellowing out! You've already made a film about incest, another about rape, a third one about drugs.

GN: Yes, but this time it's a film about love, about the harmful effects of love. [*Laughs*]

Interview: Gaspar Noé on *Love*, Sex, Masturbation, and More

Gary Kramer / 2015

From *Slant Magazine*, November 3, 2015. Reprinted by permission of *Slant Magazine*.

In case you didn't already know, Gaspar Noé is keen on outraging audiences, from the brutal rape and graphic murder portrayed in *Irréversible*, his breakout film, to the up-close-and-too-personal-for-some depiction of a penetration, as well as an abortion, in *Enter the Void*. His latest effort, *Love*, is considerably—perhaps deliberately—less shocking. The film depicts a romantic triangle that develops between Murphy (Karl Glusman), a young American (and Noé stand-in) living in Paris, his ex-girlfriend, Electra (Aomi Muyock), and his current partner, Omi (Klara Kristin). Throughout the film, Noé uses one prickly, beyond-sexually charged situation after another to tease out issues of jealousy, trust, and truth as Murphy grapples with his obsessive desire for Electra and his current unhappiness with Omi. The film undoubtedly leaves little to the imagination, which is precisely Noé's agenda as a provocateur: to be as in-your-face—cheap, scary, sexual, or otherwise—as possible. During a pit stop at this year's Philadelphia Film Festival, Noé sat down to discuss with me the making of *Love*, masturbation, playing with spectators in three dimensions, and what the different permutations of sex in the film may have to say about more than just his characters.

Gary Kramer: You like to stimulate and provoke. Watching Murphy and Electra masturbating each other in the opening scene is kind of like foreplay.

Gaspar Noé: Masturbation is one of the multiple games a loving girl and boy can play with each other. I don't see the difference between cunnilingus or a blowjob or masturbation or frontal sex. It's just, when you love someone, you play all these games. That opening scene was supposed to be in the middle of the movie, but I liked it so much that I kept the whole two minutes of it and moved it to the beginning. It made much more sense there. Instead of starting the film with Murphy waking up from the phone ringing, he's dreaming of his past before the phone rings. It was also a way of saying, "You heard what the movie is going to be about, so let's start strongly." I don't know if it gets you aroused. It could arouse the audience if I hadn't put a sentimental melody on top of it. You're used to seeing images of people having sex in seventies films with cheap disco music on top of them. The fact that I use classical music makes things more loving.

GK: Murphy describes wanting to make a "sentimental sex film," which I assume was your own intention with *Love*. For you, what makes an erotic film "sentimental"?

GN: I watched *The Dreamers*, and I thought Bertolucci was still censoring himself, maybe for commercial reasons. But I like that movie, especially for all the sexual scenes. When it happens in real life, usually, sex is very simple. You follow your instincts, and then things happen one way or the other. I don't understand why this aspect of sex in people's lives is so rarely portrayed in mainstream movies. So many films have people killing each other, cannibalism, monsters, bank robbers, all those things that rarely happen in people's lives. But something that's most relatable, like a love story of this kind, is always portrayed in a way that isn't natural. When you talk about love in movies, and the couple goes to bed, the door closes, and you don't get to see the best part. You see them the next day having coffee. When people are attracted to each other, it's natural to procreate or simulate the act of procreation. It's a simple, happy, positive thing. When it comes to the portrayal of this act, people start shaking. It's easier to show murder in a film and that doesn't disturb anyone. I've had some reactions that asked, "Are we in the nineteenth century . . . in Victorian times?" Why are people scared of sex, which is as natural as breathing or swimming?

GK: What made you decide to shoot the film in English and in 3D, and what kind of challenges did that create?

GN: The decision to shoot in English came first. French isn't my native language. I was born in Argentina. My parents moved to America; then they went back to Argentina. When I started speaking, I was speaking English at school and Spanish at home. I wanted to shoot the film in Paris, which is where I live, so I could produce the film and manage the shooting easier. English is the Esperanto of the Western world. Most people speak English, so I wanted the movie to have a wider release and not be put on the "foreign" shelf in most countries. And in 3D, the subtitles are really annoying—letters floating between you and the space that's supposed to be real. When I was casting guys, I looked at English, Irish, Canadian, and American guys, and the best actor I found to play the part ended up being American. He could have been South African.

About the 3D, I like the fact that when you see a 3D movie, it's like playing a game with the spectator: You tell people to put the glasses on and that they're going to see something more real than a regular movie. Also, three years ago, I bought a home-video 3D camera. I was filming many things and they were shaky on a handheld camera, so I wanted to do a film in 3D with a tripod or a crane with slow movements so as not to create nausea. A month before shooting, I ran into a guy who told me there were subsidies from the French government to make 3D movies, and they confirmed that I would have the money to rent the 3D camera. I enjoyed 3D because it was more intimate, and it allowed me to make a richer movie, in CinemaScope, in English, *and* in 3D.

GK: How did you first conceive Murphy?

GN: Murphy is an extension of myself. It's not autobiographical, but I relate to him because I've been through similar experiences in my life. Or my friends have. He's like my younger brother.

GK: What about the sexual tableaus in the film? Was it a question of creating emotion through sex?

GN: I wanted to portray the love addiction in all flavors. You meet a person and are really attracted to them and start falling in love. You want to spend all the time with them and try every experience you can dream of with that person. Some people think whatever you can do [within coupledom] makes you stronger, like Nietzsche said. But if you share those experiences with someone else [like a threesome], it might make them closer, but that's not always true because some experiences are risky, and there are other people involved.

GK: What can you say about working with the actors and getting them to perform some very explicit sex acts? Was it exhausting shooting all of the sex scenes? Did Karl require heavy doses of Viagra to maintain that erection?

GN: Not that I know of! The good thing about Karl was that he was young and willful. He wasn't at all a sex maniac. He had just broken up with a girl a year earlier, and he was extremely broken. He's not at all the guy who's running after his dick, contrary to almost every other guy I know. He's very handsome and had no problems with nudity. He knows that some people don't like seeing themselves naked, and he had no issues with that. Neither did the women. Some things are real, and some things are simulated in the movie, but it's not an issue as long as it looks real on screen. By starting with a scene where things really happen, you believe all the rest is real. I did not want to get into those kinds of promotional issues that *Blue Is the Warmest Color* or *Nymphomaniac* went through about the sex not being real but looking real. It's like a magician bringing a rabbit out of a hat: If the rabbit looks alive, *that's* important, not *how* it comes out. The actors were open-minded, and they weren't worried about what we did on the set. During the casting process, almost every male friend I had in France wanted to be in the film and show their dick.

GK: I understand you had a full-frontal role in the film. Why did you decide to do this?

GN: I wanted Murphy to be obsessed with the ex-lover of his girlfriend. I thought showing that he had images of the enemy's dick would make sense, and it was easier to do it than get a body double. Also, it was a way to show to Karl that it was no problem. He would show his dick, so I would show mine too.

GK: You have featured sex clubs in several of your films. What is your experience or impression of these places?

GN: [*Laughs*] I'm not a swinger. In France, Germany, and Belgium, five percent of the population likes sex clubs. I don't belong to that five percent, but I've seen parties of that kind. But maybe I'm too sentimental to enjoy those situations. It doesn't hurt my eyes. It even arouses your eyes and brain. But I'm not attracted to anonymous love or sex that much.

GK: Some folks might find the scene with the transsexual discomfiting, but the lesbianism very erotic. What are your thoughts about the two very different permutations of a threesome in the film between two women and one man?

GN: That's something I've heard many times: how a guy and a girl will have a threesome with a girl—one time out of two—and then the girl will want equality and want to have a threesome with a guy. Heterosexual men are far more competitive with guys and are scared to have another man's penis close to the object of their desire, so Murphy's reaction in the movie is very relatable. I wanted to put a twist on that compromise by having a transsexual, which might be less problematic because he would not be sharing his girlfriend with another man. The Brazilian playing the transsexual was very funny, but for Karl, that scene was riskier because he thought about the reaction of his family. As an actor, you may be exposing yourself to the whole world, but you know your mother or father will see it, too.

GK: Did you ever have the kind of despair Murphy does over a woman? How did you handle it?

GN: Time heals the scars or calms down the addiction. I think many guys have fallen for the wrong person, and guys who are strong emotionally fall in love and get addicted to a woman. But if they break up, they consider suicide because the pain was too great.

GK: There are some very interesting ideas in *Love*, as when the characters grapple with jealousy, addiction, and love.

GN: When the worm of jealousy is ruining the apple of the couple's relationship, they're playing hidden power games. The characters are afraid of each other. They end up doing things that they aren't strong enough to handle. There's not one situation in the movie that I condemn. I like my friends who are open-minded, but some people can handle monogamy. A guy can be very monogamous with one girl, and in the next relationship, he can be very different. It all depends on the starting point of the relationship, everyone's needs, and how much you trust the other person, and how addicted you are. The ultimate fear is the idea of losing that human drug that fulfills your life. You then turn jealous, and you end up losing what you desire. Jealousy never helps. In French, as in English, the word "love" contains many different meanings. There are different kinds of love. There's the love you can feel for your parents, or your kids, or your best friends, or your ex. It isn't possessive. Then there's falling in love in an addictive way and trying to possess someone. There should be a different word for that. Some people call it romantic love, but I would call it carnal addiction, and when you get into that emotional zone, you turn blank. Your house could be burning, but you don't care, as long as you're in the arms of the person that obsesses you.

GK: Can I ask you, as Murphy does Electra: What is your ultimate fantasy in terms of sex?

GN: [*Laughs*] I will not say because it's like a movie project: You don't talk about them until they're done. I have a few. But mostly, they're situations that aren't very common. I guess I have one or two that will maybe happen one day.

Abel Ferrara with Gaspar Noé

Abel Ferrara / 2015

From the *Talkhouse Podcast*, November 3, 2015. Reprinted by permission.

Hi, this is Nick Dawson, the editor-in-chief of Talkhouse Film, and you're listening to the *Talkhouse Film Podcast*. The fact that this episode of the podcast is making it out into the world is, well, something of a miracle, given the circumstances surrounding its recording. When I was digging around for ideas on someone to talk with Gaspar Noé about his great new film, the pornographic 3D romance *Love*, regular Talkhouse Film contributor Jim Hemphill suggested Abel Ferrara. Two of contemporary cinema's most controversial, boundary-pushing directors in conversation? Why the hell not? And everything went smoothly, really, until the time of the talk itself. Then it transpired that Abel hadn't been able to watch the viewing link for *Love* he'd been sent. An impatient Uber driver left without picking up Gaspar, meaning he was now running late. We were recording the conversation on both Skype and on landline, but the Skype sound quality was dreadful, and the phone call got disconnected not once but twice. At one point, there was a power surge in the room, and a bunch of lights went off, replaced by a low, persistent buzzing noise. It was one of those days. But mercifully, Noé and Ferrara prevailed over technological gremlins and an angry universe, managing to have a highly entertaining conversation despite the fact that they couldn't always hear each other. So settle in now for Gaspar and Abel talking about having their movies banned, censorship, what's sexy in Saudi Arabia, the connections between *Love* and Ferrara's first film, *9 Lives of a Wet Pussy*, porn's rightful place on the big screen, their mutual hero Pier Paolo Pasolini, and much more.

Gaspar Noé: Hey, Abel.

Abel Ferrara: Hi, Gaspar! Rock on, bro.

GN: I was thinking I'm happy you didn't see the movie on your computer because it's in 3D and it looks better on a big screen.

AF: Well, yeah, I mean, I don't have the glasses, number one. [*Laughs*] You gotta wear those glasses, right?

GN: How long are you going to be staying in Italy? You live there?

AF: I'm in Italy. I've been here for like a year and a half, you know what I mean? I just had a baby, dude. I just had a little girl.

GN: So, are you fluent in Italian?

AF: You got that? [*Laughs*] You understand that? I got a new girl and a new daughter.

GN: Uh-huh. Do you have an Italian passport?

AF: No, not an Italian passport. I'm still an American.

GN: I have one, but I don't speak Italian.

AF: Are you kidding? Well, you know. [*Speaks Italian*] No, you don't speak Italian. Alright. So, what are you doing in Brooklyn? I'm living, you know, I've been, I came to shoot *Pasolini*, and I'm staying here. I'm here, I'm like married, I got a daughter, and I'm working on, I'm doing a film about Padre Pio, on top of—

GN: About who?

AF: You know who Padre Pio is?

GN: The *papa*? *Il Papa Pio*.

AF: The monk that had—yeah, yeah. No, he's not the pope. He was a Capuchin monk that had stigmata during, you know, the early part, you know who I'm talking about, right? He's kind of like the patron saint of Italy. Anyways, so we're shooting a documentary now, and we're starting to shoot that. And I'm working on a film, another film with Willem [Dafoe]. And that's gonna be, well—

GN: Have you done documentaries already?

AF: The what?

GN: Have you done documentaries already?

AF: Yeah, yeah, yeah. I did *New Rose Hotel*. We did *Napoli, Napoli, Napoli*, I did a film about Mulberry Street, so. Have you done it? Have you tried?

GN: I did a short film about guys dying of AIDS in Africa. And the, actually, I shot so much footage that I also edited a longer version. And probably, I'm going to revisit it soon.

AF: About guys, what? About guys—

GN: It's called *AIDS*.

AF: About guys where in Africa?

GN: Just four guys who got infected by women and who were dying of AIDS. I was just filming them explaining—

AF: Which country?

GN: Burkina Faso.

AF: Did you go? Where did you shoot it?

GN: [It was] the only time I'd been to Black Africa. Actually, I'd really like to go shoot another movie there one day.

AF: You know my guy Jean Sauvaire, Jean-Stéphane? You saw—

GN: Yeah, yeah, yeah. I saw that movie he did with the young kids.

AF: Yeah, what's the name of that film? Yeah, that was pretty cool.

GN: *Johnny Mad Dog*. It's really good.

AF: Yeah, *Johnny Mad Dog*. That was a cool film. You guys should see it—anybody listening to this, Google that up. I don't know where you'd see it, Netflix, maybe. So, what are you doing in Brooklyn? What's up?

GN: I'm just promoting the movie as the movie's released here and rated; they brought me to do press and Q&As like you for every movie you do. Alchemy—I think the company used to be called Millennium—they changed the name, and now they are buying like all these art movies. They are very cool. And hopefully, in America, they have this—

AF: Where?

GN: It's at the Angelika and the Village East.

AF: Right—cool, cool. When does it happen? Today?

GN: They're playing it in that theatre that looks like a synagogue.

AF: [*Laughs*]

GN: Have you been there? It used to be a synagogue; they rearranged and put seats inside, but you have a Star of David on the ceiling. It's kind of weird.

AF: [*Laughs*] No, I don't, I don't. . . . So, how's New York? You enjoy it there?

GN: Fine, fine, fine. It's changed a lot.

AF: Are you going to go around the country?

GN: It's been released in many countries in Europe; it hasn't been bought for Italy and Spain yet. But it was even released in Ukraine, and it was banned in Russia for being too explicit.

AF: Yeah, well. [*Laughs*]

GN: I would not go to Moscow. It's not a big pain.

AF: It's not one of your places, right? So how's life in Paris?

GN: Yeah. When are you coming back?

AF: To Paris?

GN: Any coproductions?

AF: Yeah, I got to go to court. I got to go back to Paris to court, okay? There's like an inquiry on the Strauss-Kahn that Dominique is having. And I have to answer to the judge about, okay?

GN: Yeah.

AF: How do you like that one?

GN: I heard the guy, I read that the guy, that Strauss-Kahn moved to Morocco now.

AF: Did he? Well, that's where he's from. Well, there's still, you know, but I got to go to court in France over this, so you know, it's like, it's, I don't know what. [*Laughs*]

GN: You know what? In my movie, at a point, you see a dick, of course, because it's a sexual movie. And then I was saying that I don't understand why in American movies, you never see the penis of the actor; it's just part of the body, like you should see it as you can watch the hands. People said, "There are a few movies in which you can see the penis of the actors here." Just some names. And the two persons around me just said, "*Bad Lieutenant.*"

AF: Yeah, well, I mean, go see *9 Lives*. I mean, I made, you know, yeah, it's kind of, yeah, I mean, I don't know, man, it's a cultural deal. I mean, you know, they have all these sexy movies, but you want to see, you know, you want to see a fucking real dick, you know. Did you ever read Norman Mailer's review of *Last Tango in Paris*?

GN: Yeah. Yeah, but—

AF: No? So he's saying, you know, there's all this *sexuality*, but where's the fucking guy's dick, man? You know you want to see this fucking guy jamming the bitch, you don't want to see this fucking, you know, you know, like they skirt the issue to do it, you know, you want to see fucking sex. Let it rock, you know. But it's this, the big taboo, right? I mean, and how was your film? In your film, how're they relating to it? What's the press reaction there in terms of—

GN: The press is very good, very bad, but there is always in every single article, good or bad, they're talking about the visible willies, and what's the issue? Like they don't talk about—

AF: Well, the issue is that you can't see that in another film, you—

GN: When you see a war movie, you don't talk about the hands of the actors. You make a movie about love, the press shouldn't even focus on that detail.

AF: Yeah well, that's, you know, forbidden, you know, fruit, bro, you know, that's the other side of it. But then some, but I mean, they're talking about it because they can't see it in a movie theatre, right? There's no movie theatres showing porno films anymore. I mean, all the porno is online, right?

GN: Yeah. I don't even, I haven't checked for a while. I used to like it. I used to like to see it on a big screen.

AF: You know, Gaspar, when I started making films, the top, you know, the top ten of the top fifty films were all porno films.

GN: Yeah, *The Devil in Miss Jones*, *The Defiance of Good*, yeah.

AF: You know, everybody, New York was all, yeah, I mean, the whole humongous industry. Yeah, I mean, they made *Deep Throat*, they made *Debbie Does*

Dallas. Okay, *Deep Throat,* they made it for what, I don't know, fifty grand? They made seventy million dollars. Okay? And then the guys that made my first films, *The Driller Killer* and *Ms .45,* they made a film called *Debbie Does Dallas,* okay? And they made it for thirty-five thousand dollars. And the film made thirty-five *million,* okay? And, but it made thirty-five million where they owned half the theatres it played in, and like they got all, like, cash back. And then, you know, so it was a whole industry, it was all in the theatres, there wasn't any, you know, there was no video back then.

GN: But it was the same in France. When porn started being released in big theatres, it was all over the city. There were, like, the Champs-Élysées was mostly movie theatres playing porn movies, and then they added all these ratings and censoring laws that killed the mood.

AF: Yeah, but I mean, well, it's not that, I mean—

GN: But I once saw a French guy who had a copy of the first movie you ever made. And I really enjoyed it, especially that you play in the movie yourself the father of the two daughters. [*Laughs*]

AF: Yeah, yeah, yeah. That's me rock and rolling in *9 Lives.* Yeah. What was the cat—

GN: Was it ever released on DVD, or no?

AF: The what?

GN: Because I just had a VHS that was a copy of a VHS from another VHS. But was it ever released on DVD?

AF: Well, you know what happens with a film like that, bro, there'd be a 35mm print, right? And they send the print out to this kind of, like, the "track" of porno, you know, it started in New York, then it would go to Philadelphia, then it would go to Baltimore, then it would go to Raleigh, North Carolina, then it would go to some drive-in somewhere. And every time the movie played in these places, the projectionist would, like, take the best scene of the film and just clip it out of the movie and keep it.

GN: So, at the end, the movie is twenty minutes long.

AF: And then send the movie back. Yeah, okay? So by the time the film got back to New York, naturally, they didn't take out shitty scenes, they took out the best scenes.

GN: [*Laughs*]

AF: So I don't even know if there is a version of that film that, you know, I mean, it wasn't like we were keeping track back in the day. But it was one of these deals, you know, I got roped into doing that because, I mean not roped into it, I mean, we'd be doing the film, and then we'd hire the actor, right, the girls were all kind of girlfriends of ours, we didn't use like professional actors, right? They were like go-go dancers—

GN: You know what? Wait a second because the sound got disconnected. I did not get the last two sentences.

Nick Dawson: Ugh. Well, at this point, we wearily gave up on the landline, turned on video Skype so Gaspar and Abel could now see as well as (kind of) hear each other, and prayed that there would be no further obstacles.

AF: Alright. Gaspar!

GN: Hey!

AF: Hey! How are you, homeboy? You're making moves. What's going on, dog? What's going on, my man? Can you see me?

GN: Hey. I see you moving.

AF: Yo, can you see me?

GN: Yeah, I see you. It's all blurry, but I see you.

AF: Alright.

GN: It looks much better.

AF: Good.

GN: So, hey. We were talking about your movie and how it was shortened in every city, and, at the end, maybe your first feature turned into a short?

AF: Yeah, exactly. So you can imagine these projectionists cutting out the best piece of every film and putting it on a reel. I would love to see that movie, you know what I mean? Like the movie, that is, that is the best scene from every porno film that comes through Raleigh, North Carolina, you know? So you know, the odd thing about me being in it was that we were, you know, using basically our girlfriends, kind of go-go dancers, you know, but they weren't X-rated chicks, and then we hired like a professional dude, right, and we had to pay them all the money in the budget. Like these guys get like three hundred dollars a day. And the guy came, and he couldn't get it up!

GN: [*Laughs*]

AF: Can you believe this? A no-budget film. Yeah. It was a no-budget film, we're giving the guy three hundred bucks to fuck our girlfriends, and the guy couldn't even get it up. So you know—

GN: So you had to play the part. You were the lead who would play the part for free.

AF: Dig this, dig this. There was me, the writer, the cameraman, and everybody, and we, like, kind of drew straws, like one of us five, whoever lost, and I lost. So that was, that was the beginning of Jimmy Lane.

GN: The truth is that was my favorite scene of the movie. But you looked too young to be their father.

AF: Well, that, that's because you knew me. But anyway, shit, it's crazy.

GN: [*Laughs*]

AF: But yeah. I mean, you know, I mean, I don't know, how do you do it without doing it, you know? But this is all false censorship, you know what I mean? In other words, okay, you can't shoot a guy's dick, you can't shoot them fucking, you can't shoot a hard-on, you can't. . . . You start putting this in there, we're working from like, you know, telling Van Gogh he can't use blue, green, and yellow. You dig what I mean?

GN: Yeah, yeah.

AF: So at the beginning when they edged, you know, we would shoot a film like that, it's balls to balls, bro, anything goes. Even something like *The Driller Killer*, you know? And then all of a sudden, there's like the MPAA rating, and I'm being told that I can't do this, and you know, just how much blood I could show, and how much I can't, but then I realized that I'm being censored before my imagination is being censored, you dig?

GN: Yeah, yeah.

AF: So this film you're making, it's super important, you know, you've got to get, you know, because what happens with this kind of control, this mind game, this, you know it comes back to *Welcome to New York* with the edits on that. It's like, dude, you cannot edit me, you cannot touch that fucking film because I can't edit myself; otherwise, I'm already in a self-censorship mode. You know, it's up to you, dude, you know, that's your gig, Gaspar, to like, *dream* for everybody, to imagine all this shit, to come up with, to come up, if you are already thinking of "this is rated here, this is what I can show in China," this again, you know, it was funny because with these sex movies they used to say to me, even a pornographic film, they'd say, "You know, in England you can show all the . . . um. . . . It can be funny, it should be funny, but you can't have violence. You can't have the sex with the violence. But in Japan, they love the sex and the violence."

GN: [*Laughs*] They like their violence more than anything else there.

AF: Okay? So like, they don't like shit being funny. "They don't want this shit being funny. So don't be funny." But I said, "Dude, how am I going to be funny over in London, but I can't be funny in Tokyo? What am I going to do, reshoot the violence?" You know? I mean, come on. But this is the constant battle; I mean, you've got to find your personal freedom where it's not altered any. So—

GN: What do you think is sexy in Saudi Arabia? What's a sexy movie there?

AF: Um, no idea, I've never been there. I mean, I don't know.

GN: [*Laughs*] I'm sure there's a subgenre.

AF: They don't even have movies there. So that's, you know—

GN: You know, in a way, I'm proud, I'd never had a movie banned; on my last movie that is very sweet, it was banned in Russia. I wish it had been in a more daring country, but I was kind of proud that the minister of culture said,

"No, this is never going to be released here." Did you get banned? Did you get banned for movies?

AF: Banned? Yeah, yeah, yeah, yeah. All the time.

GN: It *sounds* good. Maybe it's bad for the guys who put up the money, but it sounds good.

AF: You know, back in the day, bro, you know, like when we did the film about Pasolini, these guys were not only, I mean, Pasolini's *Salò* has never even *now* been allowed to be shown. You dig? I mean, *Salò*, they wanted to burn the negative, which back then meant they were looking to destroy the film. Because you burn a negative back in 1975, that meant you're, you know, that motherfucker's gone. For good. You know, with *Last Tango in Paris*, they wanted to put fucking, you know, Brando in jail. If Brando came to Italy, he would've went to jail, okay? Never mind Bertolucci going. So you know, never mind, imagine making a film where your actor is gonna go to jail? But now I got to go to Paris on November 10 and go to fucking court and have an inquiry with the judge about *Welcome to New York*.

GN: Seriously?

AF: Can you believe this?

GN: Seriously?

AF: Yeah, *abso-fucking-lutely*. That's what I was telling you before. Absolutely, November 10. And it's not a court case yet. It's not, you know, so I got to go by myself, no, you know, none of my buddies, none of everybody else involved, and go with a lawyer that I have, and go and in front of a judge, and I don't know what the fuck the guy's gonna ask me. Now—

GN: Are you forced to go?

AF: I'm gonna go. I'm not forced to go, but I don't feel like going back to Paris. I mean, you know, I got the fucking police sending me fucking emails and calling my lawyer and, you know, and a lawyer's telling me, "I really recommend you go and show up." I mean, hey, I want a fucking decent inquiry. What are you gonna do? I mean, this is sleazy. I mean, you know, I don't want to think about his life. But I'm making movies, dude. You know what I mean? I don't get the point. I mean, I'm a filmmaker. I'm not, you know, that film's not a documentary. And I don't give a fuck about the guy other than, you know, hey, I could relate to the newspapers, right? I could relate to TV, or what do I have to do, make films about Donald Duck? What the fuck am I supposed to do? You know, you can't, trying to censor me, trying to, you know, trying to, you know it's like putting your mind in a fucking box, putting your imagination in a box. Well, I cannot think about, you know, I wake up in New York, the front page of the news is about this event. I'm supposed to what, eradicate that from my mind? When I think of a movie to make? Come on, you know? Anyways.

GN: Hey, our idol, Pasolini, who was coming to court almost every year, for one reason or another, the short film *La ricotta*, with Orson Welles, went to court over and over for insulting the church and the cross and—

AF: You know, the fortieth anniversary is tomorrow. Tomorrow is the day he was killed.

GN: Oh yeah!

AF: Yeah, yeah. So they are having all these crazy things here on Monday. I think the second? I always forget the date. He was killed on All Soul's Day. Do you know that?

GN: On what?

AF: All Soul's Day is like Halloween. It's like the feast of that. And one crazy guy who was trying to tell me that this was planned, that he was going to kill, have himself killed, that he wanted to do it when All Soul's Day, the holiday of death, you know, of the spirit, of the fucking ghost, you know, fell on a Sunday. Alright? That this was totally planned by Pier Paolo. I mean, this is just coming from one crazy friend of his. And he waited until five years before when Sunday fell on All Soul's Day, and then he came to. . . . [*Laughs*] It's crazy, man.

GN: There was an interview of the guy who was accused of killing him in that French magazine. And the interview of this guy was really creepy.

AF: I met him. We interviewed him, too. I interviewed him, too. [Giuseppe] Pelosi. We met him, I met him. I met him when we talked for the movie. We had a crazy interview with him, too. We went to this café in the middle of nowhere, right? Listen to this. So my guys here are going, "Let's not meet him, he's some gangster," but he's like a little fucking career criminal, you know, he's been in jail for thirty years, not just for Pasolini, for a bunch of shit, right? So we go to the café [where] we're supposed to meet him, and he's out in an orange jumpsuit, right? Because when he gets paroled from jail, they give him a job like cleaning the side of the highway, right? So now I know what this guy looks like, right? Like the way I know what Mickey Mouse looks like. You know, because I've seen all the videos, all the tapes, all the pictures, you know, in research, and there he is standing outside, waving to me, like "Hey, wow, we're going to meet," you know. And we sit and, you know, we start talking, and so we're going to a café, right, no one's there, you know, nobody is even behind the bar, so the place is open, like a real sketchy kind of joint. And you know, he goes, "You want coffee?" And we're like, "Yeah, coffee," and he goes in the back, he makes the coffee, you know. We're gonna get water, we go next door to get water from another place, anyway. So yeah, you know, I mean, he's told the story so many fucking times, I don't think the guy himself even remembers, you know what I mean?

GN: No.

AF: It's become such a fantasy for him, and he's told it so many times, you know, I wasn't even really interested. You know? It was more just—

GN: And also—

AF: Yeah?

GN: Also, old memories are rewritten. You know, you recreate your memories in order to feel better, so they say that all these, like, traumas from your childhood are just reinvented to justify the problems of the present time. So memories, you rewrite them, and you believe them that they were real.

AF: Yeah, absolutely. Plus, the guy's a hustler, so what's real and what's not real doesn't matter. Plus, he's getting money every time he comes up with a different story.

GN: [*Laughs*] Adding details.

AF: Yeah. So anyway, I offered him, like, money. I didn't want to ask him about the murder, right? I'm asking him like, "Well, what cigarettes did you guys smoke?" You know, he claimed actually that he knew Pasolini for months. His story was that everybody who knew [actor Ninetto] Davoli was not with him anymore, you know, they were all street guys kind of, and they were kind of like, you know, seeing if, they were just hustling the guy, he was a rich guy, they were fucking hustling. And they met the guy at Tiburtina train station a month before, and he was seeing the guy. But I also met a guy that was a professor at a university who had been seeing this Pelosi all the time, picking him up, you know. Because they used to have this place by the, you know the train station in Rome?

GN: Yeah, I know the train station.

AF: Yeah, okay, so right out front. Okay, and naturally, you know me imagining it [being] some sleazy, junky place, but it wasn't, they said, "No, this was the only place that gay cats could come, it was very festive, very wonderful, all the intellectuals would come, the police wouldn't bother anybody, it was the one place the gay guys could go." You know? And it was like a real, totally the opposite of what I'd filmed. [*Laughs*] You know? It was like a cool joint. And everybody would come, and it was, you know, because it was 1975, it was very uptight for then. Then they would take the, but then, later at night, this was '75, like, Rome is, like, really an open, you know, open city, right? *Aperta città*. They would take the kids into the Coliseum, they would break into the Coliseum, right? And all these rich guys, you know, the guys and Pasolini went every night. And they would sit up in, you know, where, you know, the fucking senators sat, and in the middle, the kids would walk around naked, in the middle of the Coliseum in the middle of the night. Can you imagine this? I mean, we should have shot that but we never, we didn't get it, you know. That was another of those stories. Like, are you kidding?

GN: There are some stories about Pasolini about when he came to New York that are quite funny. That he was all the time in the Bronx hanging out with Black guys.

AF: Yeah, when he came, they had a big thing for him at the Museum of Modern Art, okay? Dig this about art, you know, about art reputations, not showing up, coming late, or whatever. At this big fucking deal, he goes, as the guest of honor at the Museum of Modern Art, 1969, he stays for ten fucking minutes. Blows these people totally fucking off, all of these big VIPs from Italy, this and that, just blows them the fuck off, goes up to one [*thinking of the particular street*] . . . goes to fucking Harlem—

GN: Ah, it was Harlem—

AF: And this guy who was supposed to be taking care of him, the guy was like twenty-one years old at the time, he said the guy disappeared for like two days. He ended up with a bunch of Black Panthers. And you can imagine, this skinny little Italian guy couldn't speak a word of fucking English, he's up in Harlem in 1968, he's like looking to get fucking laid, you know. [*Laughs*] It's—

GN: [*Laughs*]

AF: And then Zeffirelli told me this story. He went to India with him. So Zeffirelli was saying, "It was the worst trip, man, you know, like, the *plane* is late, *this* is late, the train wasn't there," blah blah. So it takes two days of traveling, they're traveling for thirty-six hours, forty hours. He says, "But when we got there, we got there at two o'clock in the morning to the most beautiful hotel I ever saw in my life." So Zeffirelli naturally goes in and has a bath and gets in the bath. He says that Pasolini, he just put his bags down and took off into the fucking night. I mean, he's somewhere in the middle of India, never been there in his freaking life, just, he's saying, that the dude didn't come back for like two days. He said, "We were fucking worried, we didn't even know where to fucking look for him." And he says, he just came back and says, "Man, I had the time of my fucking life."

GN: [*Laughs*]

AF: Yeah, the guy never gave it up. That was his deal. He was an adventurer. You know, every night, ten o'clock, *bang*, he got in his car, and off to the fucking races. And it wasn't anything underhanded, sleazy, anything. That was his life. And everybody knew it, everybody was cool with it, and that's the way it went, man. You know.

But guys, I gotta go. So Gaspar, tell me something. Hey, everybody, go to Gaspar's film, man. You gotta go to the fucking theatre. You know, they're selling Trojans and fucking shit at the café there. I mean, what kind of people are coming to this movie? Are they wearing raincoats, they come there to jerk off, or what?

GN: All kinds of guys, but the girls like it better.

AF: Alright.

GN: So, have a nice day. Okay, see you soon in Paris.

ND: This is Nick Dawson from Talkhouse Film, and you've been listening to Abel Ferrara and Gaspar Noé on the *Talkhouse Film Podcast*. And as Abel says, go see *Love* in 3D on the big screen. It's quite an experience. This episode was engineered and edited by Elia Einhorn. For more filmmakers talking film and TV, visit thetalkhouse.com/film. Subscribe to Talkhouse film and Talkhouse music podcasts on iTunes where you can find all our previous episodes. And while you're there, please rate and review if you can.

AF: Guys, let me just look at your fucking sorry asses for one second.

Gaspar Noé Censure(s)

Mathieu Morel and Léolo Victor-Pujebet / 2017

From *Horschamp: Rencontres de cinema.* Reprinted by permission. Translated by Geoffrey Lokke.

Question: What's great about *Love* is the way it was advertised. All the publicity suggested that it was a pornographic film, which ultimately isn't the case. You've said that "porn is like sports, it sucks."

Gaspar Noé: Well, most things suck, don't they? Porn is a very particular genre, it's very coded. Nowadays, it only has girls with shaved pussies. And the guys, too, they all have shaved cocks. It doesn't look at all like it used to. So you might wonder if one can even make a sentimental film anymore, or when people make love, we might sense that they have plans for the future, whether or not they're realistic or shitty plans. Actually, porn, as a genre, is nothing like sports, except maybe at the best of times. It's all very mechanical—porn is supposed to excite, and especially excite males. And it all takes place under very unique circumstances. That's why people thought *Love* was going to be porn. I had used porn in my films when I was a teenager. Maybe because I had a lot more testosterone, and it just needed an outlet. My other films were more knowing, citational. I was always thinking of other films, articles, novels . . . but on *Love*, I said to myself: "What if we were inspired by the lives of our friends, our own lives?" It's not exactly autobiographical, like Jean Eustache's *The Mother and the Whore*, an absolute masterpiece where Eustache pours his guts out on the table as well as the guts of everyone around him. In *Love*, these are all things that I've experienced or what my friends and girlfriends have experienced. I tried to paint a portrait of the Paris of a young film student as I knew it. But the problem is that, when it comes to sex, a lot of people are becoming increasingly anxious, particularly on TV and online, now that sex and nudity are divorced from the everyday world. In reality, a naked body is much more natural and more beautiful than a clothed body. Yet you find like five hundred fashion magazines in every newsstand. I mean, what the fuck is with this obsession with *clothes*?

Q: Originally, you wanted to call the film *Danger*. How did you go from "danger" to "love"?

GN: After *I Stand Alone*, which was met with a lot of critical and festival acclaim, I was dying to do *Enter the Void*, but it was going to be a film with a lot of special effects. It tells the story of a guy, a drug dealer, who is lacking in spirituality because his material life is not giving him what he wants. Suddenly, he's set free in the afterlife, with all these astral projections and the promise of reincarnation. These are things people believe in, things people want to accept when they're teenagers. When I was twenty, I read a lot of stuff like that; I took a lot of hallucinogens, too. Most of my friends did. But later I thought, "Fuck, why isn't there a film that represents these secondary—maybe primal—states you experience through psychedelics and other substances?" It was a project very close to my heart. It's a story of someone who genuinely believes in the power of disassociation—astral projection, reincarnation. Anyways, I knew the film was going to be very expensive. I also wanted to do it without any known actors, so that made things even more complicated. I hadn't had any commercial success yet. So it seemed impossible. I decided to do something that was on a more human level. This was, I think, around the year 2000. I needed a topic I knew something about, and that wouldn't cost too much. So I said to myself: "Hey, let's make a passionate story between two young people who party, take drugs, argue, make love (and are good at it), genuinely love each other, talk about the future and children, scream at each other some more, beat each other up, etc." It's the kind of spiraling relationship that most people have known in their lives. But it's hard to present stories about real love in such a prudish society. There's so much consumption, both of people and, strangely, of divine things. This is a story of an almost impossible love. It's not because they weren't made for each other, though. It's because of the context in which they find themselves, today's supposedly idyllic and charmed Paris. It's all complicated. I could have, back in the day, made a 16mm film, which wouldn't have cost that much. I would have done it with friends, with an ultra-small crew as I had with *I Stand Alone*. But I met Vincent Cassel around that time, who asked me what I was doing. He'd just come off of *La haine* and *Brotherhood of the Wolf* and was at the height of his high-profile affair with Monica Bellucci. He said that they both wanted to make a film with me. So, I handed him the scenario for *Danger*. I told him it was a love story between two people and that I wanted to film explicit sex. But it was about the intimacy of the couple, above anything else. All of the nudity was essential to the film. He was about to read the scenario. Suddenly, out of nowhere, I had producers who said to me: "A sensual, erotic film with Vincent Cassel and Monica Bellucci? *Yes*. Let's do it. We've got the money for you." I'd found two producers who wanted to do *Danger*. But then, after reading the scenario, which was like five pages at the time, Vincent and Monica told me that it was too intimate for them. They were a very famous couple and couldn't expose their bodies on screen like that. Their privacy was the only thing they had left. On top of that, they had all of these stalkers who followed them day and night; their private moments of intimacy were their only sanctuary left. So they told me no. But since we had told the producers that we were going to make a film with them and that I was friends with [Albert] Dupontel, I pitched him the idea of *Irréversible*, a story of revenge told inside out. So I shot that film, thinking I had to rush it, but it turned out far better than I could have imagined. It went to Cannes, inspired all kinds of animosity and praise, but it was, crucially, a huge commercial success. And after that, I was finally able to do *Enter the Void*, which ultimately took me six years.

Q: *Love* has a lot of improvisation, it came out of a five-page scenario.

GN: Yes, and *Irréversible* was initially around three pages, too; it was just a synopsis. If Vincent and Monica hadn't said yes to me, the film could've never been financed based on a few pages. I obviously didn't have the clout of someone like Godard. It was because of their names that the film got moving. In terms of *Love*, I made a deliberate choice not to write any dialogue, all of which was improvised with the actors on set. It's a method I use more and more. I don't submit a full screenplay of what I'm going to film. I just describe the scenario. We shoot one take, two takes, and each time it gets richer, but it deviates. I film almost all the suggestions that are made to me on the day. Sometimes we'll do six consecutive takes without stopping the camera. This was the first time I shot digital and there was no need to reload. We could string everything together. Before the end of a take, I'd say: "Don't move! Let's go again!" And I even gave them notes during their performance. When I'd see an actor was out of ideas, I'd propose things to them in the middle of a take. That's something natural when making documentaries, and I haven't done a lot of them, but they resonate with what I'm doing. It's much more thrilling to film people experiencing drama or ecstasy without having to bring them into your own personal world. When I make fiction films, I like that there's some overlap between the two. We are always more surprised by others than by ourselves. And the fact you're surprised by the people you've chosen to film makes you want to get back to the set each morning.

Q: I gather that the scenario for *Love* was much more brutal at first. But your mother's death softened the film and gave it a sense of melancholy.

GN: I think that as long as we haven't lost someone close, we have the impression of being immortal, a deluded affirmation of one's self and life. The moment you lose a child, a brother, a sister, a lover, your mother, everything becomes different.

Q: I hear you don't like to delegate.

GN: Don't ever delegate. You have to know how to incorporate everything good that's offered to you, but never delegate. Trust is something that changes all the time in relationships. You can trust a person one day and not at all the next day. Because, I don't know, she lied to you about something. And if you have to delegate, it can only be to people who have talent. For example, with Benoît Debie, the cinematographer on my last three films, I have total confidence in him. And this has to do with taste as much as his character. He never stops coming up with ideas. So when I get to do a film with Benoît, I feel confident. And I couldn't wish for anything more. But you're best served by your own ideas. I mean, I'd love to be able to make the music for my films, but I don't know how. I'm only talking about Benoît because he's such an obviously important part of the crew, but there are other people on my team—production assistants, production directors, editors—who understand me perfectly. And I know I'm safe with them. I worked a lot with Lucile Hadžihalilović at one time, we made films together. I edited hers, she edited mine. I think you have to surround yourself with people who have taste, a passion for cinema. People who put you on the right path when you go to shoot, when you're casting . . . I really get along with Laurent Lufroy, who does my posters. Working with him is like going on vacation with a friend. And I prefer being locked up making beautiful posters than being at the beach getting drunk.

Q: Having seen your films, we didn't expect to meet someone so calm and gentle in person.

GN: Let's just say that I am aware of legal limits on behavior. I was very shy when I was fifteen, like a lot of people. It's an affliction that eventually passes. But if I think about it, it was only after seeing *Irréversible* that people started to think that I was some kind of sadist. Or sometimes people thought I was a hardcore queer, and they invited me to clubs. . . . So I realized that we often project characters from films, the good ones as well as the bad, onto directors. But no, I make films about drama that I've imagined. You have to be fairly centered to be a director because it requires a lot of diplomacy within the cast and crew. You have to be very down to earth. A junkie director doesn't make many films, neither does a depressed director. A temperamental director will get his ass kicked unless he has a lot of protection around him.

Q: You say that some people, after seeing *Irréversible*, took you for a "hardcore queer." Conversely, do people ever find your films homophobic?

GN: Well, homophobia is something that's in the air. Fritz Lang is not anyone in *M*. Just because he made a film about a guy who gets accused of pedophilia doesn't mean he's one. In my films, I try to have the characters talk like they would in real life. And characters like Karl's, I know fifty thousand guys just like him. Half of my friends, when they get angry, make racist and homophobic remarks, but I don't think that makes them racist or homophobic. Even the main character in *I Stand Alone* is not really a bad guy. He's just in a state of crisis. And in a state of crisis, even the loveliest people can turn into monsters. I don't actually know what a monster is, but in any case, it was a uniquely French opportunity to put all of that into a film without being judged. For example, in the United States, there are things you'll never see or hear in a film. Or if someone says something hideous, that character has to be punished at the end or at least be clearly identified as a "bad" character. In an interview, Douglas Sirk once said that the problem with American cinema was its Manichaeism. The characters are flat; they're either good or they're bad. Either red or green. But a man or a woman has different sides to their person. Without being schizophrenic, you can be very kind and also be incredibly cruel without even realizing it. I find it interesting that in my films, people are neither heroes nor antiheroes. They're just galley slaves who pretend they are something else. It's like *The Mother and the Whore*, the characters are very sweet yet very twisted. And it's autobiographical, given Eustache used his friends' own language. I don't know if it's still possible to paint such a precise image of human complexity.

Q: Is the final sequence of *Enter the Void*, where we see several couples having sex in a "love hotel," an introduction to *Love*?

GN: Maybe, yes. Yeah, I think so. I'd read something in a book by Michel Simon that explained how Kubrick always tried to link the beginning of his films to the end of the previous one. At the beginning of *Lolita*, for example, there's Peter Sellers dressed in Roman garb, which echoes *Spartacus*. At the start of *Dr. Strangelove*, there's Peter Sellers, once again. . . . At the end of *Strangelove*, there's the planet that explodes, and at the outset of *2001*, you see the planet from afar. He gives the impression that he's stitching together the ends and beginnings of his films in a very artificial way that presents his oeuvre as a single coherent work. At the end of *2001*, we see an astral fetus looking at the camera, and then, in *A Clockwork Orange*, we start with Alex's eye. The films, in a sense, answer themselves. You can tell yourself that the fetus has grown up. So, I thought it could be fun to copy this game that Kubrick had been playing by himself. At the end of *I Stand Alone*, we see a father who is in the process of committing suicide, saying, "soon the void, soon the void," because I was thinking of continuing with "suddenly the void, suddenly the void" (first title of *Enter the Void*). But then I didn't end up doing *Enter the Void*. So, with *Irréversible*, I decided to put Philippe Nahon in the first sequence, when there was no real reason for him to be there, talking about committing incest with his daughter. But it amused me, and no one noticed that it was just some obsessive, manic delusion on my part. At the end of *Irréversible* and at the start of *Enter the Void*, I played with a few stroboscopic effects. And *Enter the Void* ends in a love hotel where you can see the words, "love, love, love." Then the next film is called *Love*, and we also see the model of the hotel from the previous film. So I don't know what I'm going to do next. I imagine it will begin in a bathtub with two people embracing, bathed in red light, with Bach in the background.

Q: After examining loneliness, violence, death, and now love, what do you want to film next?

GN: Psychosis! Maybe. Yeah, psychosis. I've been thinking for a while that we have to make a great antireligion film. I'm very phobic about it. I bathe in total atheism, when I was a child, my mother asked me not to go near churches. . . . At one point, my Buddhist friends took me to some event and my mother almost killed me. But lately, the presence of religion is starting to rot society and the world. So making a film about religion is very fashionable. You don't have to tell people it's bad anymore because it's just so obvious.

Q: Is it true you first tested using 3D on your mother?

GN: [*Laughs*] No, I did not test my 3D technique on my mother. She was dying and I'd just bought a 3D video camera because I like 3D photos. I wanted to keep memories of this person I loved. I had fun, well . . . not fun exactly, photographing my mother in 3D, filming her in 3D. Sometimes, she came to her senses and talked to me. I'm impressed with these images when I watch them on my TV. I feel like she's in a little coffin, she's still there. Doing this during my mother's final days of agony, I realized that in 3D, the camera should not move. Because, suddenly, it doesn't work. You need a certain distance and a stable perspective, so that it feels like people are actually behind the screen. So, when I was filming, I put the camera on a tripod and told myself that if I one day made a 3D film, it would only be with fixed shots or linear movements. I would design the shots last because the problem with classic editing in terms of 3D is that you get used to a space. If everything is moving too fast, the eye won't have enough time to acclimatize.

Q [*From the audience*]: When you're casting, how do you know that an actor is right for the role?

GN: I rarely go through casting directors; I like meeting people. If I shot a film tomorrow at a police station, I'd shoot with real cops. It was the same with *Irréversible*; we found real cops to play cops, firefighters to act as firefighters, and thugs to act as thugs. It's becoming more common, especially in cinema that wants to be a little more documentary or realistic. Actors who've done theater often declaim in front of the camera. It doesn't necessarily come through when everyone on set is a pro, but when you start mixing professionals and nonprofessionals, amateurs tend to talk very low, shy and simply. It's easier to ask the actors to lower their voices than do the reverse. Now, thanks to lavalier microphones, one can work more easily with nonprofessionals.

Q [*From the audience*]: You made a video for the musician SebastiAn.

GN: I get asked to make music videos all the time. Commercials less so, because producers are afraid that I'll argue with the client. They've kept me out of advertising, just to be safe. But music videos often come from friends who offer songs to me. Like with SebastiAn. He had spoken to me about making a film with a little kid who films herself on her webcam. We thought a sixteen-year-old girl should play it, so we launched a big casting call in the United States, asking girls to dance in front of their webcams pretending to be Britney Spears. We went that route, but then an eleven-year-old girl showed up with her mother. The producer thought she was reminiscent of Jodie Foster in *Taxi Driver*. And she was awesome. But she was underage. So I came up with a scheme to make the film with two girls, but I think the older one was embarrassed to be working alongside the younger kid. Once we were done with that part, I improvised some things just with the little one. I asked her to do whatever she wanted. Her charisma shined through. I had to try and keep up with her when I was editing.

Q [*From the audience*]: Why did you shoot *Love* in English?

GN: I wanted the film to be in English because I wanted it to reach as many people as possible, without subtitles. Especially if it was going to be in 3D, I can't stand 3D subtitles. But above all, I realized after doing *Enter the Void* that films traveled better when they were in English. *Enter the Void* lost producers money and *Irréversible* made them money. But despite the success of *Irréversible*, *Enter the Void* is better known. Especially in terms of illegal downloads. A film might not work in theaters but can be a success afterward, especially if it's in English. And since I'm not French by birth, my first languages being English and Spanish, it doesn't seem unnatural not to work in French.

Q [*From the audience*]: What advice would you give to a young actor?

GN: To let yourself go. In all circumstances. Without blacking out, obviously. But don't expect anything from others. The real problem for actors has to do with waiting around. It's the same with directors, the wait can gnaw away at you. You can spend three years with a screenplay and no one wants to fund it. The trick is to not get comfortable waiting around and to do things constantly. Whether it's writing or even making music. I spent years waiting for *Enter the Void* to happen, largely driven by false hope. And it just eats away at your soul. But when it comes to actors, I'd say don't feel restrained. When you have the means to do something, just go ahead and do it. You have to be bold, daring at times.

Q: You've said you were in a bit of a rush to finish *Enter the Void*. You needed more time before you could draw any conclusions about the film.

GN: The film was released a month and a half after it was shown at Cannes. And that stage, the film was still pretty shoddy. It is surprising what my name conveys since *Irréversible*. People think a film about love by Gaspar Noé is an impossible object. Yet there is no violence in the film, except maybe the verbal assaults. It's a couple who tear each other apart out of jealousy. They love each other too much and just don't know how to manage the situation. For me, it's a very sentimental film. I thought the film was only going to be restricted for children under twelve, like *Blue Is the Warmest Color*. But the film was restricted for anyone under sixteen. Then there was this far-right politician from the south [of France], who pisses off every director who makes anything approaching a respectable film. He escalated things. The film was reclassified "under eighteen" because of some ambiguous legislation. But all of this drew attention to a secondary issue: the means of classification themselves. The movie is on Netflix now, and any kid can watch it. It's the same elsewhere on the internet—any ten-year-old who knows how to download a movie can see it as if it were *Godzilla* or *Star Wars*. So, these theatrical bans are completely outdated. It's as if an old regime wants to defend its values in a world that doesn't give a fuck about them anymore. The culture now operates elsewhere. You can see any movie today, however you'd like. The controversy surrounding the film has nothing to do with the real essence of the film. The real question is this: Can we represent today a loving relationship in a direct way? This is how you can tell that society has changed a lot. I grew up in the seventies, and I saw erotic films and read erotic magazines. I was bathed in a culture of lust. Sensuality was a natural thing and considered an integral part of life. Today, people get kicked off Instagram because they've shown a nipple, while in most French parks, there are statues with bare nipples. You can see how the world has regressed. When I released my film in the United States, for the most part, I wasn't surrounded by intelligent audiences or critics. People asked me: "Why did you need to show his penis?" And I didn't really understand the problem: Why can I show my hand but not my penis? Over time, I've appreciated this regression in terms of how we represent sexuality, and even affection, in cinema. It's worrying. Why can you show guns on Facebook, but a nipple is a problem? After the penis, a woman's nipple becomes the image of the devil. We are insane. We are slowly coming to resemble the Islamic State. It is against nature.

Q: And what do you think is the origin of this regression?

GN: Religious movements shape society. But society is becoming more and more repressive. There have been a number of revolutions: the pill in the 1970s, the moment when the internet arrived. The acceptance of homosexuals in Western society has obviously improved. It's much better to be gay today than forty years ago. On the other hand, you have aspects of life that are becoming more and more repressive. We are now censored in unprecedented ways. And as far as feelings or sexuality are concerned, if you were to go to Canal+ and say that you were going to make a film with sequences like those in *Love*, they'd much rather you make a film about a mass murderer, with a submachine gun.

Q: What recommendation would you give a young filmmaker in light of your experience?

GN: You have to be a cinephile. Nowadays, the means of distribution are different; there is no longer any need to run to the 15th arrondissement to discover a film at ten o'clock in the evening on Monday, May 1. You can find everything online and on DVD. I think that cinephilia helps a lot if you want to make good films. Just like reading makes it possible for someone to write good books. After that, it's just life; take the plunge and don't listen too much to other people.

Interview with Gaspar Noé

Pip Chodorov / 2018

At the 2018 Cannes Film Festival, Gaspar Noé received an award in the *Quinzaine des réalisateurs* selection for *Climax*. But the filmmaker was also excited by the prospect of a 70mm screening of Stanley Kubrick's *2001: A Space Odyssey* on the occasion of the fiftieth anniversary of the film's release. Pip Chodorov and Jeremi Szaniawski took the opportunity to ask him questions about Kubrick's sci-fi classic.

Pip Chodorov: Gaspar, we are at Cannes. This is the fiftieth anniversary of *2001: A Space Odyssey*, and it just got screened in 70mm. You are an avid fan of the film, do you remember when you first saw it?[1]

Gaspar Noé: I was around seven years old. It was in Buenos Aires. I went to see it with my mother and my father. I came out of the movie transfixed. I was under the impression that I had enjoyed it far more than my parents did. And I remember very well, wondering at the time, "What was that baby with a huge head. . . ." And my parents explained to me, "You know, babies, when inside the womb, have a huge head." And so they had to explain both fecundation and birth to me by the same token. So, in one go, I got to realize what a psychedelic trip could be, where life came from, and how it was conceived. The origin of life. I was so fascinated by the movie . . . it got rereleased every summer, maybe every other year, and each time, I went. Without my parents, even though I was little. I would go with schoolmates, and then as a teenager I would go by myself, and I kept seeing it, in high school, in film school . . . and I have never stopped since. I must have seen the movie fifty, maybe sixty times by now.

Jeremi Szaniawski: Are there other Kubrick movies that matter as much to you?

GN: This one stands alone, above all the others. And I am flabbergasted when critics tell me that Kubrick's greatest film is *Dr. Strangelove or: How I Learned to*

Stop Worrying and Love the Bomb [1964]. I have seen that film once. But *2001* . . . I just can't get enough of it. I even watch it sometimes when I am on an airplane. People tell me, "Come on Gaspar, there's tons of new films," but I say, "They are showing *2001*; I am going to watch it one more time."

JS: Your film *Enter the Void* [2009], with its "ultimate trip" dimension, its color patterns, the way it deals with death and resurrection, its camera movements, is very ostensibly influenced by *2001*. But in general, your whole oeuvre seems to be informed by the film. For instance, in *Irreversible* [2002], the red tunnel, the poster of *2001* on the protagonists' bedroom wall, the flicker at the end of the film, revealing a subliminal outer space and the black monolith . . . and I have a sense that your oeuvre as a whole engages with a phenomenology of drugs, just as *2001* clearly engaged with the effects and hallucinations of psychedelic drugs . . .

GN: The poster at the end of *Irreversible* has to do with the fact that the Vincent Cassel character is a cinephile, but the film was also shot in the year *2001*, so it's a reference to that, a way of dating the film . . . and also a way of announcing that Monica Bellucci's character is pregnant: we see the Star Child, a fetus, on the poster on the wall. The camera pans, and we can see the characters and the poster in one movement. I have this poster at home, by the way, and it's my favorite of all the many *2001* posters that have been released. I believe I have the largest collection of *2001* posters and publicity paraphernalia in the world. It felt good to be able to put the poster in the film. We got the clearance to do that . . . but indeed, for me, the influence of *2001* is more explicit in *Enter the Void*, this tendency toward experimental filmmaking and psychedelic representations . . .

JS: Would you say that there is a Kubrickian tradition in your cinema?

GN: I am not fascinated by Kubrick's oeuvre as a whole. I am fascinated by R.W. Fassbinder, by Kenneth Anger, . . . and then, there are distinct films that I am obsessed with. *Salò* by Pasolini [1975] is one. *2001: A Space Odyssey* is the other big one. I just am the opposite of Kubrick. . . . I am incapable of doing anything serious . . . even if I wanted to do a serious documentary or psychological drama. . . . I can film people getting beaten to a pulp, and it's always derisive in the end; it ends up being funny one way or another. What I make will always be closer to a Buñuel than a Kubrick film.

PC: When did you start collecting posters of Kubrick's film?

GN: I always had this drive to collect. It's a mental disease. Since I was a child, I collected stamps, comic strips . . . it's pathological. I don't know. It's as if in order to possess something, you had to have the totality, the product as a whole. The latest and longest lasting manifestation of this *maladive collectionitis*, in my case, is my obsession with *2001*. That is clear.

JS: In Kubrick's films, in *2001* particularly, there is a worldview, a philosophy. Do you think that your films have a philosophy, a worldview?

GN: I am a dwarf . . . a flea . . . compared to the giant. . . . You can't compare. Kubrick made *the* film. The film where you can wonder how could someone do something so utterly majestic and ahead of its time. When you see *Metropolis* [Fritz Lang, 1927], you know it's the major, the ultimate work of art made by a filmmaker. When you see *King Kong* [Merian C. Cooper and Ernest B. Schoedsack, 1933], you ask yourself, "How is it possible to accomplish something so perfect technically, with such special effects, at that period in time?" When you watch *2001*, made in 1968, it's sublime. It's unthinkable that someone managed to pull off a film like that before any form of CGI. . . . It was a period when people still believed in cinema. This film is the absolute and ultimate manifestation of the power of the mind over matter, over technology. In cinematic terms, *2001* is that manifestation. I was fortunate enough to meet Douglas Trumbull, who was only twenty-four when he did the effects on that film. I did an interview with him for *Premiere* magazine. His work is a feat, an intellectual but also an existential feat. The whole film is. It is visionary. And deep, so deep. It's a mix of depth and lucidity in the analysis of the past but also of the future.

JS: Is there a final goal, a telos in Kubrick, in your view?

GN: When he spoke of his films, they were almost all on the same level. He conceived of them as a continuity. And, indeed, there is a continuity in his approach, an approach you can see in the evolution he describes in *2001*, of man as animal, even a reptilian creature, evolving to a higher stage. But the film also deals with many more things. It is far broader in its scope, it deals with the inner world as much as with the outside world. We spend one-third, maybe even more, of our life sleeping. So there's conscious and unconscious life, and to me, the last third of *2001* deals with the unconscious, the great, vast unconscious, as vast as outer space . . .

PC: Is there a final goal to your cinema?

GN: In Kubrick's, there is. In mine, no.

JS: Would you like to express something about Kubrick's legacy? What's the most important aspect that he has left behind him in our life?

GN: When you make a film, the film is the most important thing. That's it. After that, to each their own method, their relational approach. Kubrick would seek isolation, even on the set, he was reserved . . . he used to say that it was a great weakness to get upset on the set, to show your emotions. He would play chess with people and would keep calm to get the best of everyone. I learned that from him, from an interview where he said this: "It is a weakness to get upset with your collaborators."[2]

PC: Do you think young viewers today understand and respect the legacy of Kubrick?

GN: I don't know if it's a question of respect. . . . People simply have moved away from cinema . . . from the temple. The temple of cinema that we used to know. I was born in 1963. I knew the time before the DVD, even before the VCR, no Blu-ray, no internet. When you wanted to see a film, you would go to this place, often majestic, called a movie theatre. Today, you can see your films on your smartphone. Kubrick's films, and particularly *2001*, don't do well on small screens. You have to see *2001* on the big screen. It's a sign of the times . . . all films are accessible, in a way that is just so far less majestic than fifty years ago.

PC: Peter Kubelka said the same. You can't own a film. Nowadays, people say they buy, own a film, meaning they acquire a piece of plastic that is the DVD. But Kubelka has memories from his childhood, seeing a great film, and then lying in bed and just thinking about it, and reliving the film, this fugitive experience, which you can't "own" . . .

GN: [In the theatre] you are sitting in the dark, among many other people. When I make a film nowadays, Vincent Maraval from Wild Bunch, who produces and sells my films, tells me that ninety-five percent of people see the film on their laptop or their smartphones. So, the perception is different. And so a film composed mostly of long and wide shots, with few close-ups, registers differently, and to the detriment of the film, because, at the end of the day, surface matters.

PC: Do you change your approach to filmmaking based on this factor?

GN: I don't change mine because I conceive my films to be seen in a movie theatre, but mine may be a vintage state of mind and approach.

PC: Anything else you would like to say about *2001*?

GN: Everything has been said and written about *2001*, and yet the film retains its mystery. It took me at least forty years to sort of get what the film was about, I read all the interviews by Kubrick, articles in magazines. . . . I bought a VCR of a documentary that your father made, Pip, where Keir Dullea explains the film . . . it's terrific stuff.[3] That's how we met! You should put that stuff on the net; it's terrific. It should be on a DVD/Blu-ray bonus of the film, when they release it in 4K or 8K.

PC: Have you read the book *The Astral Fetus* [*Le foetus astral: essai d'analyse structurale d'un mythe cinématographique*, Jean-Paul Dumont and Jean Monod, 1970]? It's a structuralist, Levi-Straussian analysis of the film. For example, the authors explain how, at the beginning of the film, everything is craggy; nothing is straight, no straight lines except for the monolith. At the end of the film, it's the other way round—everything is straight, smooth and geometrical, except for the broken glass. There's symmetry and inversion. At the end of the film, Dave Bowman loses his spacecraft, then his suit, then the broken glass . . . it's the last layer of technology, the last surface of glass that gets shattered.

GN: And you can't tell his age either. He is outside of space and time . . . is he in a Martian zoo, perhaps? That amazing Louis XVI space, lit from underneath . . .

JS: The final membrane, as Deleuze taught us, is the brain . . . and so all of Kubrick's cinema is a mise-en-scène of the brain, of the noosphere as Deleuze put it. . . . Enter the brain.

PC: I also have a theory about the construction of the monolith; the music by Richard Strauss used in the film, *Thus Spake Zarathustra*, is tonic: 1, 5, 8 . . . very tonic. Harmonics. And the geometry of the monolith is 1, 4, 9. One squared by two squared by three squared. Strauss's music comprises in itself the three phases of the film: the ape, the man, and the superman. And in Nietzsche, you have a similar three-stages evolution of man.

GN: You are being a bit Kabbalistic!

PC: Maybe a little bit. Every person has an interpretation of this film.

GN: For me, it's about evolution . . . at first animal species, with a reptilian brain, then they develop a mammal's brain, and then a neocortex . . . the human brain. And so we have three brains, with the neocortex, which is a bit like a computer. And so perhaps the ultimate stage of evolution is when we are only left with a neocortex under dematerialized, digital form: artificial intelligence, in short. A superior form of intelligence would be man without the animal. But then there is the danger of the glitch or the bug. Computers bug and crash. They go psychotic, like HAL 9000. Humans do, too . . . and more often, perhaps.

Notes

1. The film was shown in the frame of the Cannes Classic section, at the Debussy Theater, on May 13, 2018. In the end, however, the announced remastered print didn't make it to Cannes, and a slightly scratched print was shown instead. The Cannes program announced that the remastered print would have a running time of two hours and forty-four minutes, meaning this would be the longer, original release version, which Kubrick later discarded in favor of a shorter, two-hours-and-twenty-nine-minute version.

2. Still, in the making-of [feature] of *The Shining* directed by his daughter Vivian, Kubrick is seen losing his temper on the set, getting mad at Shelley Duvall, who has recounted working on the film as an often difficult, even traumatic, experience.

3. Noé is talking about an American television program, narrated and hosted by Keir Dullea, which features excerpts from Kubrick's film. The program was written by Stephan Chodorov for the Camera Three CBS weekly show and broadcast in 1971. It includes some behind-the-scenes information and references to material not included in the final cut of the film.

Interview: Gaspar Noé Talks *Climax*

Ulkar Alakbarova / 2019

From *Movie Moves Me*, March 1, 2019. Reprinted by permission.

Collective madness. Craziness. Something that you don't know may happen, and when it does, what do we do to avoid it? How about things which take away our ability to control ourselves? What would we do if we find ourselves with a group of people that we barely know and have no idea if we can trust them?

Gaspar Noé's *Climax* is not just about people who, after having LSD mixed with their sangria, became high; it's about individuals who not only started acting strangely due to hallucinations, they begin seeing an enemy in every single one of themelves, turning a seemingly fun night into a nightmarish one where some of them never make it through.

As I can speak a lot about *Climax*, it's that strange yet paralyzed experience that you should put yourself through as a viewer. Yes, it may be uncomfortable at times, but remember, good movies are not there to comfort us; its main job is to displace us from our comfort zone to live a life we otherwise would not in real life.

During my phone interview with writer and director Gaspar Noé, I came to know more about *Climax* than has been written about the film anywhere else, the details of which I have no doubt you also would like to learn about.

Ulkar Alakbarova: How did you manage to fit the entire story into five pages of screenplay?

Gaspar Noé: My first feature was written, the one called *Enter the Void*, and I made it over a long period. Shooting one day here, one day there. But then, when I was proposed to do a movie with Monica Bellucci; we started *Irreversible* with just a three-page script and no dialogue. And probably until now, that's my biggest commercial success, although the movie was very violent.

I dropped one idea, I wrote three pages. We prepared the movie. Five weeks later, we were shooting. We were shooting five and a half weeks. And then it made a real movie. Also, it was easy because the whole story was taking place over one single night. And we shot it in chronological order. Then, in postproduction, we reversed the scenes. And the whole story is shown backwards in the film.

But last January, in January 2018, I had this idea for a movie that could take place in one single space with dancers. And I said, "Oh, probably, I can shoot it very quickly if I get the money. Because once you put the lights on and once you have dancers, you can hold them for fifteen days. Let's do it like an experiment. Let's create the movie altogether in fifteen days." And that's what happened. We prepared it in one month with one location and the twenty-three dancers.

Then we shot it in fifteen days. And we edited in two months. And what you can feel when you see the movie is the energy that was present on set. And yeah, everybody was really happy. There were no fights. No one was drunk; no one was wasted. They were happy to participate.

UA: After watching *Climax*, I really must ask if you have any empathy towards the characters you created for the film? Or was it all about testing their (the characters') limits?

GN: Actually, I like all the characters the same. Then, when I was choosing the dancers and actresses who were going to be in the movie, I made sure that they were people I really related to. In the first half of the movie, you like them all. There's not one that's a bad character or a despicable character. They are all full of energy. They are creative. And building this collective project in the most constructive way.

Then what happens is an accident. It's induced by one of the members. And the whole collective project starts collapsing. And you realize people have multiple faces. Everybody is sweet with his kids or can be sweet with his kids. His parents are the ones he loves, and they can all be regular people. But in the case of this movie, they all turn paranoid and start becoming destructive. Because they don't want to just control, they feel endangered, so they become angry and cruel.

But even in their anger, there's not one that is more despicable than the others. And when people in the movie become paranoid against those who didn't drink, it's not because they didn't drink or because of the reasons why they didn't drink. It's just because they think they're responsible for reducing the collective madness. Again it's not . . . most people who have kids, their favorite character is the young kid. I know each person probably would relate to one person more than the others. But I liked working with all of them. I also like all the characters the same.

UA: The "readiness" of actors, or whether it was improvisation, felt so real. You'll probably find it a funny question, but how about the state of mind of actors? Was there any kind of check done before and after the filming concluded?

GN: No. I told them the storyline in advance. I told them, "This is how the movie's gonna start. You're gonna be dancing toward the beginning. Then you're gonna improvise your dances. Then you're gonna be chatting, making projects about the party night. And then I'm gonna put the credits in the middle of the movie. And we go, after the credits in the middle of the movie, we go to the rest of the night. Like thirty minutes later or one hour later. And you're all turning psychotic." And they were all very clean on the set. They weren't drinking, they weren't doing any chemicals. They really enjoyed portraying some kind of craziness. And I showed them a lot of videos from rave parties, mental hospitals, people on drugs being arrested. And for them, it was a lot of fun to represent that. The kid who appears in the movie, he was there for just three days because we weren't allowed to have a young kid around for more than three days.

And then he's put in a closet. And you hear him screaming, but he wasn't on set. And when the movie was finished, every single dancer was as happy as the producers or the members of the crew. We just made the movie a catastrophic movie, in the best mood. And I don't think anybody regrets anything. They're all so happy that the movie exists. And most of them now want to become directors or actors. It was a pleasure to make the movie and it was a collective pleasure to show it and film it.

There's another thing. I think, in France, the issues are different. And even when I shot the movie, I didn't have in mind how many men or women I wanted on screen. I just wanted to have the best dancers. I didn't care at all about racial issues or sexual issues. I just said, "Oh, I want to have the most diverse people on set." And then, when the movie was finished, I got the best people I could get for the movie.

And then, yeah, you see something that probably could happen in France. Because the whole perception of the time is of a less communitarian people. People who were born in France, they all speak French. And that's why I included that sign that says the movie's French and proud of it. I'm happy the movie was produced here because it would not have been produced anywhere else.

UA: I'm sure, based on what I saw, it wouldn't have been produced in the United States.

GN: No. United States, no way. The producers would have reedited every single scene of my movie. In America, producers consider the movie as their own product. In France, producers finance, and the directors are proud of them because of this history of protecting painters, writers, whatever. And people still believe in like, believe in art. I don't know if art . . . if cinema is an art, it can be. But mostly, it's not. I feel that there's more respect for the final cut of the director in this country.

UA: What about the books presented during the interviews—the audition tapes seen in the film?

GN: Those were the books I was reading at the beginning of the nineties. And initially, that scene was shot in an old video format with a ratio of 1:33. And the cinema script screen is 2.35:1. I said, "Oh, that's not gonna look good, to put a square image inside a large image." And then I said, "Why don't I just put it inside the TV? Like if someone was watching those casting tapes in an apartment at that time?" And yes, that apartment is actually my apartment. All those books and those VHS were the ones that I had in my apartment. The books or videos that inspired me to make such a movie twenty years later.

UA: Going back to your work before *Climax*. All the characters you've written can be hardly considered as "normal." In fact, they are all rather extraordinary. But many people might also be scared of them.

GN: I don't know many people who are normal, or who consider themselves normal, or if anybody considers themselves normal. It's kind of scary. You know people have their own lives, they have their own traumas. Everybody has their traumas in childhood. Everybody has traumas in adulthood and some later. But I would say all these people that I filmed they mostly represent people who struggle to do things right, even when they do them wrong.

UA: As an editor of *Climax*, how many scenes did you decide to leave behind?

GN: I almost didn't cut anything. I just cut one dance scene in this movie. When I started shooting the movie, my producer asked, "Can you make a nineteen-minute movie in fifteen days?" And then I decided to cut it. But I didn't cut much. On the other hand, all those master shots that you see, those long takes, I shot them each up to eighteen times. And mostly it was the last two takes that were good. And all the previous that were just rehearsals for the final take.

UA: What do you think is the main takeaway viewers should be looking out for?

GN: It's about . . . I would say the movie is about construction, fragility, and destruction. I've seen so many couples, so many love-strong couples, suddenly breaking up because one day they got too drunk. And the reptilian, hidden face came up and they started openly insulting each other. And then the whole love story that was constructed. It's about the fragility, the chemical fragility of the human brain. I would say "losing control." It's like, this is the shiny side of the moon, and there's the dark side of the moon. When people go out, and they party and say, "Oh, this is controlled." At the beginning, it's great. And then usually it's a nightmare. Then after, it turns into a nightmare.

Gaspar Noé: Director

Frédéric Polizine and Alexis Veille / 2020

From *Le temps détruit tout*, August 24, 2020. Reprinted by permission. Translated by Frédéric Polizine and Alexis Veille.

Here it is. After more than forty interviews, coverage of each movie since 2003, and important updates to the website, we had to go back to our roots—just as *Irréversible* gave birth to us—to finally offer you an interview with Gaspar Noé. We deeply thank Gaspar Noé for his availability and Isabelle Sauvanon, without whom we couldn't have made this. Happy reading!

Question: If you could reshoot one sequence from one of your movies, which one would it be?

Gaspar Noé: I don't really have any regrets on a specific sequence. Maybe because I never watch my old movies because I always want to reedit, regrade, remix it . . .

Q: After the loss of Philippe Nahon, which deeply moved us, have you considered making a cinematic tribute to him?

GN: I wrote a tribute letter to my friend when he died, which was published in *Libération*. . . . Since then, his ashes were thrown in sea, and it makes me want to swim there. The next tribute will be when the 2K/4K digital master of the two movies we made together will be done and so that the movies can finally be rereleased in theaters and on Blu-ray.

Q: You shoot more regularly. Is it because you have more opportunities or simply because you are more conscious of passage of time?

GN: I shoot when I'm given the money to shoot. *Enter the Void* and *Love* were very difficult to finance, especially the first one, which was really expensive (€12M) and with a very atypical style. But I didn't want to scatter by directing projects that mattered less to me. Today, now that those teenage dreams are accomplished, I'm more willing to seek where the money is in order to do a movie

I can enjoy myself directing, and on which I won't be bothered too much. If it has to be shot within fifteen days, I'm sold! Give me the money. And if it has to be done within five days, it's all the same. . . . And if I'm given money for shooting a movie over four months or longer, like *Enter the Void*, of course I'm in. But the freedom given is always more precious than the budget.

Q: Which recent work—film, books, music—affected and inspired you and even opened up new horizons?

GN: Technically speaking, the first thirty minutes from *Gravity* astonished me. Six months ago, I was in the hospital, stuffed with morphine, and the movie was broadcast dubbed in French on the little TV at the other end of my room. And I loved it as much as when I watched it the first time in the best 3D theaters in Paris. . . . Except that I took advantage of my recovery, and particularly quarantine, to watch many great movies I had never seen before: *Andrei Rublev*, *The Rules of the Game*, *The Ballad of Narayama* (the one from 1958 directed by Kinoshita), *Sansho the Bailiff*, and *The Life of Oharu*. Discovering such masterpieces makes you want to direct new movies . . .

Q: Have you considered someday adapting a book or some other work with a screenwriter?

GN: Yes, for sure. But I don't have any particular novel to adapt or a coscreenwriter at the moment.

Q: How do you calm down your anxiety?

GN: Watching classic movies and falling asleep.

Q: In your career, most of your projects came from past ideas: *Pulpe amère* presaged *Carne* with its ever-present voiceover, and at the time of *Carne*, you already had *Enter the Void* in mind as much as *Love*, which was nearly produced by Dario Argento. *Love*, a project from 1992, was then known as *Danger*, and it's the plot you offered to Vincent Cassel and Monica Bellucci before you chose to make a rape-and-revenge movie with long shots. . . . Were you inspired by *Memento* to make the movie in a nonchronological order?

GN: Dario Argento never nearly produced *Irréversible*! I don't know where this fake news comes from.

However, he did come into my editing room when I was editing the movie. I showed him the very first part, and I stopped when Monica's character enters the tunnel. I wanted him to watch the whole movie on the big screen. . . . Except that, when I saw *Memento*, I felt lost in its maze-like temporal structure, made of sequences going backwards and others in the other way around. But watching this film reminded me of another film I had missed in theaters and on TV, but which was told backwards. It was *Betrayal*, based on a play by Harold Pinter. So I wrote a "rape-and-revenge" (missed revenge in this case) story, happening in one night with twelve sequences we could edit backwards. I wrote each sequence on a separate page, and reversing the order once, then twice, I could see if the movie would be clearly understandable—and if it was logical—in both orders. We shot chronologically in a bit less than six weeks, but I knew at the very beginning that the movie would be edited backwards. It was my wish. Seventeen years later, when we remastered it in 2K/4K, when I had the movie back in my editing room, I thought I should try an alternative cut for the Blu-ray extra features. This new chronological cut, quite quickly made, was actually way more interesting than I had ever imagined. It was screened in Venice, and it is finally being released in theaters, too. But I deeply advise everyone to watch the 2002 cut first, then watch the "Straight Cut" from 2020. The first one asks a lot of questions; the second brings some not-so-gleaming answers.

Q: During your masterclass in Lyon, Cyril Roy [actor in *Enter the Void*] told me that in Asia, *Irréversible* was recut in its chronological order for DVD extra features. You then explained to me that it was made without your agreement, and instead, you probably would have added black title cards between each scene, a bit like *Love*. That's not what we see in the "Straight Cut," for which you and your crew remade each transition in order to keep invisible cuts. Why?

GN: Indeed, in Korea, they tried a recut for their bonus features, but when I started to watch it, the cuts were so poorly done that I stopped after twenty minutes, and I never watched it again. In the straight cut that I edited, we made sure that every splice between sequences remained as enjoyable as in the original version.

Q: Back in 2016, StudioCanal was supposed to rerelease the movie in Germany with a new master. In the end, it was on an Italian Blu-ray that we discovered this master in 2017. Is there any difference between the 2017 and the 2020 masters?

GN: I think that the *Irréversible* Blu-rays already available (Italian, Japanese, etc.) are all frauds in fake high definition, made from poor masters used for TV and DVDs in 2002. . . . No, I absolutely changed nothing to the original cut by doing, in 2019, the new master of the movie.

Question: Is the period between this 2017 master and the rerelease due to the fact that you wanted to do the "Straight Cut" for the Blu-ray extra features? Otherwise, why has there been such amount of time while the master seemed ready and most likely approved?

GN: The only master we approved was the one we started in 2019, which is finally ready to be commercialized in 2020. No others were ever approved. And it's nice to go from "2002" to "2020," it's like a partial reversal of reading direction, just as in the new cut.

Q: *Irréversible* was remastered in 4K, but StudioCanal will edit both versions in one double-disc "standard" Blu-ray combo pack. Is it only because of the lack of popularity from the UHD format?

GN: The truth is that the film was originally shot in Super 16mm, postproduced in HD video, but not at all 4K, and after the grading, reshot on 35mm film. We saw the 16mm grain, and it was part of the charm of the picture. If the film is upscaled in 4K, the original image is in a lower definition than 2K anyway. To release 4K Blu-rays, they have to be made from 4K masters or 35mm or 70mm films. Otherwise, it's pointless. But if theaters' projectors are 4K, it's normal to deliver a 4K DCP, even if the original film hasn't the right definition.

Q: It's no coincidence that I talked about *Pulpe amère* earlier: the first DVD of *Irréversible* should have included it in its extra features. Although it's mentioned on the DVD cover, your short film is completely absent. Can we expect to see it in its entirety, maybe in the Blu-ray features?

GN: *Pulpe amère* won't be part of the Blu-ray because, rewatching this very short film, we all thought it didn't belong in the video edition. And yes, I had shot this short with my friend Maxime Ruiz in his photo studio at the time. Since then, he has been a still photographer on *Irréversible*, and he is fabulous in my last medium-length film, *Lux Æterna*.

Q: A few months ago, Albert Dupontel told us a story about *Irréversible*'s success. In the US, he didn't have any ID and in order to buy something with his credit card, he had to show a DVD of the movie. . . . What impact did the movie have on your career?

GN: Me too; when I was arrested by the cops and had to tell them my name and job, I told them I'd made *Irréversible*, and all of them had seen it. Same for the taxi drivers and bouncers. It helps a lot.

Q: You shot unused footage of Monica Bellucci on her hospital bed. One could have expected that the "Straight Cut," more focused on Alex who opens the movie, would have ended up with this footage, or at least have shown some never-before-seen footage. But that's not the case. Did you consider using any unused footage?

GN: Indeed, I considered using this cut scene, but it would have been used at the very end as a happy ending, revealing that she was still alive. I thought it was stronger and more anxious not telling what happened, and I gave up the idea.

Q: *Climax* and *Lux Æterna* didn't provoke any outrage (well, we remember the authorities coming in at the end of *Lux Æterna*'s Cannes screening); some film critics think you're wiser now. Is this rerelease a way to remind them you haven't lost anything despite your earlier projects supposedly being darker and more vicious?

GN: Being wiser or not isn't the issue. We shoot films about more or less problematic themes. We should never force ourselves to shock people, just as we should not be afraid of doing so. Personally, only the news is still able to shock me. Not fiction movies with actors.

Q: *Irréversible* is a turning point in your career: your first feature with complex camera movements and invisible cuts, your first collaboration with poster designer Laurent Lufroy and cinematographer Benoit Debie. How do you expect your career and style to evolve in the next ten years?

GN: I hope I'll continue shooting films with my gifted friends. It's the collective competition that makes us want to shoot these movies and to show them.

Inside Gaspar Noé's Head

Marc Godin and Laurence Rémila / 2020

From *Technikart*, September 16, 2020. Reprinted by permission of *Technikart*. Translated by
Geoffrey Lokke.

By the end of 2020, we'll have received a double ration of Gaspar Noé, who returns with the "Straight Cut" of *Irréversible* (in theaters starting August 26), a film
more radical than ever, as well as *Lux Æterna* (September 23), a mind-bending,
instinctual film—this time without any of the drugs or violence. Following his
brain hemorrhage and months living under quarantine, Noé talks to us about
Netflix and Philippe Nahon, morphine and Yves Saint Laurent, the dollar and
Professor Choron . . . basically, an interview unlike any other.

Since the release of his film *Carne* in 1991, Gaspar Noé has been one of the
most dazzling talents in contemporary cinema. A provocative, vanguard artist,
Noé is an indelible inventor of new forms, yet a markedly laconic *auteur* (only
six feature films in nearly thirty years) who has dug a unique, deep trench for
himself, irrigated with blood, semen, and tears.

At fifty-seven years old, the former *enfant terrible* of French cinema has never
garnered even the most minor César. But his influence is palpable from Ari Aster's
film nightmares to a number of Kanye West's music videos. A director who has
made Pasolini's motto ("Why deprive yourself of the pleasure of shocking, why
deprive the public of the pleasure of being shocked?") his own, Noé has returned
in 2020 with no fewer than two new films. He has put the sulfurous *Irréversible*
(2002), starring Vincent Cassel and Monica Bellucci, back in chronological order,
which turns out to be an even more despairing and radical experience than what
we remember. He's also given us *Lux Æterna*, starring Charlotte Gainsbourg and
Béatrice Dalle, a story of witches with the kind of forceful staging that manages
to tear up everything in its path.

For *Technikart*, Gaspar Noé, in his YSL jacket and glasses, takes off his mask
and throws it away, all in his little nasal voice and his machine-gun delivery. We

discuss the death of his favorite actor, his cerebral hemorrhage and his convalescence in hospital, Netflix and the supposed end of cinema, the secret of his mustache, and his love for Professor Choron. All of this is bookended by fits of laughter. Because Gaspar Noé likes nothing more than to laugh, especially by watching . . . *Mr. Bean.*

Question: This year, 2020, in our collective period of confinement, seems to have transformed every person on the planet. But you experienced this feeling a few months ago when you suffered a cerebral hemorrhage.

Gaspar Noé: Fortunately, I had the accident on a Sunday last December, before the appearance of COVID. If I'd called the emergency number ("15") on any other day of the week, the ambulance would have been stuck in traffic jams due to the strikes. I would have arrived at the hospital too late, and I would have died, like fifty percent of the people this happens to, or I would have had cerebral sequelae, like thirty-five percent of the others. Around noon, I noticed I had a rapid heartbeat, which was followed by a sort of dull explosion in my skull. I knew what it could be, given a friend had once described these sensations to me. I knew I had only five to ten minutes to act before I'd slip into a coma, so I ran to a bar asking for help and to call the SAMU [Urgent Medical Aid Service]. By that time, I no longer could hear anything; I was shaking, sweating, and, among other things, I couldn't synchronize my right eye with my left anymore. The ambulance arrived quickly, and a few minutes later, I was under a scanner with streams of blood flowing into my increasingly less-than-gray matter. And just like that, I was saved. The happy or fatal outcome of these episodes plays out within minutes. Then I spent the month of January in hospital, followed by another month of convalescence. When I was supposed to get back to work in March, lockdown happened. So I thought: "Great, I'm going to be able to watch DVDs and Blu-rays at home." I crisscrossed Paris by bike, and if there's one thing that still makes me melancholy, it's seeing a deserted Paris without any alcoholics in the street. . . .

Q: And you immersed yourself in classic cinema?

GN: I watched a dozen or so by Mizoguchi because I'd only seen one. It was a perfect opportunity to catch up on a lot of stuff. I'd never seen *The Rules of the Game* by Renoir, *Andrei Rublev* by Tarkovsky, nor the incredible *Ballad of Narayama* that Kinoshita made in 1958, long before the terrible remake. I turned to films that everyone considers to be masterpieces that I'd missed out on. So I deepened my knowledge of the classics . . .

Q: Did the accident make you go back to *The Tibetan Book of the Dead*, which you directly reference in *Enter the Void*?

GN: I had incredible hallucinations due to the morphine. And that was all pretty great, to be honest. The only thing I was able to watch during the three weeks at the hospital was *Gravity*, in French, on a tiny TV hanging at the other end of the room. I was tied to the bed, stuffed with blood thinners and morphine, and this viewing was one of the great cinematic experiences of my life. I have now reconciled myself with public television, with Hollywood, with NASA. Near-death experiences can lead to unexpected enchantments.

Q: You discovered morphine when you were in hospital—a very easy-going drug . . .

GN: It's a very sweet drug. Above all, you no longer feel any pain, you float . . . Then afterwards, you don't remember anything . . . I only have a very vague memory of my first week in the hospital, and given the constant explosions that I heard in my skull, I only slept for around thirty minutes each day. I had the impression that the battle of Verdun was replaying in my head.

Q: Does this episode make you want to produce films more quickly than you have before? You usually take three to four years between each feature film.

GN: No, because I like to make films that I haven't seen before, films that are a little different, atypical. This way of doing things courts financial setbacks that push you to struggle for months, even years. *Climax* and *Irréversible* were financed at the whim of their producers, but films like *Love* or *Enter the Void*, which I'd written long before, were almost impossible to get made because of the sex, the glorification of drugs, or the cost of visual effects. You sit there waiting a couple of years until one day, by some miracle, you're told that money is available but only if you can shoot right away. And then you have barely two weeks to find the actors and start filming.

Q: Philippe Nahon, a major actor in your career, died due to complications after contracting COVID. How did you process this loss?

GN: I'd intended to shoot an epilogue with Philippe that would have been a third part of a trilogy with *Carne* and *I Stand Alone*. I had lots of ideas for this generous and touching person, but I was too late. He'd suffered two strokes already that caused him to lose some motor skills, part of his memory, his vocabulary; I wanted to take more time with him to improvise something appropriate. When I was finally ready to get to work, using a very small crew, Philippe was hospitalized again, and he died a week later. Things only get made when the people and the locations are ready. Otherwise, there are only regrets . . .

Q: Your relationship with him dates back to 1989.

GN: It's funny, from the inside, you never feel like you're getting old or growing up. And as you move forward in life, you forget most of the path you've traveled. But there are a few encounters you remember in detail. With Nahon, I remember the moment he opened the door when I came to see him for the first time. I'd chosen him based on a photo. Charisma always plays a role, of course, but it's amazing how your brain can imagine someone's personality just from an image. For me, he represented a bit of what Jean Gabin represented at one time, this kind of French bonhomie that we all love. But what I didn't expect was his voice, which was as rare as it was marvelous.

Q: When you first saw his photo, was this at the start of your career?

GN: When I met Philippe, I was twenty-five or twenty-six years old. I was about to start shooting *Carne*, which was ultimately forty minutes long. *Carne* was a hit at festivals in France and also in Japan. Out of that success came the desire to make a sequel, except that I had run out of time and money. I wanted to do a second part, as a diptych—a little unbalanced, I suppose—with a forty-minute first part followed by another ninety. But it was Agnès B. who swooped in and saved the film by offering her help.

Q: And now you find yourself working in another "bastard" format with *Lux Æterna*, a fifty-two-minute, medium-length film that comes out September 23.

GN: There are no bastard formats, only bastard commercial conventions. When we talk about fifty-two minutes for TV, we are not talking about a bastard format but a TV format. Luis Buñuel's best-known film is *Un chien Andalou*, which is only sixteen minutes. Among moving-image exhibitors, there are very calibrated distribution systems, kind of like shoe sizes. But let's be clear: any work, from one minute to ten hours, is a film. There are filmmakers like Tarantino who make extremely long films, and no one blames them. Personally, I can make a two-hour-forty-minute film with the same enthusiasm as one that's fifty minutes. I just want to say, "Leave me alone. You can go piss off others but don't piss me off."

Q: Except you're the only one who still wants to make fifty-minute films.

GN: No, there was Buñuel and Renoir, with their unfinished projects *Simon of the Desert* and *A Day in the Country*. And, of course, there's Eustache! Speaking of masterpieces and the great masters of cinema. Eustache made both feature films and medium-length films. And when he shot *A Dirty Story*, it was conceived as a diptych (twenty-eight minutes plus twenty-two minutes). It's just that when people have traveled thirty minutes on the subway to go see a film, they prefer a longer format because then it feels like a more worthwhile investment. But today, with streaming platforms like Netflix, it doesn't matter anymore how long anything is. Some short- and medium-length films are financed with a lot of money by these new platforms. Whether it's Paul Thomas Anderson's musical short for Netflix or whatever, there is now a market to produce things that people can watch on the subway or on the bus. When everyone watches films on their tablet or on their phone, why limit yourself to ninety minutes? Streaming television exploded film runtimes. You watch *Chernobyl*, it lasts for four hours. So, if it's episodic, it's okay. But it's a film, really. When we look at the Kechiche trilogy—*Mektoub, My Love: Canto Uno*, *Intermezzo*, and the next one—some people say, "Damn, it's too long." But if you have them split into several one-hour episodes, the same people would say it's perfect for a Netflix or Amazon series.

Gaspar Noé: An Exclusive Interview on Creativity and Life

Ronit Pinto and Sam C. Long / 2021

From *Honeysuckle*, June 16, 2021. Reprinted by permission of Ronit Pinto, founder and publisher, Honeysuckle Media. @honeysucklemagazine, honeysucklemag.com.

The first monster that an audience has to be scared of is the filmmaker. They have to feel in the presence of someone not confined by the normal rules of propriety and decency.

—HORROR MASTER WES CRAVEN

Gaspar Noé does not make horror films per se, but . . . some sequences are like cutting off your eyelids and packing the sockets with salt. The filmmaker Just. Does not. Cut. The camera is not going to pan away. No one is holding your hand. You are just going to have to sit and watch the horrors of life: rape, murder, psychedelic trips gone wrong (and the eventual end of the Vincent Cassel/ Monica Bellucci marriage).

Beyond story the camera sometimes seems like it's glued to a broken car-assembling robot. There's the movie told backwards *(Irréversible)*. There's the movie shot on two cameras at once *(Lux Æterna)*. How about a movie, told from a ghost's POV, where the character gets reincarnated, or not, depending on the cut you see?

Gaspar represents that pinnacle of filmmaking: You just sit down, buckle your seatbelt, and give up. You are not in control; there is a mad man at the wheel. A real leery psychopath. So when *Honeysuckle* flew to Paris, what could we possibly expect for our interview, only confirmed at 10 p.m. the night before?

Gaspar . . . total fucking sweetheart.

Maybe it was the themed "LA MORT N'OUVRE AUCUNE PORTE" shirts we had made for the trip. Maybe it's that Ronit and I are also total cinephiles.

Gaspar was literally skipping out on preproduction for his next film, a companion piece to *Lux Æterna*. Very pressed for time. But once we sat down, we chopped cheese—for hours.

Our only regret was when he asked us for the inside scoop into contemporary American films; we admitted we don't really watch them. Actually, we watch a lot of French films.

Gaspar, notorious filmmaker, secret sweetheart, sat down with us for the following interview on life, movies, and his early creative life.

The following interview has been condensed and edited for clarity.

Ronit Pinto: The first movie you ever saw was in New York?

Gaspar Noé: Yes, because my parents moved to New York when I was a few months old. I don't remember the first movie I saw in the theater, but I know that the first memory I have is watching *2001: A Space Odyssey* when I was six. . . . Certainly, I had seen other movies before, but I don't remember. The problem with memory, it's very selective. It's like a hard drive. You have to empty [it] every week, every year, because you can't keep all the useless memories. They say that the memories you have from your childhood are the ones that have been reactivated every three or four years. If you stop reactivating a memory, it disappears.

RP: How do you reactivate it?

GN: Each time you think of the past, and you talk about it, you rearrange it, so after many years, the memory of you talking about something creates memories. The past is very blurry unless you have photos. . . . If one day you were in an amusement park and you had a toy and you were photographed with [it], many years later when you see the photos [you go], "Oh yeah, I had that toy." But you had certainly forgotten the toy.

RP: Did growing up with an artistic father influence you?

GN: Yeah, of course. Actually, when you have a father who's a painter or who's bringing you as a kid to all these exhibitions, openings, etc., and everybody's happy and they're drinking. . . . He had all these books of art [and] he was also teaching painting to younger painters at my home . . . I was watching all the time.

I think my visual education comes from my father, but the real cinema buff in the family was my mother. She was bringing me to see [the films of Rainer Werner] Fassbinder when I was nine because she wouldn't want to leave me alone at the house. . . . That's how I learned what lesbians were, [from the movie] *The Bitter Tears of Petra von Kant*. I was probably nine. . . . [My mother is] the one who brought me to see [Pier Paolo] Pasolini's *Salò* when I was eighteen. She's the one who brought me to see *2001*. She loved literature; she loved movies.

Also, we had a cinematheque three blocks away from my house. My father met the guy who was selling tickets. Then we became friends . . . I would go almost every two days to see what was going on in there. If the movie was forbidden [to kids under eighteen], the guy would still let me go in.

Sam Long: That's awesome.

GN: Yeah, movies are addictive. We're all addicted to something. Some people are addicted to food, alcohol, social working. I got addicted to cinema very early. I was also addicted to comic books, but then I said, "No." Probably because it's closer to life, I switched to movies.

RP: Why do you think you were addicted?

GN: It's like dreaming. A movie's a conducted dream. Then, you choose your channels.

RP: Do you have a favorite part of filmmaking?

GN: I like showing the movie. I don't like the preproduction. I like shooting. I like editing, but the problem with editing is that when you get there, you already have some pressure for delivering the movie. . . . You have the material, and you can't relax and do it at your own pace because they say . . . "You have to deliver the movie before Cannes." They were psychotic about that. Also, when you make a movie, and you're broke, when you get your salary, you're so happy. You go to eBay and buy all the movie posters on the planet, and then you're broke again [*Laughs*]

RP: What about the idea, the inception?

GN: I don't really believe in inspiration. You're inspired by other people's words, by drama in your own life [and] your friends' lives. Sometimes you go, "Well, I have to do a movie" because you have to pay your rent. . . . Also, because people say, "You're good, so you should do another movie." You say, "Well, I'm going to get again into a tunnel of work."

Mostly, you know what you don't want to do for a whole year. People say to you, "Why don't you do a bad, crappy movie?" I say, "No way, I'd rather stay at home watching DVDs and eating sandwiches than do a bad, crappy movie." . . . You exclude all those things you don't like and because you're a filmgoer and a DVD addict, you end up finding scenes in some movies and say, "I really like this moment in this movie. One day, I should put something similar in my own movie." Or you just open the newspaper, and there's a drama that you have never seen onscreen, and you say, "Why has no one ever done a movie about [this]?"

Nowadays, I'm more fascinated by documentaries than by feature films, probably because I'm a filmmaker myself, so you see all the tricks. You see the people acting; you can even sometimes feel the makeup. There's so many elements that seem fake to your eyes. . . . Movies are flat. It's not like being with people or doing psychedelics that blow you away. You are in front of a big screen or a small screen, but it's just a flat screen with people pretending to do scenes that you know are fake. At least when you watch a documentary, you know that the point of view of the director is always fake, but what is portrayed mostly is not.

RP: What happens if you are in a situation where you don't want to do it, but you have to?

GN: Why? When do you have to do things that you don't want to do?

RP: You don't. But just for work, or something like you were saying.

GN: The good thing about shooting movies in France is that legally, the director has the final cut. There's always tension with the distributors. There's always someone who comes from a business school who tells you how you can make your movie better and more successful, but you just don't listen to them, and they get angry and say, "I have the final cut. Shut up." . . . That's why I feel safe making movies with French production companies, is that you have the law on your side.

In which situations can you cut? Sometimes, if the financiers don't raise enough money to do a movie the way you want it, they ask you to cut a quarter of your script. Then you have to make the decision: "Should I cut a quarter of my script or not do the movie?" Of course, you cut a quarter of your script, but it's not about censoring. . . . You have fewer toys, but sometimes it gets better.

SL: I think my favorite edit of all time is when you just cut a whole reel out of *Enter the Void* for the theatrical showing.

GN: There are moments you say, "Well, I'm inspired." They were putting me [under] so much pressure when *Enter the Void* was released because the movie . . . the original cut was two hours and thirty-five minutes. Nowadays, it would be distributed later because of all these TV series and also because of some blockbusters that were three hours long—people considered that a movie that's two and a half hours can be successful—but the movie was so weird as a product when it was shown at Cannes. . . . It was not fully completed, by the way. It was a first mix, first edit; I was still working on everything when it was shown at Cannes.

I had so many film critics hating me since I'm born that the first thing that would come was, "This movie is too long." At that moment, I was showing an unfinished version in Cannes. So then the financiers said, "Oh, you have to cut the movie down." In my contract, I had the final cut for the French version, but it was written in [that] if the movie was above two hours and thirty minutes and the foreign distributor asked for a [shorter] copy, you have to deliver a copy of two hours and twenty minutes maximum.

They didn't know how to cut because also, at that time, the movie was probably the last I had printed on 35mm. It was the first year that I discovered the existence of DCPs and all the digital projections. So I said, "If I cut the movie, I'll never see my cut anywhere because the negative is going to be cut." They said, "Well, you have to listen to us. You signed the contract." I said, "No, I signed the contract for the foreign release, but in France, I can do two hours and forty minutes."

Finally [I found] probably one of the solutions that I'm most proud of in my whole career. I [reconstructed] the whole movie. On film cans, the maximum is twenty minutes. The movie . . . was made of nine cans. Then I checked how I could cut the cans, and I compressed some. Some of them were twelve minutes . . . in order to say, "Okay, we print the nine cans, but if you want to pull out reel number seven, you can screen the movie without one reel. . . . But you have to deliver my whole movie to everybody."

It worked. It's very weird, but I couldn't believe that it would work so well. In Japan, they released it with eight reels. In America, they initially released it with eight reels . . . then, two weeks later, they said, "And now we have the director's cut!" They already had the reel in their projection room, but—

SL: They weren't playing it.

GN: Yeah. Sometimes, even, on the DVD, you have the short version and the long version. It's just that there is a seventeen-minute cut.

RP: That changes the entire film—that scene.

SL: But what I enjoy about the movie with the different reels is that it does become another movie, like *Possession*.

RP: Like completely. . . . How do you get into the psychology of your characters?

GN: You just pick up people [who] have the charisma needed to portray a character, but then you let them by themselves inside their own characters. I'm not pushy with actors. Just people that I think are funny, talented, whether they're professional or nonprofessional. It's just some people grab your eyes and your brain in a particular way, but it's always better to make movies with people you really like, even if they're very different from you. Then, let them find their own words.

Even if I wrote some film scripts that were long, like for *I Stand Alone, Irreversible,* or *Enter the Void,* I never wanted to give the screenplay to the actors. I was refusing. I said, "No, you're going to learn the lines. Those lines, I wrote them, and I don't have your language, so please, once you read the script, give it back to me." I seriously didn't want anybody to learn any lines because I like scenes happening on the set because it's fresher. You're not doing a documentary, but you create the scenes with a group of people that you selected.

RP: But in terms of the characters, the inner dynamics, and psychology—do you intend it to be so subtle? I don't know if you intend it, but sometimes it's almost like a statement. *Irreversible* was all about different kinds of men, like male toxicity, I thought. And it landed on one woman, but it's different versions of male—

GN: Monsters. Yeah. In my movies, the male characters are mostly more stupid than the women. At least, you can tell that they're driven by their hormones in a more predictable way.

SL: And definitely love.

GN: No, but the. . . . Then you ask people who know how to portray the characters.

RP: Why do you think that's important to you as a filmmaker to bring that out, highlight it?

GN: You know which movies touch you, which things in life touch you. Then there are things that don't touch you. I don't like filming dialogue, for example . . . I think it's boring to film dialogue. If on the set, you don't feel you're filming dialogue, it's just people that are being, then you edit whatever is good, whatever is bad. You can tell, for example, in *Enter the Void*, most dialogue [is] useless. I think literature is great for dialogue. But then it's just how people portray the situation . . . but the body language is more important than the words.

Pasolini was saying the audience isn't stupid. You can ask any actor to say anything where people watch a movie, or as they do in real life, they consider people for their acts, not their words. So someone can say, "I'm going to save you." If he looks tricky, if he's a greedy character, he can talk about the Bible, but life is the same. Some people talk about the future of this planet. They can be vegan; they can be humanist, whatever, but you know, behind that, they [can be] just as evil as the worst cop of the town . . .

I like movies like [Carl Theodor Dreyer's] *Day of Wrath*. It's a movie about inquisition. . . . There are many characters involved in the story, and there's drama. You can understand the psychology that it's not made of white or black. There's always gray and brown in all the characters, and how they fight for their own survival and drama appears. Mostly, people behave in a way because of their traumas, because of their education, but they're all part of the same humankind [regardless of] color, gender, etc. American cinema is far more. . . . How do you say?

RP: Binary.

SL: Black or white.

GN: *Oh, mon Dieu*, since the first scene, you know who's the good guy and who's the bad guy. Mostly in commercial movies, you know that the bad guy is going to be destroyed, so people come out happy.

SL: That's like in the old Westerns. The person wearing the white hat was the good guy, the person wearing the black hat was the bad guy. You just had to look at the color of your hat.

GN: Then even in the storyline, for example, in a Hollywood movie, you know that anybody who misbehaves will have bad luck at the end of the movie. . . . In

· real life, the people who survive are the strongest ones or the most manipulative ones, but people don't want to see that in a movie theater. In America, and in the rest of the world . . . people will go to the movies to relax. If you want to learn about life, you watch a documentary, but sometimes people want to forget. They don't want to learn.

RP: Well, I don't [want to forget], and that's why I'm extremely engaged when I watch your movies because it's like I'm there. Are you nervous your audience won't get it because you're not selling them? Do you assume they're intelligent, or you don't even care?

GN: Most people understand it. I don't know if they're intelligent or not. I don't think I'm intelligent, but I see many stupid people around all the time. It's just like you don't do a movie for an audience. You do it for your friends, for yourself . . .

In my case, I have one obsession. When I make a movie, I think, "I'm going to show it to Scorsese [and] Cronenberg." Show it to your idols. I don't have an edit complex besides with the film directors that I admire, even if they're younger. . . . It's not an art, but you are kind of professionally or humanly competing and sharing with people who do the same kind of things that you're doing. But for me, the ultimate spectator of my movie is not a film critic. It's probably, of course, the people who are close to you and then the directors you admire.

SL: Have you had any feedback from directors who have seen your work?

GN: Yes, I'm not good at names, but my favorite liked my last movie, so . . .

RP/SL: [*In unison*] That's awesome.

GN: When I see a movie with someone that I know, or I don't know, immediately I want to call the person or send him a message even if I don't know him. Just to go, "Congratulations. You surprised me." . . . It's good to compete in a happy way, a nondominant way.

RP: Do you relate to the movement Cinema of the Body, the French extremes?

GN: I don't know what that is. I know that some critics . . . invented a genre called the New Extremity. Let's just say that in France, the production system gave more freedom to directors than the TV channels were giving or that some American producers were giving to their own cinema. So, some scenes happen in the French cinema because you could go with a project like *Irreversible.* . . . French people are more selfish, not in a financial way, but in a mental way. Everybody in France thinks he's one of a kind and that his movie has to be different from all the others. It's not a commercial issue; it's more like an ego issue.

Not pretentious, because pretensions [can] fail, but that's also why artists like coming to France because it's about developing your own identity. People don't want to be part of a group. . . . Most of the people here want to be just the king of themselves.

RP: I have to ask about the sex. That's a big part of your movies. Is it just part of everyday life that you're exploring?

GN: You don't have sex every day.

SL: I wish.

[*All laugh*]

GN: Sometimes, yes, by periods. But I don't see why things that are essential in everybody's life should not be portrayed. There are things that you don't want to portray for legal reasons or emotional reasons. The good things in life, why would you prevent yourself from showing them, giving to other people? I loved erotic cinema when I was a kid . . .

I have memories of watching naked couples or naked women. I think that's missing now. The fact that even *Playboy* magazine now puts bras on every girl. I say, "What the fuck?" It's like they're demonizing something that made my childhood and my adolescence happy. I would masturbate a lot, but I felt better after masturbation. When you masturbate, you release serotonin, endorphins. I know nowadays, teenagers masturbate on a cellphone or watching gangbangs on YouPorn—what I experienced in the 1970s and '80s was far more rewarding and fresher.

RP: They lost the art.

GN: [On the other side], if a girl puts a nipple on Instagram, she gets banned. I can't believe that nipples are banned nowadays. You see nudity in every part, and you see pornography in the old Indian temples, and nowadays, nudity is the representation of evil. We're getting back to an old way of thinking.

RP: Do you think that will affect film?

GN: Of course.

RP: Does that make you angry?

GN: No, because I live in France. I make my way, but the planet is becoming more Victorian or religious or this or that. There's so many ways of controlling people, of mass controlling. . . . Demonization. Demonization of sexuality. It's so weird. It's the source of life.

RP: What's next for you?

GN: I don't know.

RP: Do you ever know?

GN: Probably an atomic bomb. [*Laughs*]

RP: But if you could do anything, your dream.

GN: One thing is the scenes you want to see . . . the projects that you can think you're strong enough to do. Like, for example, *Enter the Void* took me such a long time that I don't want to get into a process of two years of preproduction, one year of shooting, the effects, then, one year of promotion. I didn't know at the time that it would take me six years, but I like things that are short because

I want to be free to move around. Nowadays, I'm doing short films, or feature films, but in a short time because I don't want to get stuck for two and a half years on a project. The ones I dream of seeing, they're complicated, so probably I have one day to—

SL: To do it?

GN: To get the cross again and carry it on my shoulder and go to the cornfield.

Gaspar Noé: Interview with the Director of *Vortex*

Juliette Reitzer / 2021

From *Trois couleurs*, July 16, 2021. Originally published in French as "Gaspar Noé, entretien avec le réalisateur de *Vortex*." Reprinted by permission. Translated by Geoffrey Lokke.

Juliette Reitzer: *Love*, *Climax*, *Lux Æterna*, and now *Vortex*—since 2015, you have been going through a very productive period.

Gaspar Noé: Well, *Enter the Void* was difficult to finance and it took a long time to prepare, shoot, and postproduce. But I've always wanted to shoot more quickly and close to home in Paris. We shot *Love* in five weeks and *Irreversible* in five and a half weeks. Beyond that, I get exhausted. *Climax* was shot in fifteen days, *Lux Æterna* in five days, and *Vortex* in just twenty-five days. I am, alas, not as prolific as someone like Fassbinder or any of the great masters of Japanese cinema who could make two, three, four films a year. But if I managed to make one film a year, I'd be happy.

JR: The cast of *Vortex* is pure cinephile fantasy with Françoise Lebrun and Dario Argento. Are the two of them idols of yours? They sit at opposite ends of the cinephile spectrum.

GN: They didn't know anything about each other! They met on set. I've always been fascinated by both of them. When I asked myself which actress could interpret this character, a retired psychiatrist who's losing her mind, the first person that came to mind was Françoise Lebrun. I am obsessed with one of her films . . .

As for Dario Argento, I'm as fascinated by his work as filmmaker as I am his person. I remember once at the Cinémathèque Française, he presented *The Phantom of the Opera* and for an hour just monologued. People died of laughter, applauded at the end. What a performance. What charisma! I'd first met him in Toronto when I presented my film *Carne* (1991), and we've remained friends since. He also visited me in the editing room when I was working on *Irreversible*. Afterwards, I've hung out with his daughter a lot [actress and director Asia

Argento], so I've seen him fairly often. But I wasn't sure that he would agree to act in the film, especially since I knew that he was starting to prepare one of his own. When we were ready to shoot *Vortex*, his production got delayed. So I called his daughter, and she helped me convince him.

JR: Does Dario Argento improvise in the film?

GN: He improvises, but everyone improvises. There was very little dialogue in my original "microscript," the dialogue was just there to help people understand what the movie was about, and it wasn't ever meant to be followed. Dario, given he's a director, knows how to direct actors, but he knows how to direct himself even more. So, he took charge of his own direction. Alex Lutz took on his own direction, too, because he's a great performer.

[Lutz] had shot his film *Guy*—that's how I'd discovered him—from just ten pages of script. He likes when things are created on the spot. As for Françoise, having myself seen close-up how people have trouble expressing themselves due to age-related problems, my main note was to have her stammer. Afterwards, like the other two, she was a master of her own character. It's almost a coauthorship in terms of the writing.

When she starts crying because her grandson is banging his toy cars on the table, I hadn't asked her for anything at all. The kid hit the table so hard that after a while, it created all this tension and Françoise just burst into tears. When I saw that, I also cried behind the camera. It was so moving. It's good when you can get closer to shooting a documentary. Everything is still artificial, but by not imposing dialogue, I can achieve a certain degree of naturalism. I showed the film to Barbet Schroeder, and he said to me, "I can't stand improvisation on the screen, but here, I had the impression of seeing real life." Going forward, my job was just to hold one of the cameras. The other was held by Benoît Debie, my usual camera operator.

JR: It's characteristic of your films—the form is delirious, conceptual, but the content is very close to reality. We almost exist in real-time throughout the first part of the film.

GN: Yes, but it was still a hill we needed to climb. Sometimes, I try to make films in sequence shots, but we always know that a sequence shot, whether it's from a fly's point of view or a man's, is artificial. I don't know which camera position best approximates the human eye. But for this film, which is the story of shared solitudes, I said to myself, "Let's try to do it in split screen and always be on one side with the father and on the other side with the mother."

The result, which is very conceptual, works because the concept enters the mind in a very direct way. I don't feel like the concept weighs down the film. I feel like it flows naturally, that in an unconscious way, we understand exactly what it represents: two entwined solitudes that come together and then come undone.

A film, anyway, is just a game using an artificial language called cinema. We are very, very far from real life.

But when we manage to approach a film properly because the situations seem believable and the form allows us to see them from a point of view that we haven't before, we manage to create states of hypnosis in the viewer. The film is hypnotic because of the split screen. We do not know whether to look left or right. People who have seen the film several times have told me that they felt like they were seeing different films. The gaze sweeps from right to left or remains fixed on one side, but you cannot see the entire film at once.

JR: There are also times when the two cameras film almost the same thing, almost in the same axis, which creates an estrangement, a distortion.

GN: I've been told that the film is very psychedelic. But that was not the intention. It's like when you see someone, and then you see an X-ray photo of that person. It's the same person, but it's a particular point of view. We are not used to seeing the world this way. As soon as we put the points of view side by side, there are quirks that are unnatural but can also be playful.

I started playing with split screen on *Lux Æterna*, and then in an eight-minute spot I did for Yves Saint Laurent, and I sometimes would see things that worked that I hadn't imagined. For *Vortex*, I hadn't initially planned to do the whole film in split screen. We started by shooting sometimes with one, sometimes two cameras. But when I started editing, and I realized it was working well, we turned things around to ensure that I could get the film in split screen from A to Z. I'm happy I made that decision.

JR: As you often do in your films, you start off by telling us that it's going to end badly, which creates a strong hold on the viewer. Here is this dedication: "To all those whose brain will decay before the heart."

GN: The dedication is to be taken at face value. I think that among viewers of the film, a good third of them will experience cognitive difficulties linked to Parkinson's, Alzheimer's, or other diseases of this type before they die. Within a family, you don't ever know who is going to get cancer, who is going to spend ten years completely losing control over reality . . . it's Russian roulette. It's always very, very unexpected and, honestly, an absolute nightmare.

Even chemical-related nightmares, like in *Climax*, are less worrisome than problems related to brain degeneration. There have been plenty of films lately that have tackled these subjects, like *The Father* or *Amour*, but maybe they were more *written* and had a more typical form. In my film, as it's in split screen and the way people speak is a bit more documentary, it is more of a challenge. On the other hand, there's a film about old age that really inspired me, a 1958 film by Keisuke Kinoshita called *The Ballad of Narayama*. Like Kinoshita's other films, it's very conceptual but very moving. He's a master of both melodrama and the cruelty of the human experience.

JR: Why make this film about old age now? Does it scare you?

GN: No, I'm fine! Although, people are much more affected by this kind of subject at fifty because we have known a father, a mother, a stepfather, an aunt, or other people who've found themselves in this situation. I'd watched my maternal grandmother lose her mind when I was a child. When I saw my mother thirty years later in the same situation, it was a different story . . . the interactions that emerge out of these circumstances are . . . really disturbing.

At some point, I asked myself what I could've shot with Philippe Nahon. [The actor, who appeared in *Carne* and *Irreversible*, died in April 2020.] He had suffered two strokes; he'd partly lost his speech, and I really wanted to make a film in which he'd have been free to perform what he could, to use or invent whatever words he could. . . . But in the end, it didn't happen, and maybe not being able to make this improvised or semi-improvised film with him pushed me to make a film of the same nature with Françoise Lebrun, even if she, of course, doesn't have these problems. But these situations are all very sad and very violent.

JR: There is a deep melancholy in the film, which passes through the film posters and the books piled up in the couple's apartment. At the end, there's a series of static shots of the emptying rooms that is heartbreaking.

GN: Anyone who has lost their parents has experienced this; it's a common feeling. You don't know what to do with the books, so you put them in a storage unit, but after six months, you part with them. . . . The objects are linked to people, and when people are no longer there, they no longer have any real value. The interiors of a leftist psychiatrist, sixty-eight, and a film critic obsessed with Fritz Lang, Federico Fellini, and Luis Buñuel—I wanted it to be a very messy apartment.

I had in mind the apartment of a friend and film critic, Jean-Claude Romer, who died this year. It's the most book-filled apartment I'd ever seen. We discovered a building that was for sale and had been used for filming, and on one floor, there was this apartment with a very low ceiling that was like a labyrinth. I thought it was good because it was completely gutted. For this story of two people whose lives are coming to an end, the idea of having such a low ceiling excited me from the start; it reminded me of the low ceiling from the apartment in Orson Welles's *The Trial*.

JR: Through Alex Lutz's character, who is a former junkie, the film evokes the lives of drug addicts in Stalingrad [a Paris neighborhood] that the media often talks about lately.

GN: What I really liked about filming his particular relationship with drugs, even if it's a secondary element of the film, is that sometimes drugs or alcohol can destroy people physically and intellectually in a dramatic way. From having burned so much energy using chemicals, some people age faster. Most drug users, whether it's crack or heroin, can be heartbreaking . . .

The character, played by Alex Lutz, is very sociable. He tries to do his best to help people live a more comfortable life, just like his mother, the psychiatrist, has tried to help people. These neighborhoods that have been infested by the drug trade, which have long been found in Brazil and the United States, are now in Paris. It's got a lot worse over this year of isolation. At one point there was no one really left in the street, but you could see all these people who were in need, who were out looking for drugs. The trade has developed, and drug use grown; perhaps with isolation, demand has increased. When I asked myself which district of Paris I wanted to film, I chose this one because it reminds me most of this last year of isolation.

JR: There is also a little boy in the film, the couple's grandson. What does he represent?

GN: I really wanted to have a very young child in the film who hasn't yet mastered language, just as his grandmother is losing hers. Somehow, they are almost on the same level of dialect. But he is so cute that you also tell yourself that there must be a future that could be happy. He brings a ray of light at the end of one era, during this end-of-life scenario.

JR: Finally, can we get back to Françoise Lebrun? You said you were obsessed with a particular movie of hers.

GN: *The Mother and the Whore*, I have seen it maybe ten, twelve times in my life, and it still remains for me the most impressive French film of the 1970s . . .

JR: Her role in your film, almost silent, is the opposite of the one she played in Eustache's film, very talkative and cerebral.

GN: Yes, her character is the opposite, but my approach is the opposite of Eustache's method, which was to enforce each and every comma that had been written and inspired by real life. For me, it's the reverse. But I think that when you make a film, you have to surround yourself, both in front of and behind the camera, with the most intelligent people that you can find, the most inspired. And I was incredibly lucky to have had a cast of this magnitude here. They are so inspiring, all three of them. . . . It's strange that the film is not being screened in competition at Cannes. I think that if it had been, there might have been an acting award for one of them. They are that good.

Gaspar Noé on *Vortex*

Sonia Shechet Epstein / 2021

Originally published on Museum of the Moving Image's online publication, *Sloan Science & Film* (scienceandfilm.org), by Sonia Shechet Epstein, October 4, 2021. Reprinted by permission.

Gaspar Noé's (*Enter the Void*, *Climax*) new film *Vortex* tells the story of a couple whose ability to care for one another becomes compromised as they age and one develops dementia. Starring Françoise Lebrun (*The Mother and the Whore*), Dario Argento (writer, *Suspiria*), and Alex Lutz (*Guy*) as their son, the film is primarily presented in split screen. It made its world premiere at Cannes and its North American premiere at the New York Film Festival in the main slate. We spoke with Noé over Zoom during the New York Film Festival. (His screenname was "fritzlang"—the filmmaker who may have killed his first wife, Noé told us.)

Science & Film: I love the moment at the beginning of the film when the split screen drips down and disconnects the couple. Why did you choose a split screen?

Gaspar Noé: I [filmed] that shot from above thinking that probably I would use the split screen. If you're dealing with someone who has dementia, you know that person is perceiving things you don't perceive. You don't know what's going on in their head. It even happens on a much smaller scale when you're talking on the phone to a friend, or a boyfriend, girlfriend, and their voice and questions are weird, and you say, "Hey, have you smoked a joint?" And they tell you, "Yes, how did you know?" And you say, "Because I cannot understand what you are saying, and you don't understand what I'm answering." People can get disconnected with a small amount of THC. When senility hits people, they get disconnected in a much harder way [and you end up] sharing the space with someone who is actually in another world.

My mother, eight years ago before she died, was in a very similar situation [to the characters in *Vortex*]. There are moments in the movie that I experienced personally. I would talk to her, and because I have a face that is quite close to my father's when he was young, for a moment she would think I was my father. Or I would talk to her, and she would look away watching the window, then I would say, "Mom, mom, mom!" And she would turn to me and say, "I heard Gaspar's voice!" She would not recognize my face but could recognize my voice.

The generation that is portrayed in the movie is the generation of my parents. I remember when my mother started losing her mind, we connected through Skype so she could see me—I was in Paris, and she was in Argentina—and she didn't connect at all because she would just see a guy on a screen and say, "That looks like Gaspar." She was very pissed off; she didn't enjoy it at all, so we stopped using Skype because she could not connect with the screen. My father is eighty years old, and every morning, he buys three newspapers because he wants to compare the information. That's a scene; I don't know anybody who is twenty or thirty years old nowadays who is buying three newspapers to compare the information.

S&F: Did you do any sort of research into dementia?

GN: My grandmother had dementia, and my mother had dementia. I knew the subject. I had been to some funerals last year of people dying of COVID. The presence of death was around me, or the nonpresence, because death is not a presence; it's the things that happen around someone's death that we're representing.

Everything [about this film] was conceived very naturally, smoothly, and quickly. I had the idea of this movie in January of this year; we started trying to find money in February, we found a location, then I found the actors, then in April, we were shooting. We finished on the tenth of May and had two months to edit the movie, mix it, and show it in Cannes. So, the whole creative process took six months. What actually helped was that there was a confinement in Paris [because of COVID], so you were very concentrated; you're not partying, the nightclubs are closed, the cinemas are closed, so what can I do? Also, I had to pay my debts, so I had to work. I said, "Let's do a simple movie in a small apartment with two vaccinated actors."

S&F: I noticed that in the film, on the television, there were a few natural history shows or something that looked like that, and also in the beginning of the film the radio broadcast is speaking about memory and the brain. Where did those come from?

GN: That [radio broadcast] is a very famous one in France by Boris Cyrulnik. I didn't write it; we just found those podcasts on the internet, and they fit to the movie, so we used them. The underwater spiders and crabs come from a French movie called *Oceans*. We shot the TV with nothing on the screen, then, during editing, decided what we'd put. I had tried many storms, Hollywood movies, other documentaries, and they didn't work. Suddenly, when I tried that scene from *Oceans*, it did work. At that moment in the movie, her husband has already died, and she's alone. Those images are really creepy. They remind me of this feeling when you're really sad or melancholic, you feel like you have a spider inside your body. She's watching a documentary, but to use those underwater crabs or spiders is also a perception of her inner feeling.

S&F: Among other things, *Vortex* seems to be about the relationship between identity, memory, and place. The house, in particular, is such a character. Did you find that place as is?

GN: The art director and production designer of the movie, Jean Rabasse, is by far the best one in France. It was an empty apartment [when we found it]. He brought all the furniture, books, posters, and in one month, he created a whole life. You see the father's death, the mother's death, then the apartment's death.

What's really sad about [the father's] speech about movies and dreams, a quote by Edgar Allan Poe, is that at the end, you see what was going to be his intellectual testament disappear. It's just put in a garbage can. Not only do his memories disappear with the house, also his thoughts or what was going to be his intellectual testament disappears too.

S&F: That is very sad when his life's work gets tossed in the trash.

GN: Into the toilet! [*Laughs*] Flushed like a piece of shit.

S&F: Does that say something about how you feel about the importance of leaving your mark?

GN: My father is a famous painter in Argentina; he believes in leaving marks. In my case, I know it's almost impossible nowadays to show a 35mm print, so now you have DCPs, but probably in fifty years, no one will have the code to open the DCP. I don't know how sure you can be about the marks you are leaving. It's easier for an architect, it's easier for a painter, probably. If you have sold a big painting to a museum and the painting becomes famous before your death . . . okay. But there are so many movies that have disappeared totally from this planet. Some of them I have on VHS that you cannot find anymore, but they are unwatchable because my VCR is not working anymore. [*Chuckles*] People like leaving marks by making babies, but the babies are so different from the parents. I don't know. I don't think cats want to leave a mark. Plants neither. So why should we?

S&F: Has your father seen the film?

GN: My father hasn't seen it. I'm supposed to go to Argentina to show it to him. If there are similarities between situations that I lived through with my mother, it is an invented story out of situations that happened in my family or other families. I lost some other close friends from COVID last year; I was assistant director to Fernando Solanas, and he was like a second father to me; he died in Paris of COVID. The actor of my first two films [Philippe Nahon], who was also eighty years old, died of COVID last year. People come and go, but then, some-times, when they're gone, there is a VHS or DVD left—that's the mark. [*Laughs*]

Event Horizon: Gaspar Noé on His Devastating End-of-Life Drama, *Vortex*

Scott Macaulay / 2022

From *Filmmaker Magazine*, April 14, 2022. Reprinted by permission.

In 2012, after months in Buenos Aires helping care for his Alzheimer's-afflicted mother, Gaspar Noé traveled to Cannes and saw Michael Haneke's *Amour*, about a husband dealing with his wife's stroke. "Oh my god, I cried watching that movie," he says. "Even if that movie had nothing to do with my personal life, it was about someone who needs to die, and at that time, we were considering how my mother could die peacefully." After the festival, Noé returned to Argentina; his mother died a few weeks later. When the Palme d'Or–winning, and quite brutal, *Amour* went on to international success, Noé realized "that these movies could exist, could be financed and that, after these experiences with my family, I wanted to do a movie about these difficult days and do it like De Sica did in *Umberto D.*, Kinoshita in *The Ballad of Narayama*, or Haneke in *Amour*. Why should I keep on doing movies just with teenagers who learn how to do drugs or have sex? There are other things in life that are more common, more dramatic and more interesting than that."

A decade later, following his erotic 3D melodrama *Love*, dance musical hell-scape *Climax*, and *Lux Æterna*, a medium-length, darkly self-referential fashion film for Saint Laurent that is part *Day for Night*, part Paul Sharits-influenced experimental movie, the Paris-based director returns with that last-days drama, *Vortex*. Shorn of shock effects, acts of explicit cruelty, and on-screen sex, it's nonetheless a work that encapsulates much of Noé's overall cinematic project, carrying forward oft-used stylistic devices, an existentialist viewpoint, and a commitment to filmmaking that's as much about its story as the sensations induced by the act of watching. Starring the Italian *giallo* maestro Dario Argento as an aging film critic with a weak heart and the great French actress Françoise Lebrun (*The Mother and the Whore*) as his wife, a psychiatrist who now spends her days in the haze of dementia, *Vortex* follows this couple—left-wing members of the May '68 generation—as they shuffle around their spacious yet cluttered apartment in Paris's Stalingrad neighborhood, tending to matters ambitious (Argento's critic is quixotically working on a book about dreams and cinema) and quotidian (Lebrun haltingly navigates a daily life that has been made irreparably strange by her illness). Actor, director, and comedian Alex Lutz plays the couple's son, a recovering addict who evinces the alternating bouts of resolve and anguish that come with dealing with intransigent aging parents clinging to a way of life they can no longer honestly claim.

If this all sounds quite bleak, well, it is. But it's also riotously funny at times—in one moment, Noé literalizes the idea that one's life work turns to shit in the end—as well as formally thrilling. Noé shoots almost the entire movie in split screen, a frame divider slowly descending, like some Barnett Newman zip, early in the picture as Argento and Lebrun start their day. Each character occupies his or her own frame, allowing the viewer's eye to dart back and forth when they are separated and take in uncanny moments and perspective shifts when they share the same scene. At times, the camera leaves the parents to follow the son, capturing at one point a heartbreakingly despairing moment that Noé scores to Ennio Morricone's triumphant theme from *Mon nom est personne.*

"When my father saw the movie, he told me that for him, it's my most violent movie." When Noé tells me this, I agree. In the end, all stories come down to a variation of the one Noé tells here. As someone whose own mother died from Alzheimer's, I appreciated and even found consoling the astringent clarity of Noé's vision, as well as the ways the film formally evoked how consciousness warps during periods of confusion and loss. I spoke to Noé via Zoom, discussing the technical aspects of his use of split screen, making a largely improvised film off a brief treatment, and, to start, his health crisis, which occurred just before the COVID pandemic. *Vortex* will be released by Utopia on April 29, and *Lux Æterna* will have its own theatrical run in May.

Filmmaker Magazine: I have to tell you, I didn't really know about how sick you were until I saw your postings just before Cannes.

Gaspar Noé: It happened suddenly. In the middle of an afternoon, I had a brain hemorrhage. When that happens, you call 911, then at the hospital, they give you morphine. They gave me so much morphine they turned me into a junkie. I came out three weeks later and had cold turkey [withdrawal]. I was back at my place and couldn't sleep at all. Then, as I began to recover, the COVID virus appeared. There was a confinement, so I spent almost the rest of the year at home watching Blu-rays, DVDs. I had seen only one movie by Mizoguchi until then, so I got all the DVDs and bootlegs I could find and watched them all. There is something about the Japanese melodramas of the 1950s and '60s that is really hardcore—they are very mature and philosophical. The movies of Naruse, Kinoshita, Mizoguchi—they're great cinema and extremely touching. You cry watching them. I thought, that's the kind of movie I would like to do after doing kind of "cult movies" for decades. By having Dario Argento in it, and by calling the film *Vortex*, some people are going to think it's a horror movie, but it's more like a Japanese melodrama from the 1950s.

[During the pandemic,] I was taking my bike and riding around the empty city. The feeling was very dreamy. For years, I had this recurring dream of walking in an empty Paris, as if a nuclear plant near Paris had exploded or, like in the movie *Threads*, as if a nuclear war had begun. I never thought that I could see the city this empty. It was very trippy and nice, but then the streets became more desperate and full of junkies. There are so many more crackheads nowadays in Paris than two years ago. Especially at night, the empty streets felt more dangerous, and I show that in *Vortex*. The neighborhoods I like in Paris are the African neighborhood, Barbès, and Stalingrad, which is also the crack town of the city. Many hipsters were buying apartments in that area five years ago, and now they're trying to sell them for half the price—it's kind of evil. I thought if I was making a movie about the last days of a left-wing couple who are falling to pieces, the danger should be not only in the house but also outside. It's not a psychological horror movie, but there's a feeling of fear everywhere they are. There is no safe place for them.

FM: I was going to start by asking you about the Edgar Allan Poe poem, "A Dream within a Dream," which is really central to the film. The line has a metaphysical meaning, and it relates as well to cinema as you are just talking about. When did you encounter that poem, and when was the idea to make it so prominent in the film?

GN: The Edgar Allan Poe quote Dario Argento says in the movie comes from him—I didn't ask him to say it. He said it once during a scene; I loved it and kept it in the editing. And on the last day of the shooting, I asked him to say it again for the joyful prologue of the movie. Dario improvised all his lines, the guy who plays their son also improvised all his lines, and Françoise also improvised all of her lines. I asked her to mumble most of them, so you just understand one word out of every two or three.

FM: That's very interesting because some of these improvised dialogues are like philosophical debates, such as Dario talking about his worldview that fate moves within a city and his son arguing against that, or Françoise saying that people are fundamentally kind and Dario disagreeing. Did these conversations arise out of improvisation, or were you guiding them?

GN: No, I wasn't really guiding them. On the first day, if they would do something that I wouldn't like, I would tell them so they wouldn't do it again on the next take. But they were all very playful. To succeed in a collective project, like an [improvised] movie, you need to work with people who are inventive and playful. So once I'd created the context, the apartment, and told them the subject of the scene, I would let them go their way, which is why, at moments, it feels almost like a documentary—they were not remembering lines that someone else wrote. We'd shoot it once, twice, three or four times, but rarely more than four. But, contrary to other movies that I did with long master shots, I knew that, for this one, I would edit the scenes. So I told them, "As long as it's good, I'll keep it. And if at any point it gets bad, we'll just put a blink, and we will jump to another take or to a few seconds later in the same take."

FM: I love that you have the blink going back to your first feature, *Carne*—an editorial device you've stayed with since.

GN: Yeah, a psychotic gimmick I cannot get rid of.

FM: What does that blink mean to you? It's the opposite of making the cut invisible, but it also references the viewer's perception because the viewer could be the one blinking.

GN: As you say, it feels like a blink, and at the same time, it's just pretending that you did not do a cut and being clear about that. Sometimes, when I do posters, we talk about that with the graphic designer. He does an image he likes, and I say, "Okay, let's put a little frame around it." And he says, "You don't need the frame—just put the image to the limits of the [page]." But I like it with a frame, and it's the same with the blinks between the takes. It's like putting the same black line around your visual to mark the borders of what it is.

FM: When there were three or four takes, would the dialogues evolve? Or were they very different from take to take?

GN: I don't rehearse, so the first take is like a collective rehearsal. I see if the mic or the other camera gets inside the frame. It starts getting good on the second take. If it's a dramatic scene, you can stop after you do the third one, but if not, you can do a fourth. When I was doing *Climax*, I was shooting up to twelve, fifteen takes because there was a big mess that I had to handle and also because I knew I could not cut inside the takes, so I wanted the take to be perfect. But *Vortex* was almost like doing a documentary: whatever was good, I would keep, and whatever was bad, I'd cut off. When I started shooting the movie with a ten-page script, I thought it would just be ninety minutes long. Also, I didn't really imagine that I would keep this split-screen for the whole movie. But, once you get the material and like it, you discover the final length of your movie because there are scenes you just don't want to cut because you like them too much. There used to be this big thing that the movie should be ninety minutes long because that's what the audience wants, and that's what the distributors propose to the audience. But now, everybody's used to [watching] TV series. Some are nine hours long, and I have friends telling me they saw them all in a day. So, I don't think people complain as much as before about the length of a movie. But there is a natural inherent pace—when the movie doesn't want to be cut, respect the movie.

FM: Was there much debate about the length of the film after it was finished?

GN: Actually, no. It took me five weeks to shoot the movie in March and April [2021]. There were rumors that year that the Cannes Film Festival would be delayed until November, so I thought, "Oh, I have all my time to edit the movie." But they changed the date to July, so I had just three weeks to complete the editing and May and June to do all the postproduction. So we did everything very quickly. Ten days before showing it in Cannes, the movie was twenty minutes longer, and I reduced it, but I am very happy with the result. I like working at this speed. If the editing becomes too long, you get bored by your own movies. It's like dinners that last all night long—they're fun at the beginning, then they get boring.

FM: Could you talk about the origins of your work with split screens, which you've now done with *Lux Æterna* and this?

GN: There's a Paul Morrissey movie that I saw many years ago, *Forty Deuce*. It's a split-screen movie made out of a theatre play, but the split screen that lasted through the whole movie wasn't very effective. It was kind of dysfunctional, although he had done it before with *Chelsea Girls*. I thought the split screen was a great cinematic idea that someone should do better. With *Lux Æterna*, the long master shots I was trying to do, like in *Irreversible,* were not working, so I said, "I'll have to over-edit the movie," and I had many cameras. I started having fun with two and three images [at the same time] that I all edited inside the same final CinemaScope frame. So, you learn how to use the gimmick, the language of split screen, by playing with it. You use the sound mix, so you listen to one of the two screens or the other. Also, if on one side the frame is not shaking, it's annoying that the other one shakes. If you do handheld camera, you should do two at the same time, or else still images at the same time. And when you have one character on one side [of their frame], it looks better to have the other character on the other side [of their frame] with a similar composition.

When I started *Vortex,* I thought I'd play with the double screen for half or two-thirds of the movie. But as we were watching the first day's material, it became evident that the scenes that we could see with the double screen on the two characters were more interesting than the ones that included the two characters inside the same frame. So, on the third day, I reshot some things I had shot the first day just to make sure I could have the possibility of keeping a split screen during the whole feature. I was holding one camera, and [DP] Benoît [Debie] was holding the other. As Françoise is shorter than Dario, I said to Benoît, "You're tall, so you follow Dario, and I follow Françoise." Both cameras had a wide angle, and both frames were reframed in postproduction to make them more precise. There are interesting accidents, like when Dario sees Françoise Lebrun crying—she was not supposed to cry—and he takes her arm with his own hand. And then the arm seems very long, crossing the two screens. I thought, "Wow, it's so *pretty!*" But I never asked him to touch her. There are many accidents like that.

FM: When Dario and Françoise are apart but in the same apartment, were you ever filming those at the same time?

GN: No. We'd shoot one of them the first day, then before the following day, we would decide which take we were keeping, then edit it to have the precise length of the shot we needed on the other side.

FM: Were you then doing playback of those previous takes when shooting so as to match the timing?

GN: No, but we would know that Dario should go to his office, and then, fifteen seconds later, he should be opening the door going back to the living room. Then, he would finally get back into the room, where his wife was waiting for him fifty-five-and-a-half seconds later. There was a countdown: my assistant director would say, "Dario, come back to the room . . . five, four, three, two, one, zero!" And at zero, he would open the door so it was all synchronized.

FM: Tell me about the production design and the apartment. It's so overstuffed! There is so much physical media, so many books, VHS [tapes]. And Françoise's closets are so packed, and she has that giant rack of necklaces.

GN: Some things were inspired by my parents' house. They're leftist intellectuals. [Françoise's character] was a psychiatrist, and my mother was a social worker. In the 1970s, neohippies were [wearing] all these necklaces. All the posters that you see in the apartment are of 1968. The posters in Dario's office are posters from my collection that I photocopied because I don't want to put my originals on the walls. Dario said he wouldn't mind playing a film critic because he was a film critic before he was a director. I said, "Okay, you'll be a film critic, and you'll be writing a book about dreams in cinema." So, their apartment in the movie was a mix of references from apartments of older friends in Paris and my parents' apartment in Buenos Aires. [Production designer] Jean Rabasse and his team did a great, great job. When people would come to the set, they could not believe it was a recreated set. They really thought that we invaded the house of an old couple.

FM: What did Dario want from you as a director?

GN: He's playful, so he wants to have fun. And if there was anything that could be shocking, of course, he wanted it to be shocking. When he was supposed to portray a heart attack, I never expected him to be that good. He created his own asthma crisis—he had a microphone under his shirt that was recording his lungs, and it really felt like he had Darth Vader inside.

FM: He definitely had that phlegmy morning cough. I don't know how much of that was added in postproduction . . .

GN: It was not done in postproduction, it was done on the set. He wanted [the scene] to be shocking. He did the scene twice, putting himself in a trance [each time]. When I ask people who watched the movie when is it that they cried, for most of the women, it was when the father has a heart attack, and it sounds so terrifying.

FM: The scene with Dario and Françoise waking up at the start of the movie is soundtracked to a radio interview on grieving and the internalization of grief. That has the effect of making the whole movie almost like an experience of anticipatory grief.

GN: I thought I would put something under [that scene] from radio, probably music. But in the editing process, I thought it could be a podcast about aging or loneliness. There is a very famous psychoanalyst in France that everybody reads, everybody respects. I thought, let's just put [a recording] of his voice here in a podcast, and there was one about grief. So, we added it to the scene, and it worked perfectly. It was the first one we tried—I couldn't believe it; it's almost as if we [recorded it] according to the screen, and we got the rights immediately. And the image of Françoise Hardy singing at the beginning of the movie was the kind of happy accident that happened during the editing process. I wanted to get that song to try it on the balcony while they're having their cocktail. So I said to my editor, "Can you download from YouTube the song about the rose?" ["Mon amie la rose"]. My editor [downloaded] it, but he took the image at the same time—a version that was recorded on film for Swiss TV in the 1960s, just a close-up of Françoise singing. And she's so beautiful and so charismatic that I said, "Let's put it inside the movie after the opening scene." It makes no logical sense, but emotionally speaking, it's perfect. It's like a satellite that cuts the movie in two pieces.

At the end of her life, my mother had memory problems. She had a kind of short Alzheimer's in terms of months, mixed with nonconvulsive epilepsy, so she really lost her mental capacities over six months. I went to Buenos Aires to be with her, and many details in the movie are inspired by scenes that I experienced personally. The movie's not [based] on my parents, and the son is not me, but I saw what Alzheimer's could be. There are moments that are so tough for the person who goes through it that the days seem endless, both for the person and for the family. At a point, the suffering, the fear, the terror is so intense that everybody agrees that it would be better if the person dies, and you have to wait until, someday, it happens. And the day it finally happens, everybody cries.

But the weird thing that happened to me is that when I lost my mother, I really felt this empty hole next to me—in front of me, behind me, on my left or right side. It's like something missing in space. And I thought having half the screen black was a simple way of representing that emotional feeling. That's what grief is. And then the split screen could start working again, and you say, "Oh, that's normal life." A normal scene in this movie should be with two [images] in the same screen. Then, one of the images is missing, and there is a black half. You say, "Oh, that's what it feels like when someone else dies."

Also, [filmmaker and Noé's partner] Lucile [Hadžihalilović]'s father died the year before I shot this movie, and Fernando Solanas died in Paris of COVID a few months before I shot this movie. And Philippe Nahon [the star of Noé's *Carne* and *I Stand Alone*] died of COVID also a few months before I shot this. So, I saw three men who I really loved with all my guts, who were almost fathers to me, die in a row in the same year. I saw the whole process of the funerals again and again. So, it was a very sad year and very emotional because in death, there is not only sadness, there is a lot of humility—you learn about how useless life can be.

Interview: Gaspar Noé on the Split-Screen Spectacles of *Lux Æterna* and *Vortex*

Marshall Shaffer / 2022

From *Slant Magazine*, May 7, 2022. Reprinted by permission of Marshall Shaffer and *Slant Magazine*.

Conceived and created at two radically different times, the two latest works by Gaspar Noé will wash up on American shores in consecutive weeks. The first, *Lux Æterna*, began as a Saint Laurent-commissioned short film project that spiraled outward into a fifty-two-minute meta-movie about the connection between witchcraft and filmmaking. The second, *Vortex*, arose from COVID-related restrictions confining his camera to a limited scope.

While worlds apart tonally, *Lux Æterna* and *Vortex* function in a complementary fashion, just like the split-screen technique employed in both films. Noé remains acutely aware of the sensory impact that his imagery has on viewers, using his signature aesthetic to overwhelm eyes and ears alike. This is most immediately evident in *Lux Æterna*, in which the director harnesses the full power of light and sound to conjure the agony and ecstasy of filmmaking.

But if *Lux Æterna* finds Noé in a familiar mode of provocation, *Vortex* makes for a counterbalancing emotional evolution. His somber survey of senility, starring Dario Argento and Françoise Lebrun, locates an invigorating avenue through which he can keep surprising audiences, as formally unexpected as it is thematically unsettling.

I spoke with Noé while he was in New York to promote the openings of both films. Our conversation covered a range of topics, from how he determines the duration of his projects, why he chose to use split screen for both *Lux Æterna* and *Vortex*, to what he thinks about death after grappling with it so directly across his work.

Marshall Shaffer: Does it feel weird that *Vortex* and *Lux Æterna* are being released almost like a double bill in the US?

Gaspar Noé: Nah, I'm happy they'll release at the same time so I can do the promotion together! [Publicity] isn't the most boring part of this process, but sometimes it's the most repetitive. So if you can promote two movies in a row, then you can you can start working on another one. But the weird thing about *Lux Æterna* is that it's just fifty-two minutes. It was fully financed and produced by Saint Laurent. They gave me money to make a movie that would be six to ten minutes in length. I never expected the movie to get so much attention by being released theatrically in France, Russia, Spain, Japan, and now in the States and the UK as a feature film. I like it for what it is. I like it for its length. And it has some similarities with *Vortex*: Both are French and use split screen. But one of them is very funny, and the other one is as sad as a movie can be.

MS: How do you determine the right length for the stories you want to tell?

GN: When I finished *Lux Æterna*, many people said, "Why do you use a split screen? If you would just put the scenes one after the other instead of putting them on the right and on the left side, we could have a feature." I said, "I don't want to have a feature. I want to have a good movie!" I decided I'd rather have a movie with two things going on screen simultaneously. The movie has a perfect length. It could have been longer if we had more days of shooting, but *Lux Æterna* was improvised out of a three-line script. We had five days of shooting, so it's really magic that we managed to do such a good thing in such a short time.

But when it comes to *Vortex*, it made more sense to have it shot with two separate screens telling the interlinked lives of these two members of a normal couple who live under the same roof but are disconnected by some mental disease. So, in that case, I didn't know because I did not write the dialogue, and we could not measure the demands of the scenes beforehand.

I thought the movie would be eighty or ninety minutes long. It ended up being two hours and twenty minutes long with two screens, so if you add the two sides, it's like four hours and forty minutes of images. But the movie, from my point of view, is perfect at two hours and twenty minutes. Some of the movies I admire the most in my life don't have that common, traditional length of ninety minutes. *2001: A Space Odyssey* is very long, and *Un chien Andalou* is seventeen minutes, and that's my favorite movie. The French movie that I'm the most obsessed with from the 1970s, *The Mother and the Whore*, is three hours and thirty minutes long, and I can watch it over and over. If the movie was six hours long, I would enjoy it even better.

MS: Did you start *Lux Æterna* not envisioning that it would utilize split screen?

GN: I think I envisioned it at the end of the first day of shooting. When I started shooting, I thought I would do it like *Climax*, with long master shots that I would match with invisible cuts, and like Iñárritu did for *Birdman*. But we were so unprepared that the result after one day of shooting wasn't catastrophic, but I could not keep the whole take. I wanted to do a four-minute master shot at the beginning. But I had evidence that the discussion starting the movie with Béatrice and Charlotte was not very good. So, at the end of the first day, I decided that from the next day on I would shoot the whole movie with two cameras so I could edit it.

Lux Æterna is a movie that's over-edited, and the idea of using the split screen came in the process of preediting it. And there are moments that have a triple screen. On the very last day of shooting, I begged Charlotte to stay an additional thirty minutes, and she said, "No, I have to go run to a dinner!" I said, "No, please stay!" And we reshot the dialogue that we did on the first day because it wasn't very good. She finally agreed to arrive thirty minutes later to her dinner. And the scene we reshot that day was really good.

I think if I hadn't done that with *Lux Æterna*, I'm sure that *Vortex* wouldn't be shot with two cameras. But the dialogue between Béatrice and Charlotte was so funny that I kept to twelve out of the thirty minutes of the improvisation, and the result was so good that I saw that I could do another movie using that same technique. Dario Argento is extremely charismatic, very inventive; Françoise Lebrun too. I like going to the set as the documentary directors go to location. You don't know what's going to come out, but you know [you're] going to scratch the surface to see which essential things can be captured by the camera.

MS: And for *Vortex*, it's my understanding that you also didn't start out shooting in split screen and needed some reshoots?

GN: Because it was a really low-budget movie, it came out of my producer saying, "Do you have an idea for a movie with two or three characters in a single location that you could shoot during the confinement?" I said, "Yeah, but I want to make a movie with an old couple. And if they're not vaccinated, it's gonna be difficult because I want them to be close to one another." The two of them and the young actor [Alex Lutz] were vaccinated, but all the rest of the crew was not. There was a paranoid feeling during the whole shoot because everybody was afraid of COVID. We had two COVID inspectors on the set, and they were the first two to get infected! The mood on the set was very good, but it was very claustrophobic. On the first day of shooting, we were not ready. We rehearsed something just with the camera to see how we worked. Then we had nineteen days of shooting, and it was really stressful to try to do the whole movie in chronological order. On the second day, we started with a scene that I shot with one camera, and then we had another scene with two cameras. It became evident that morning that we had to shoot the whole movie with two cameras, so we reshot the scene that was one camera.

MS: Does shooting in split screen affect the way you compose a shot? Are you thinking about the ways in which the panels will play off each other, such as the moment when the man reaches out across the frame to hold his wife's hand?

GN: I didn't expect that to happen! In that scene, I asked the kid to hit the car with all he's got, and I even promised him a gift if he would just smash the car into the other car. During the second take, he became so psychotic that Françoise started crying for real. Everything becomes very touching, and Dario felt worried for her so he moved his hand to touch her. And on the real take, he even said, "Are you okay, Françoise?" Since she's not supposed to be called Françoise in the movie, I had to erase the word with "mon amour." But that was a joyful accident of shooting with two cameras because [his arm] looks elastic. I had another surprise when editing the scene in which the father and son are discussing the institution they could go to. I put the mother in the middle, and when she moves back on the sofa, she has two heads instead of one. That was also a very joyful surprise that I had envisioned. I thought, "Well, I didn't expect this to happen." But once I had put the two images next to each other, I discovered that.

MS: You've described committing to split screen for *Vortex* as a choice to be "playful." Why was that important to you in a movie that can be quite grim?

GN: It's playful because most people don't do it. On an emotional level, it's evident that it works. You understand the concept without even seeing it as a concept. Every spectator who sees the movie will see the split screen and say, "Okay, it's gonna be like that." And then you don't pay attention to the split screen anymore. One side of your brain is following one screen, and the other is following the other. And also, the fact of having the two screens inside the screen, especially when you're in a big theater, creates a rapid eye movement. Now, these are things that they are using in post-traumatic therapy, where your eyes are moving from the left to the right, and it creates a state of hypnosis that makes the movie seem shorter than two hours and twenty-two minutes. Some people have seen the movie twice, and they say, "It's weird, I felt like the second time I was watching almost a new movie because I was watching the other side."

MS: Are you doing scientific research into how movies act on the brain, or are you going purely off instinct and artistry?

GN: [*Shrugs*] It's overwhelming if you see it in a movie theater. But probably, if you watch the same movie on a laptop, it will not be overwhelming. It'll just be another movie. Nowadays, people are used to multiple screens because of Zoom, since COVID appeared. Every day, you're dealing with two, three people inside the same screen. When you see something that's "eye-blowing," you remember it. I'm the kind of filmmaker that avoids classical movies. I never watch TV. I like watching documentaries. But if anybody says, "Oh, there's a movie with very strange editing effects or sounds," of course, I run to see it. But there are so few around.

MS: You thank Dario Argento in the credits of *I Stand Alone*. What was his role?

GN: He had seen my [short film] *Carne*, and he said to me, "Oh, you have to make a feature out of it! Can I help you?" He proposed coproducing a feature version of *Carne* that actually became a separate movie, *I Stand Alone*. I had met him in Toronto in 1991 during the film festival, and I have photos of me and him having dinner for the first time. He was lovely to me. Since then, we have become very close friends.

MS: How do you think now having outright collaborated will affect or inspire your work moving forward?

GN: With the help of his daughter, Asia, we managed to convince him to be in the movie, and he's extremely happy that he did this movie. He says, "I'm not gonna play in another movie because I'm not an actor, but I did it for my friend Gaspar." Also, I think he did it because he really loved Italian neorealism. He has a particular affection for *Umberto D.*, as I do. When I proposed the part to him, he said, "Well, I'm young!" I said, "You're young, but remember the movie *Umberto D.*?" And then we started talking about it, and he said, "Okay, I understand."

He was also going to start a feature film, and his movie was postponed for COVID reasons. He had two months free before getting back to his preproduction. Very happily for me and the movie, he could accept the part. He's so charismatic that now I cannot imagine who else could have played that part. And initially, I said, "Oh, I probably should call the movie *Dementia*." There was a really good movie from the 1950s called *Dementia*. But this dementia is about senility, the state of mind of the woman. The whole situation is very demented, so it could have been called *Dementia*. But imagine a movie by Gaspar Noé, the director of *Enter the Void* and *Climax* called *Dementia* and starring Dario Argento. Everybody would have thought it was a horror movie! Then I decided on this other title that makes more sense.

MS: Speaking of *Climax*, do you feel any differently about its title card reading "death is an extraordinary experience" after the experience of making *Vortex*?

GN: That is not a joke. I don't know why people are so afraid of this. Death is nothing. We hit a wall, and then it's over. The *New York Times* review of my movie said, "We dream for a while, and then we sleep." Death is just the underlining of a sentence. There's a starting point, and there's an end point. There's nothing before, there's nothing after, there's nothing below. Our whole life, our dreams, are floating like a cloud above the void. I like saying, "Is there life before death?" Because there's no life after death . . . but is there one before? [*Laughs*]

MS: If you have no belief that life exists beyond this and no faith that even the work of someone as accomplished as yourself will live on, what's the point of it all?

GN: No, we're not creating pyramids. The movies will survive for a few years, as long as people have [something to play them on] . . . and as long as World War III doesn't destroy them. When you see what's going on today, it teaches you to be humble. Because you should do things for the present time and not for posterity if it seems right to you. But even if you have kids, your kids are not like you. They probably have part of your genes, but they're so different that you're not surviving through them. Take the dream for what it is and enjoy it for as long as it lasts.

MS: You've mentioned having an interest in pushing the envelope aesthetically. Is there anything catching your eye right now?

GN: For a moment, people were excited about virtual reality. But the helmets are a bit funny when you see a guy from the outside. Probably there's going to be some kind of new cinematic art coming soon, but it's not really created yet.

MS: Are you watching anything like TikTok where people are composing for vertical frames with rapid cuts?

GN: Uh, no. I like the square format. People don't play too much with the format, but I like CinemaScope because it's closer to human perception than the 1.33 format. For example, when I collect photos or paintings, I like the square format. But if you put a square inside a CinemaScope frame, it's like, "Why do you have so much black on both sides?"

Gaspar Noé and Françoise Lebrun on Their Dementia Psychodrama, *Vortex*

Alex Denney / 2022

From *AnOther*, May 13, 2022. Reprinted by permission.

At the age of fifty-eight, Gaspar Noé is still taking the kind of cinematic trips lesser filmmakers don't come back from. In his sixth feature to date, *Vortex*, he casts French new wave legend Françoise Lebrun and Dario Argento (yes, that Dario Argento) as an unnamed elderly couple nearing the end of their lives in their Paris apartment. Lebrun's character is living with Alzheimer's; her husband, who suffers from a heart condition, dodders against the dying of the light by persuading his son (Alex Lutz) that all is well at home and secretly bunking off to his office to make calls to his mistress. In one sense, it's a story that sits squarely in a recent trend for films—*Amour, Relic, The Father*—that deal with the subject of Alzheimer's. But Noé, who has firsthand experience of the subject through his own mother, makes it his own by presenting the film almost entirely in split-screen.

In placing these two characters in their little prisons of subjectivity, he subtly positions his story as part of a career-long obsession with the outer limits of consciousness—only this time, he's looking at the theme via the lens of old age, rather than hellish acid trips (*Climax*) or a drug dealer's ghost (*Enter the Void*). In fact, the void very nearly struck back shortly before shooting began on this film, when Noé suffered a brain hemorrhage that left him hospitalized for three weeks at the end of 2020. For a director whose work often seems to converge in the fuzzy spaces between life and death, it could have been the moment he's been training for all his life. And in a sense, aren't we all.

We spoke with Noé and Lebrun about the film, which was made over five weeks in the locked-down early months of 2021.

Alex Denney: Gaspar, your own mother was diagnosed with Alzheimer's before she passed away. How much did you draw on personal experience for this film?

Gaspar Noé: It's not based on my own story, but I know what it is to have a mother with Alzheimer's. And it's such a nightmare for the person [who has it] and also for the people around them. It's a very simple disease that hits almost every family on this planet, and it's still a kind of taboo, because I think that [many] people are more afraid of having Alzheimer's than dying. Old age ain't no place for sissies, like Bette Davis said.

AD: Do you think that films like *Amour* and *The Father* have played a part in unlocking those taboos?

GN: Yes. Especially since *Amour*, because in many ways it was the first movie on old age that was commercially successful. But old movies like [Vittorio De Sica's] *Umberto D.* make way for tomorrow, even when they're not successful. I saw that movie when I was a kid and it really touched me. It's like there was some kind of old-age misery that was rarely portrayed [on screen].

AD: How did you develop the idea for *Vortex*?

GN: During lockdown, my producers asked me if I had an idea for a movie that could take place in one apartment with just two or three characters because it was impossible to shoot in the streets or in clubs. And I said yes. Everything happened very quickly. But the good thing is there was some kind of joyful energy in the filmmaking that was probably more powerful than the subject itself, because the [circumstances were] very sad, shooting in confinement with COVID masks in a very small apartment for five weeks.

AD: How was the film cast?

GN: Dario Argento I've known for the last thirty years and I knew he would be great, even if he's never really acted [before]. And I was really lucky that Françoise [agreed] to do the movie, because she was also my first idea for the character. It was very improvised on the set—I just gave them ten pages of script, but they all agreed it was simpler not having any dialogue prewritten by me.

AD: Françoise, were you familiar with Gaspar's work when he approached you about the film?

Françoise Lebrun: Not at all. No, I knew his reputation. I mean, who doesn't? I'm not sure if I had met him before. We live in the same area in Paris, so maybe we have friends in common, but it was the beginning of the relationship.

AD: Did you know you'd be working with Dario from the outset?

FL: No. Gaspar told me he'd put my picture on his wall, and the next question was, "Who would be the husband?" He hoped Dario could do it, but Dario was preparing his own film, which was delayed because of COVID. So Gaspar went to Rome to propose the film and to show him [Noé's 2015 film] *Love*. And Dario said, "Aha, yes!" Because it's quite a pornographic film in a way. And so he said, "I'll do it, but I want to have a mistress!"

AD: That was his condition! Gaspar, Dario hasn't really acted much before, has he?

GN: No, not at all. Mostly, he enjoyed playing the killer's hands [in his own films]. It's funny when you look on IMDb, it always says, "Hands of the Killer, Dario Argento." His hands are more famous than his face.

AD: Why did you want him for this role?

GN: Because he's so funny, so talkative and joyful in many ways that when I was trying to figure out who could play the part, the first idea that came to me was him. I once saw him speak for one hour [at a screening of] *The Phantom of the Opera*. There was no time for the Q&A afterwards! Everyone was applauding; it was like seeing a great comedian on stage. I always wished I could do a one-hour introduction [to my films] without taking a single question. And I thought, if we put someone like that in front of the camera, you could do a take that lasts one hour and probably fifty minutes of it will be perfect.

AD: Françoise, Alex Lutz plays your son in the film, who is a recovering drug addict. Am I right in thinking Alex has worked mostly in comic films up until now?

FL: Alex has worked on mostly comic films up until [recently], but he made a very good film about a seventy-year-old singer called *Guy* [in 2018], which was a new face for him in a way. And Gaspar told me he had chosen Alex because he looked so melancholic.

AD: Gaspar, Alex's character, really struggles to deal with his parents' declining health, doesn't he?

GN: Yeah. Until that moment he's been the kind of "old baby" that everyone had to take care of, and then suddenly the situation changes and he has to take care of his parents, especially his mother.

AD: In what ways do his experiences in the film mirror your own?

GN: Well, I've been living in France for the last forty years, so when my mother started losing her mind, it was my father taking care of her. At the [end] it was really crazy, because she also had something called nonconvulsive epilepsy, which means you have epileptic brain waves that turn your brain into a volcano, and you cannot sleep. The last six months of her life were extremely painful and shaky; they looked like the end of my movie *Climax* when you had these dancers whose drinks had been spiked with LSD. It's just, like, you don't know what reality is around you, and it's just sheer terror or confusion. And when someone is really confused, it's very contagious, and people around them get confused.

AD: So much of the film is just a very ordinary lived experience for these characters, but there's this constant background note of anxiety that the situation could blow up at any minute. Like when she puts the coffee on the hob to boil . . .

GN: Yeah, it's like a psychological horror movie. Because it's a survival situation, but from the beginning, you know that everything is gonna go wrong. It's more about how people experience their own tragedy.

AD: Françoise, you've been celebrated in your career for your facility with words but there's very little dialogue here. Does that present its own kind of challenge?

FL: It was a relief.

AD: What, less lines to remember?

FL: No, no, I'm joking. It was another way of discovering something. Because with that kind of disease, only the present instant is important. So you react to everything, but only to that moment; you don't project. There's no judgment, no preconceived ideas. Nothing. Honestly. It's just me in the moment.

AD: Did you think a lot about what the character was like before she was ill?

FL: There are these old reflexes that [sometimes] come to her. When her husband has a heart attack, she calls her son and tells him to call the ambulance. And she writes prescriptions for herself which the chemist would never accept. Her reflexes are inbuilt, even if they are no longer adequate. Sometimes [it's like] she has lost everything, and sometimes [there is a] little light.

AD: Gaspar, towards the end of the film we get what we might assume to be Dario's character's death scene, which is awful. While I was watching it I was thinking there is something funny about having this guy who has imagined some of the most beautiful death scenes in movie history and putting him through one of the worst.

GN: And the sound of his breathing—it sounds like Darth Vader is having a heart attack. We didn't add that in, it was his real lungs doing that noise. You really felt like he was dying. We had to bring down the sound of his breath because it was too much.

AD: You also had a near-death experience shortly before making this film.

GN: I had a brain hemorrhage on a Sunday afternoon, probably because I'd been drinking too much for Christmas, and I was poisoned with oysters. I don't know what happened. I called 911 immediately and went to the hospital, and I ended up spending three weeks [there] on morphine with IVs and so on. And I was lucky because they say that only one in six people survive this thing without brain damage. But I survived.

AD: What do you remember of the experience?

GN: I enjoyed the morphine. All my life, I wanted to buy morphine. But then the doctors told me I had to quit all kinds of drugs; I had to quit alcohol and cigarettes. So now I have a much cleaner life. What also happened during that year is that I lost three guys who were very close to me, two from COVID and another from a heart attack. These men were almost like stepfathers to me, so I was in the middle of a whole process of life and death interlaced.

AD: Why did you decide to present the film in split-screen?

GN: Just before having the stroke, I did this short piece for Saint Laurent called *Summer of '21*, which I edited with split-screen. So when I started this movie, I thought it would make even more sense [here].

AD: Do you worry it might be a device that's off-putting for some viewers?

GN: No, because, in this case, it makes sense. Emotionally speaking it's very clear, very transparent. You're following two lives; it doesn't seem artificial. It could seem like an arty gimmick, but in this case, it has an emotional meaning. It's like each life is inside of a tunnel, and the tunnels never melt.

AD: It's interesting because even when the two screens seem to present a unified picture, they're never quite aligned. So you get this odd moment where Dario's character reaches over the table to his wife, and his arms look unnaturally long.

GN: That shot was an accident because I didn't expect the actress Françoise Lebrun to cry during the [scene]. I was really moved; I felt some tears behind the camera. And Dario just moved his hand towards her to calm her down. When we were editing, we found out that effect, which was so great, but it was an accident.

AD: Françoise, can you take us through that scene?

FL: Yes, it was unbearable. I just wondered what could that woman do with that noise? If I were in a normal mood. I could say, "Stop it, take your cars and play outside." But I thought, "This woman cannot do that." And [the crying] was not expected at all. It was not a conscious reaction. And the best thing that happened to me was to abandon my conscience.

AD: The film begins with a video of Françoise Hardy singing "Mon Amie la Rose," which is really beautiful. Where did the idea come from?

GN: She's so gorgeous in that [video], and the song is so touching. We were testing music for the balcony scene, and I asked my editor to take [that song] from YouTube. And he imported this video made for Swiss TV to get the music, but when I saw the image I couldn't believe how beautiful it was. So I said, "Hey, instead of putting the music on the balcony scene, why don't we just put the whole video inside the movie?" And it made sense. It was like the last idea. But once again, it was an accident.

AD: Françoise has been in the news recently talking about assisted suicide. Is this a subject you feel strongly about?

GN: If people want to die, of course, they should be helped to die. In France, it's still not legal, so when people want to have an assisted death, they mostly go to Switzerland or Belgium. And that's one of the things that Françoise talks about, you know, "When I want to die [I should be able to die] in my own country; I can't see why I should have to move to another country."

AD: Is there still a lot of resistance to the idea in France?

GN: There's resistance from the Catholic groups, but also among doctors. When my mother was sick, we didn't know how to deal with her suffering. But what doctors always say is *We came to this profession to save lives, not to kill people.* So many of them don't want to participate in euthanasia. But having seen this from up close, it's evident that when people cannot be saved, at least they should be helped not to suffer.

AD: I love the ending of the film, with the empty spaces. It was moving.

GN: Because their lives are erased. You always think that after someone is dead, they leave behind some footprints, but it's like the footprints are being erased just a few days after they're gone.

AD: That's pretty bleak, isn't it?

GN: It's realistic. There's one small detail; you probably didn't catch it. But among the things on the floor that are going directly to the garbage at the end, there [are the manuscripts for the book] that Dario's character has been working on, *Psyche*. It's there on the floor! [*Laughs*]

AD: The "death mask" shots in the film are an interesting choice. They remind me of those Victorian photos of dead family members "posing" next to their surviving relatives, which people used to keep as mementos. It seems creepy now, but I guess that's how they rolled back then.

GN: You know, in some cemeteries, people don't put photos on the [headstones]; they put a small screen with a loop of someone walking or whatever. That's so creepy.

AD: Would you like that for yourself?

GN: No! Once I'm gone, I wanna be burned. I want my ashes to disappear in the ocean or the river or the wind.

Additional Resources

Books

Palmer, Tim. *Brutal Intimacy: Analyzing Contemporary French Cinema*. Middletown, CT: Wesleyan University
Press, 2011.

Palmer, Tim. *Irreversible*. London: Palgrave Macmillan, 2015.

Taylor, Alison. *Troubled Everyday: The Aesthetics of Violence and the Everyday in European Art Cinema*.
Edinburgh: Edinburgh University, Press, 2017.

West, Alexandra. *Films of the New French Extremity: Visceral Horror and National Identity*. Jefferson, NC:
McFarland & Company, 2016.

Book Chapters

Frey, Mattias. "The Ethics of Extreme Cinema." In *Cine-Ethics: Ethical Dimensions of Film Theory, Practice,
and Spectatorship*, edited by Jinhee Choi and Mattias Frey, 145–62. New York & London: Routledge, 2013.

Hickin, Daniel. "Censorship, Reception and the Films of Gaspar Noé: The Emergence of the New
Extremism in Britain." In *The New Extremism in Cinema: From France to Europe*, edited by Tanya Horeck
and Tina Kendall, 117–29. Edinburgh: Edinburgh University Press, 2011.

von Brincken, Jörg. "Phantom-Drug-Death Ride: The Psycho-Sensory Dynamic of Immersion in Gaspar
Noé's *Enter the Void*." In *Immersion in the Visual Arts and Media*, edited by Fabienne Liptay and Burcu
Dogramaci, 111–35. Leiden, NL: Brill, 2016.

Interviews with Gaspar Noé

Aguilar, Carlos. "Of the Same Matter: Gaspar Noé on *Vortex* and *Lux Aeterna*." *Roger Ebert*, 11 May 2022,
www.rogerebert.com/interviews/gaspar-noe-vortex-lux-aeterna-irreversible-interview-2022.

Belpeche, Stéphanie. "Gaspar Noé: 'On repart pour une bonne année de poise.'" *Le journal du dimanche*,
25 Sep. 2020, www.lejdd.fr/culture/gaspar-noe-repart-pour-une-bonne-annee-de-poisse-30388.

Berman, Eliza, "The Director of the Year's Most Sexually Explicit Movie Is on a Quest to Redefine *Love*."
Time, 30 Oct. 2015, time.com/4093000/love-gaspar-noe-interview/.

Buckley, Heather. "Interview: Director Gaspar Noé on *Love* (2015)." *Diabolique Magazine*, 21 Feb. 2017,
diaboliquemagazine.com/interview-director-gaspar-noe-love-2015/.

Dale, Martin. "Gaspar Noé Sets His Goals for His Next Film Project after *Vortex*." *Variety*, 8 Dec. 2022. variety
.com/2022/film/global/gaspar-noe-2-1235454739/.

Delorme, Gérard. "Interview Gaspar Noé: Entretien avec cinéaste sur *Vortex*, son film le plus émouvant."
Chaos Reign, 9 Apr. 2022, www.chaosreign.fr/vortex-gaspar-noe-interview-dario-argento-francoise
-lebrun-film-festival-de-cannes/.

Ebiri, Bilge. "Gaspar Noé Is Not in Control." *Vulture*, 20 May 2022, www.vulture.com/2022/05/gaspar-no-on
-vortex-and-lux-aeterna.html.

Fletcher, Rosie. "Gaspar Noé Interview: 'American Horror Movies Are More Moralistic.'" *The Dark Carnival*,
17 Sep. 2018, www.darkcarnival.co.za/gaspar-noe-interview-american-horror-movies-are-more
-moralistic/.

Foster, Simon. "One from the Heart: The Gaspar Noé Interview." *Screen-Space*, 16 Sep. 2015, screen-space
.squarespace.com/features/2015/9/16/one-from-the-heart-the-gaspar-noe-interview.html.

Gavillet, Pascal. "Gaspar Noé sublimele chaos dans *Climax*." *Tribune de Genève*, 17 Sep. 2018, www.tdg.ch
/gaspar-noe-sublime-le-chaos-dans-climax-347756178974.

Hoad, Phil. "Gaspar Noé: 'As Soon as People See a Penis in the UK, They Think They've Seen the Devil.'"
The Guardian, 9 May 2022, www.theguardian.com/film/2022/may/09/gaspar-noe-vortex-interview.

Hoffman, Matt. "Cannes 2018: Gaspar Noé on Dancing, Tripping, and Preparing for Death." *Film School
Rejects*, 26 May 2018, filmschoolrejects.com/gaspar-noe-interview-climax/.

Hooton, Christopher. "Gaspar Noé Interview: 'The Demonisation of Nudity Is Sending Western Society
Back to the 19th Century.'" *The Independent*, 21 Sep. 2018, independent.co.uk/arts-entertainment
/interviews/gaspar-noe-interview-climax-director-new-film-sofia-boutella-dance-sex-acid-a8546541
.html.

Howell, Peter. "Disgusting, and Proud of It: *Irreversible* Often Sparks Walkouts, 'I Reflect Raw Reality of
Life,' Director Says." *Toronto Star*, 7 Mar. 2003, p. B01.

Leigh, Danny. "Interview: Gaspar Noé." *Financial Times*, 13 Nov. 2015, www.ft.com/content/aca4da5a-830f
-11e5-8e80-1574112844fd.

Lupini, Ben. "Entretien avec Gaspar Noé: 'C'est universel, cela arrive dans toutes les familles, alors, il faut
en parler!'" *Cineman*, 16 May 2022, www.cineman.ch/fr/article/entretien-avec-gaspar-noé-cest-univer
sel-cela-arrive-dans-toutes-les-familles-alors-il-faut-en-parler.

Mathieson, Craig. "Noé's 'Crime' Pays Off." *The Age*, 7 Dec. 2018, p. 3.

Moreno, Victor. "Gaspar Noé: Collective Meltdown." *Metal*, 29 Nov. 2018, metalmagazine.eu/en/post/inter
view/gaspar-noe-collective-meltdown.

Morgan, Maybelle. "Gaspar Noé: The Master of Provocation on His Trippy Dance Masterpiece, *Climax*."
Wonderland Magazine, 20 Sep. 2018, www.wonderlandmagazine.com/2018/09/20/gaspar-noe-climax
-interview/.

Morrow, Finoa. "I Am Not the Antichrist." *The Independent*, 17 Jan. 2003, pp. 10–11.

Mottram, James. "Gaspar Noé on His Haunting New Film *Vortex*: "I Could Have Died, I Could Have Been
Brain Damaged." *NME*, 13 May 2022, www.nme.com/features/film-interviews/gaspar-noe-interview
-vortex-near-death-experience-3224971.

Nugent, Annabel. "Gaspar Noé: 'Watching *Gravity* on Morphine Was the Best Cinematic Experience of My Life.'" *The Independent*, 15 May 2022, www.independent.co.uk/arts-entertainment/films/features /gaspar-noe-interview-vortex-irreversible-b2078607.html.

Olsen, Mark. "The Sunday Conversation: A Most Natural Thing," *Los Angeles Times*, 8 Nov. 2015, p. E3.

Ortiz Garcia, Eric. "*Vortex* Interview: Gaspar Noé on Making a 'Cruel but Warm' Film about Aging, Illness and Death." *Screen Anarchy*, 9 May 2022, screenanarchy.com/2022/05/vortex-interview-gaspar-noe-on -making-a-warm-and-cruel-film-about-aging-illness-and-death.html.

Peacock, Graham. "Gaspar Noé: Crafting the Modern Cult Cinema." *Metal*, 24 Nov. 2020, metalmagazine .eu/en/post/interview/gaspar-noe.

Pedrero-Setzer, Nicolas. "Q&A: Filmmaker Gaspar Noé Knows He Won't Be Remembered and Doesn't Care." *Washington Square News*, 2 May 2022, nyunews.com/arts/film/2022/05/02/gaspar-noe-vortex -interview/.

Romanazzi, Alexandre. "Interview: *Enter the Void*." *Abus de ciné*, 5 May 2010, www.abusdecine.com /entretien/abus-de-cine-entretiens-enter-the-void-gaspar-noe-nathaniel-brown-paz-de-la-huerta -cyril-roy/.

Sadat, Yal. "Un trou dans la tête: Entretien avec Gaspar Noé." *Cahiers du cinema*, Apr. 2022, pp. 44–45.

Shawhan, Jason. "Talking to *Climax* Director Gaspar Noé About Cameras, Disaster Films and More." *Nashville Scene*, 13 Mar. 2019, www.nashvillescene.com/arts_culture/film_tv/talking-to-i-climax-i -director-gaspar-no-about-cameras-disaster-films-and-more/article_92909c38-3484-50e6-9c62-57e9 h83632a8.html.

Smith, Neil. "Gaspar Noé: *Irreversible*." BBC, 22 Jan. 2003, www.bbc.co.uk/films/2003/01/22/gaspar_noe _irreversible_interview.shtml.

Stone, Jay. "Censor Board Will Have Trouble with *Irreversible*: Rape Scene Sickens, but Also Seems True." *Ottawa Citizen*, 30 Sep. 2002, p. B1.

Tallerico, Brian. "Interview: French Filmmaker Gaspar Noé Dares to *Enter the Void*." *Hollywood Chicago*, 22 Sep. 2010, www.hollywoodchicago.com/news/11867/interview-french-filmmaker-gaspar-no-dares -to-enter-the-void.

Wallenberg, Christopher, "Outrage and Praise in His Direction." *Boston Globe*, 7 Nov. 2010, p. N11.

Weston, Hillary. "Gaspar Noé's Movie Mania." *The Criterion Collection*, 18 Nov. 2015, www.criterion.com /current/posts/3802-gaspar-no-s-movie-mania.

Journal Articles

Angelo, Adrienne. "From Spectacle to Affect: Contextualizing Transgression in French Cinema at the Dawn of the Twenty-First Century." *Irish Journal of French Studies* 12, no. 1 (December 2012): 157–78.

Birks, Chelsea. "Body Problems: New Extremism, Descartes and Jean-Luc Nancy." *New Review of Film and Television Studies* 13, no. 2 (February 2015): 131–48.

Brinkema, Eugenie. "Rape and the Rectum: Bersani, Deleuze, Noé." *Camera Obscura: Feminism, Culture, and Media Studies* 20, no. 1 (May 2005): 33–57.

Brown, William, and David H. Fleming. "Voiding Cinema: Subjectivity beside Itself, or Unbecoming Cinema in *Enter the Void.*" *Film-Philosophy* 19, no. 1 (February 2015): 124–45.

Caires, Carlos Sena. "The Interactive Potential of Post-Modern Film Narrative: Frequency, Order and Simultaneity." *Journal of Science and Technology of the Arts* 1, no. 1 (May 2009): 14–25.

Donnelly, Paul B. "Liberation through Seeing: Screening *The Tibetan Book of the Dead.*" *Religions* 9, no. 8 (August 2018): 1–24.

Keesey, Douglas. "Split Identification: Representations of Rape in Gaspar Noé's *Irréversible* and Catherine Breillat's *A ma sœur!/Fat Girl.*" *Studies in European Cinema* 7, no. 2 (December 2010): 95–107.

Gazi, Jeeshan. "Blinking and Thinking: The Embodied Perceptions of Presence and Remembrance in Gaspar Noé's *Enter the Void.*" *Film Criticism* 41, no. 1 (February 2017): 1–14.

Hainge, Greg. "To Have Done With the Perspective of the (Biological) Body: Gaspar Noé's *Enter the Void*, Somatic Film Theory and the Biocinematic Imaginary." *Somatechnics* 2, no. 2 (August 2012): 305–24.

Hainge, Greg. " 'Un film francais et fier de l'être': Gaspar Noe's *Climax* in Context." *Australian Journal of French Studies* 58, no. 1 (April 2021): 100–113.

Mazin, Viktor. "Techniques for Masturbating: The Impossible Sexual Relationship as Prescribed by Gaspar Noé's Film *We Fuck Alone.*" *European Journal of Psychoanalysis* 30 (September 2018): 85–105.

Morgan, Jules. "Spiralling Towards an Ending." *The Lancet Neurology* 21, no. 11 (November 2022): 969.

Palmer, Tim. "Frontier Poetry: New Adventures in Contemporary French Horror Cinema." *Modern & Contemporary France* 30, no. 1 (November 2021): 1–17.

Palmer, Tim. "Style and Sensation in the Contemporary French Cinema of the Body." *Journal of Film and Video* 58, no. 3 (September 2006): 22–32.

Schwartz, Maxwell R. " 'On Looking Away': *Vortex*, a Film by Gaspar Noé." *Journal of the American Geriatrics Society* (February 2023): 1–3.

Sirmons, Julia. "Bad Trips: Spiritual Agonies and Ecstasies in the Films of Gaspar Noé." *PAJ: A Journal of Performance and Art* 45, no. 2 (May 2023): 48–55.

Smith, Gavin. "Live Flesh." *Film Comment* 34, no. 4 (July 1998): 6.

Video Resources

"BFI Masterclass—Gaspar Noé (2009)." YouTube video, 1:29:46, posted by "Squirt Reynolds," June 12, 2022, www.youtube.com/watch?v=zjzDl-Jrw8w.

"*Enter the Void* with Gaspar Noé, Excerpt from Conversation." YouTube video, 20:46, posted by "Sarajevo Film Festival," March 28, 2011, www.youtube.com/watch?v=CW9tedAvirU.

"Gaspar Noé on His Musical Influences." YouTube video, 58:02, posted by "Red Bull Music Academy," December 16, 2016, www.youtube.com/watch?v=sZiT7tEbsLw.

"Gaspar Noé on *Vortex*: NYFF59." YouTube video, posted by "Film at Lincoln Center," October 1, 2021, www.youtube.com/watch?v=zXtkuWMe1Tw.

"Gaspar Noé Talks about His Career, Including His New Film *Vortex*: BFI Q&A." YouTube video, 1:05:03, posted by "BFI," May 18, 2022, www.youtube.com/watch?v=_Cli5f3rCy4.

"Home Cinéma: Gaspar Noé (27.01.2019)." YouTube video, 26:30, posted by "Be tv," January 28, 2019, www
.youtube.com/watch?v=BsOjnvA5m40.

"Interview: Gaspar Noé—*Enter the Void*." YouTube video, 15:47, posted by "IONCINEMA," May 29, 2018,
www.youtube.com/watch?v=IbGNy9ZoNgA.

"Interview med Gaspar Noé." YouTube video, 40:23, posted by "Blockbuster," November 10, 2018, www
.youtube.com/watch?v=MVmxpDonguk.

"Nicolas Winding Refn in conversation with Gaspar Noé." YouTube video, 27:56, posted by "Space Rocket
Nation," January 18, 2015, www.youtube.com/watch?v=u2aZdzB8TnE.

"#SemanaCineCannes2015: Gaspar Noé (MasterClass)." YouTube video, 31:59, posted by "INCAA
Argentina," May 10, 2016, www.youtube.com/watch?v=XjIBop1DyPM.

"The Modern School of Film with Gaspar Noé: 'My Films Are Not Art.'" YouTube video, 14:36, posted by
"The Modern School of Film," 25 January 25, 2013, www.youtube.com/watch?v=ImO1OF-BRrQ.

"Why Gaspar Noé Shoots His Movies on Drugs: Locarno 2016." YouTube video, 4:00, posted by
"celluloidVideo," August 19, 2016, www.youtube.com/watch?v=7KrQ9tzgiyI.

Index

About the Editor

Photo by Lachlan Brooks

Geoffrey Lokke is a PhD candidate in theatre and performance at Columbia University. His work has appeared in such publications as *PAJ: A Journal of Performance and Art*, *TDR: The Drama Review*, and *Textual Cultures*.

Printed in the United States
by Baker & Taylor Publisher Services